AICPA

AF718371

Guide

Preparation, Compilation, and Review Engagements

June 1, 2017

Copyright © 2017 by
American Institute of Certified Public Accountants, Inc.
New York, NY 10036-8775

All rights reserved. For information about the procedure for requesting permission to make copies of any part of this work, please e-mail copyright@aicpa.org with your request. Otherwise, requests should be written and mailed to the Permissions Department, AICPA, 220 Leigh Farm Road, Durham, NC 27707-8110.

1 2 3 4 5 6 7 8 9 0 AAP 1 9 8 7

ISBN 978-1-94549-838-1

Preface

(Updated as of June 1, 2017)

About AICPA Guides

This AICPA Guide is issued under the authority of the AICPA Accounting and Review Services Committee (ARSC) to assist accountants in performing preparation, compilation, and review engagements of financial statements in accordance with the Statements on Standards for Accounting and Review Services (SSARSs). ARSC is the senior committee of the AICPA that is designated by Council to issue pronouncements in connection with the unaudited financial statements or other unaudited financial information of a nonpublic entity. The "Compliance With Standards Rule" of the AICPA *Code of Professional Conduct* (AICPA, *Professional Standards*, ET sec. 1.310.001) requires a member who performs compilation, review, or other professional services addressed by SSARSs to comply with standards promulgated by ARSC.

AICPA Guides may include sections at the end of individual chapters or following the last chapter. These sections will be entitled either "Supplement" or "Appendix."

- A supplement is a reproduction, in whole or in part, of authoritative guidance originally issued by a standard setting body (including regulatory bodies) and applicable to entities or engagements within the purview of that standard setter, independent of the authoritative status of the applicable AICPA Guide.
- An appendix is included for informational purposes and has no authoritative status. However, any preparation, compilation, or review guidance in an appendix is considered other preparation, compilation, and review guidance. In applying other preparation, compilation, or review guidance, in accordance with paragraph .19 of AR-C section 60, *General Principles for Engagements Performed in Accordance With Statements on Standards for Accounting and Review Services* (AICPA, *Professional Standards*), the accountant should, exercising professional judgment, assess the relevance and appropriateness of such guidance to the circumstances of the engagement. Although the accountant determines the relevance of other preparation, compilation, and review guidance, such guidance in an appendix to a guide or a guide chapter has been reviewed by the AICPA Audit and Attest Standards staff and the accountant may presume that it is appropriate.

This guide is an interpretive publication pursuant to paragraph .07 of AR-C section 60. Interpretive publications are recommendations on the application of SSARSs in specific circumstances, including engagements for entities in specialized industries. Interpretive publications are issued under the authority of ARSC only after all ARSC members have been provided an opportunity to consider and comment on whether the proposed interpretative publication is consistent with SSARSs.

In accordance with paragraph .18 of AR-C section 60, an accountant should consider applicable interpretive publications in the performance of his or her engagement in accordance with SSARSs. If the accountant does not apply the guidance in this interpretive publication, the accountant should document how the requirements of SSARS were complied with in the circumstances addressed by such guidance.

Conforming changes made to the guidance contained in this guide are approved by the ARSC chair (or his or her designee) and the director of AICPA Audit and Attest Standards staff. Updates made to the guidance in this guide exceeding that of conforming changes are issued after all ARSC members have been provided an opportunity to consider and comment on whether the guide is consistent with the SSARSs.

An appendix and a glossary of terms have been included in this guide to provide the reader with additional sources of information related to engagements performed in accordance with SSARSs. The additional material includes the following:

- Appendix A, "Overview of Statements on Quality Control Standards," which discusses quality control standards as required by QC section 10, *A Firm's System of Quality Control* (AICPA, *Professional Standards*)

Lastly, this guide also includes two indexes, "Index of Pronouncements and Other Technical Guidance" and "Subject Index," to assist readers in locating discussion of a specific topic within the guide.

Any guidance in a guide appendix, although not authoritative, is considered an "other preparation, compilation and review publication." In applying such guidance, the accountant should, exercising professional judgment, assess the relevance and appropriateness of such guidance to the circumstances of the engagement. Although the accountant determines the relevance of other guidance, such guidance in an appendix to a guide or a guide chapter has been reviewed by the AICPA Audit and Attest Standards staff, and the accountant may presume that it is appropriate.

Recognition

Accounting and Review Services Committee

Mike Fleming, *Chair*
Denny Ard
Sheila Balzer
Jimmy Burkes
Jeremy Dillard
David A. Johnson
Dustin T. Verity

2017 Guide Edition

AICPA Staff

Michael P. Glynn
Senior Technical Manager
Audit and Attest Standards
and
Staff Liaison
to the Accounting and Review Services Committee

Weiwei Tang
Technical Manager
Accounting and Auditing—Member Learning & Competency

 ©2017, AICPA

2015 Guide Edition

(Updates to this edition exceeded that of conforming changes.)

Michael Brand, *Chair*
Joseph S. Beck
Jeremy Dillard
M. Aron Dunn
Mike Fleming
Janice Gray
Kelly J. Hunter

The AICPA thanks Kelly J. Hunter for his invaluable assistance in developing the 2015 edition of the guide, completely revised by the issuance of SSARS No. 21, *Statements on Standards for Accounting and Review Services: Clarification and Recodification* (AICPA, *Professional Standards*).

The AICPA also acknowledges the contributions of the late Dr. Thomas A. Ratcliffe in the development of the previous editions of this guide—much of which is retained in this edition. We are forever grateful for his assistance.

Guidance Considered in This Edition

This edition of the guide has been modified by the AICPA staff to include certain changes necessary due to the issuance of authoritative guidance since the guide was originally issued, and other revisions as deemed appropriate. Authoritative guidance issued through June 1, 2017, has been considered in the development of this edition of the guide. However, this guide does not include all preparation, compilation, review, accounting, reporting, and other requirements applicable to an entity or a particular engagement. This guide is intended to be used in conjunction with all applicable sources of authoritative guidance.

Authoritative guidance that is issued and effective on or before June 1, 2017, is incorporated directly in the text of this guide. Authoritative guidance issued but not yet effective as of June 1, 2017, but becoming effective on or before December 31, 2017, is also presented directly in the text of the guide, but shaded gray and accompanied by a footnote indicating the effective date of the new guidance. The distinct presentation of this content is intended to aid the reader in differentiating content that may not be effective for the reader's purposes.

Authoritative guidance issued but not yet effective as of the date of the guide and not becoming effective until after December 31, 2017, is referenced in a "guidance update" box; that is, a gray shaded box that contains summary information on the guidance issued but not yet effective.

In updating this guide, all guidance issued up to and including the following was considered, but not necessarily incorporated, as determined based on applicability:

- SSARS No. 23, *Omnibus Statement on Standards for Accounting and Review Services—2016* (AICPA, *Professional Standards*)

Users of this guide should consider authoritative guidance issued subsequent to the authoritative guidance previously listed to determine the effect of such guidance on their preparation, compilation, and review engagements. In determining the applicability of recently issued guidance, consider the effective date of such guidance.

FASB standards quoted are from the FASB *Accounting Standards Codification*® 2015, Financial Accounting Foundation. All rights reserved. Used by permission.

GASB standards quoted are from the GASB Statements, Concepts Statements, Interpretations, and Technical Bulletins© 2015, Governmental Accounting Standards Board. All rights reserved. Used by permission.

References to AICPA Professional Standards

In citing SSARSs and their related interpretations, references use AR-C section numbers, as appropriate, within AICPA *Professional Standards* and not the original statement number.

Applicability of Quality Control Standards

QC section 10 addresses a CPA firm's responsibilities for its system of quality control for its accounting and auditing practice. A system of quality control consists of policies that a firm establishes and maintains to provide it with reasonable assurance that the firm and its personnel comply with professional standards, as well as applicable legal and regulatory requirements. The policies also provide the firm with reasonable assurance that reports issued by the firm are appropriate in the circumstances. This section applies to all CPA firms with respect to engagements in their accounting and auditing practice.

Paragraphs .20–.21 of AR-C section 60 address the accountant's specific responsibilities regarding engagement level quality control procedures for preparation, compilation, and review engagements. Because of the importance of engagement quality, appendix A has been added to this guide. Appendix A summarizes key aspects of the quality control standard. This summarization should be read in conjunction with QC section 10 and paragraphs .20–.21 of AR-C section 60, as applicable.

Defining Professional Responsibilities in AICPA Professional Standards

Pursuant to paragraph .15 of AR-C section 60, SSARSs use the following two categories of professional requirements, identified by specific terms, to describe the degree of responsibility they impose on an accountant:

- *Unconditional requirements.* The accountant must comply with an unconditional requirement in all cases in which such requirement is relevant. SSARSs use the word *must* to indicate an unconditional requirement.
- *Presumptively mandatory requirements.* The accountant must comply with a presumptively mandatory requirement in all cases in which such a requirement is relevant, except in rare circumstances. In such rare circumstances, the accountant should perform alternative procedures to achieve the intent of the requirement. The need for an accountant to depart from a relevant, presumptively mandatory requirement is expected to arise only when the requirement is for a specific procedure to be performed

 ©2017, AICPA

and, in the specific circumstances of the engagement, that procedure would be ineffective in achieving the intent of the requirement. SSARSs use the word *should* to indicate a presumptively mandatory requirement.

If a SSARS provides that a procedure or an action is one that the accountant should consider, the consideration of the procedure or action is presumptively required. Whether the accountant performs the procedure or action is based upon the outcome of the accountant's consideration and the accountant's professional judgment. The professional requirements of a SSARS are to be understood and applied in the context of the explanatory material that provides guidance for their application. The specific terms used to define professional requirements are not intended to apply to interpretative publications issued under the authority of ARSC because interpretative publications are not SSARSs.

AICPA.org Website

The AICPA encourages you to visit its website at www.aicpa.org and the Financial Reporting Center (FRC) at www.aicpa.org/frc. The FRC supports members in the execution of high-quality financial reporting. Whether you are a financial statement preparer or a member in public practice, this center provides exclusive member-only resources for the entire financial reporting process and provides timely and relevant news, guidance, and examples relevant to accounting, preparation, compilation, and review engagements, as well as audit, attest, assurance, and advisory engagements. Certain content on the AICPA's websites referenced in this guide may be restricted to AICPA members only.

Selected Recent Developments Significant to This Guide

On September 14, 2017, the ARSC exposed for public comment a proposed SSARS *Omnibus Statement on Standards for Accounting and Review Services* (www.aicpa.org/research/exposuredrafts/compilationreview/downloadabledocuments/20170914a-ed-omnibus-ssars-2018.pdf). If the proposed standard is issued as a final standard, the 2018 edition of this guide will be updated to reflect the requirements of the standard, as applicable. The following summarizes the proposed standard:

- The proposed standard would result in a new AR-C section that provides requirements and guidance when an accountant is engaged to perform a compilation or review of financial statements prepared in accordance with a financial reporting framework generally accepted in another country or in accordance with both SSARSs and another set of compilation or review standards.
- The proposed standard would result in revisions to AR-C section 90, *Review of Financial Statements*, to substantially harmonize the requirements with respect to the accountant's consideration of an entity's ability to continue as a going concern with those in AU-C section 930, *Interim Financial Information*, resulting from the issuance of SAS No. 132 and to include a specific written representation regarding disclosure of all information relevant to the use of the going concern assumption in the financial statements.

- The proposed standard would result in revisions to AR-C section 90 with respect to using the work of other accountants as part of the accountant's review of financial statements.
- The proposed standard would result in a technical correction to the requirements in paragraph .39 of AR-C section 90 regarding the content of the accountant's review report in order to make the requirements consistent with the illustrative accountant's review reports included in Exhibit C to AR-C section 90.

FRF for SMEs™ Accounting Framework

Users of this guide are encouraged to consider the benefits of the AICPA's *Financial Reporting Framework for Small- and Medium-Sized Entities*. More than 20 million privately owned small- and medium-sized entities (SMEs) in the United States that are not currently required to prepare U.S. generally accepted accounting principles (GAAP)-based financial statements now have a streamlined and cost effective financial reporting framework available to them. Released in June 2013, the FRF for SMEs accounting framework is a special purpose framework which offers SMEs a reliable, relevant, and simplified financial reporting solution that addresses marketplace demands.

The AICPA's FRF for SMEs accounting framework is a less complicated and less costly system of accounting for SMEs that do not need GAAP-based financial statements. The framework is a cost-beneficial solution for owner-managers and others who need financial statements that are prepared in a consistent and reliable manner in accordance with a framework that has undergone public comment and professional scrutiny. The accounting principles composing the FRF for SMEs reporting option are intended to be the most appropriate for the preparation of SME financial statements based on the needs of the financial statement users and cost-benefit considerations. Accounting principles in the framework are responsive to the well-documented issues and concerns stakeholders currently encounter when preparing financial statements for SMEs. For more information on *Financial Reporting Framework for Small- and Medium-Sized Entities*, visit www.aicpa.org/frf-smes.

 ©2017, AICPA

TABLE OF CONTENTS

 ©2017, AICPA

 ©2017, AICPA

Chapter 1

Review of Financial Statements

Introduction

1.01 AR-C section 90, *Review of Financial Statements* (AICPA, *Professional Standards*), applies when the accountant is engaged to review financial statements. When performing a review of financial statements, the accountant's objective is to obtain limited assurance as a basis for reporting whether the accountant is aware of any material modifications that should be made to the financial statements for them to be in accordance with the applicable financial reporting framework, primarily through the performance of inquiry and analytical procedures. AR-C section 90 may also be applied, as necessary in the circumstances, to engagements to review other historical financial information, excluding pro forma financial information. Reviews of pro forma financial information are to be performed in accordance with *Statements on Standards for Attestation Engagements No. 18* (AICPA, *Professional Standards*, AT-C sec. 310). Examples of other historical information that an accountant may be engaged to review include, but are not limited to, the following:

- A single financial statement
- Specified elements, accounts, or items of a financial statement such as schedules of rentals, royalties, profit participation, or provision for income taxes
- Supplementary information
- Required supplementary information
- Financial information contained in a tax return

1.02 A review engagement is substantially less in scope than an audit engagement, the objective of which is the expression of an opinion regarding the financial statements as a whole. A review engagement does not contemplate obtaining an understanding of the entity's internal control; assessing fraud risk; testing accounting records by obtaining sufficient appropriate audit evidence through inspection, observation, confirmation, or the examination of source documents; or other procedures ordinarily performed in an audit engagement. Therefore, the accountant does not express an opinion in the accountant's review report regarding the financial statements.

Applicability

1.03 An accountant performing a review of financial statements of a U.S. entity is required to follow the review standards as promulgated by the AICPA Accounting and Review Services Committee. However, those standards do not prohibit an accountant from indicating in the accountant's review report that the review also was conducted in accordance with another set of review standards (for example, International Standard on Review Engagements (ISRE) 2400 (Revised), *Engagements to Review Historical Financial Statements*, issued by the International Auditing and Assurance Standards Board). In circumstances in which the accountant's review report states that the review was conducted in accordance with Statements on Standards for Accounting and Review Services (SSARSs) and another set of review standards, the accountant should comply with both sets of standards. An example review report in which the review was conducted in accordance with both SSARSs and ISRE 2400 (Revised) is included in paragraph 1.239.

Consideration of Materiality in a Review Engagement

1.04 As a practical matter, an accountant cannot perform a review engagement without determining materiality for the financial statements as a whole and applying this materiality in designing the procedures and evaluating the results from those procedures. As stated in paragraph 1.01, the accountant's objective in a review engagement is to obtain limited assurance as a basis for reporting whether the accountant is aware of any material modifications that should be made to the financial statements for them to be in accordance with the applicable financial reporting framework, primarily through the performance of inquiry and analytical procedures. Without a determination of materiality, the accountant is unable to meet the objective of the review engagement. For example, the accountant is required to consider materiality when,

- in accordance with paragraph .17 of AR-C section 90, designing and performing analytical procedures and making inquiries and performing other procedures, as appropriate, to obtain limited assurance as a basis for reporting whether the accountant is aware of any material modifications that should be made to the financial statements in order for the statements to be in accordance with the applicable financial reporting framework.
- in accordance with paragraph .28 of AR-C section 90, evaluating whether the practitioner is aware of any material modifications that should be made to the subject matter in order for it to be in accordance with (or based on) the criteria or the assertion in order for it to be fairly stated.

1.05 The accountant's consideration of materiality is made in the context of the applicable financial reporting framework. Some financial reporting frameworks discuss the concept of materiality in the context of the preparation and presentation of financial statements. Although financial reporting frameworks may discuss materiality in different terms, they generally explain that

- misstatements, including omissions, are considered to be material if they, individually or in the aggregate, could reasonably be expected to influence the economic decisions of users taken on the basis of the financial statements;
- judgments about materiality are made in light of surrounding circumstances and are affected by the size or nature of a misstatement or a combination of both; and
- judgments about matters that are material to users of the financial statements are based on a consideration of the common financial information needs of users as a group. The possible effect of misstatements on specific individual users, whose needs may vary widely, is not considered.

1.06 If present in the applicable financial reporting framework, a discussion of the concept of materiality provides a frame of reference to the accountant in determining, as required by paragraph .28 of AR-C section 90, whether there are any material modifications that should be made to the financial statements

 ©2017, AICPA

in order for the statements to be in accordance with the applicable financial reporting framework. If the applicable financial reporting framework does not include a discussion of the concept of materiality, the characteristics referred to in paragraph 1.05 provide the accountant with such a frame of reference.

1.07 The accountant's determination of materiality is a matter of professional judgment and is affected by the accountant's perception of the needs of the financial statements' intended users. In this context, it is reasonable for the accountant to assume that users

- have a reasonable knowledge of business and economic activities and accounting and a willingness to study the information in the financial statements with reasonable diligence;
- understand that financial statements are prepared, presented, and reviewed to levels of materiality;
- recognize the uncertainties inherent in the measurement of amounts based on the use of estimates, judgment, and the consideration of future events; and
- make reasonable economic decisions on the basis of the information in the financial statements.

1.08 Further, unless the review engagement is undertaken for financial statements that are intended to meet the particular needs of specific users, the possible effect of misstatements on specific users, whose information needs may vary widely, is not ordinarily considered.

1.09 The accountant's judgment about what is material in relation to the financial statements as a whole is the same regardless of the level of assurance obtained by the accountant as a basis for expressing a conclusion on the financial statements. That is, for the same intended users, materiality for a review engagement is the same as it is for an audit engagement because materiality is based on the information needs of intended users and not the level of assurance.

1.10 The accountant's determination of materiality for the financial statements as a whole may need to be revised during the engagement as a result of one or both of the following:

- A change in the circumstances that occurred during the review (for example, a decision to dispose of a major part of the entity's business)
- New information or a change in the accountant's understanding of the entity and its environment as a result of performing review procedures (for example, if during the review it appears actual financial results are likely to be substantially different from anticipated period-end financial results that were used initially to consider materiality for the financial statements as a whole)

Requirements

General Principles for Performing and Reporting on Review Engagements

1.11 In addition to complying with AR-C section 90, an accountant is required to comply with AR-C section 60, *General Principles for Engagements*

Performed in Accordance With Statements on Standards for Accounting and Review Services (AICPA, *Professional Standards*). AR-C section 60 requires

- the accountant to comply with relevant ethical requirements;
- the accountant to exercise professional judgment in the performance of the engagement;
- the accountant to perform the engagement in accordance with SSARSs;
- the engagement partner to possess the competence and capabilities to perform the engagement and competence in financial reporting, appropriate to the engagement circumstances; and
- the engagement partner to take responsibility for certain quality control matters.

AR-C section 60 also includes certain preconditions for the performance of the engagement.

Professional Skepticism in a Review Engagement

1.12 As a practical matter, an accountant would exercise professional skepticism in a review engagement.

1.13 Professional skepticism is necessary for the critical assessment of evidence in a review engagement. This includes questioning inconsistencies and investigating contradictory evidence and questioning the reliability of responses to inquiries and other information obtained from management and those charged with governance. It also includes consideration of the sufficiency and appropriateness of review evidence obtained in light of the engagement circumstances.

1.14 Professional skepticism includes being alert to, for example,

- evidence that is inconsistent with other evidence obtained.
- information that calls into question the reliability of review evidence.
- any other circumstances that suggest the need for additional procedures.

1.15 Maintaining professional skepticism throughout the review engagement reduces the risk of

- overlooking unusual circumstances.
- overgeneralizing when drawing conclusions from evidence obtained.
- using inappropriate assumptions or developing unrealistic expectations in determining the extent of analytical or other procedures performed and in evaluating the results thereof.

1.16 The practitioner cannot be expected to disregard past experience concerning the honesty and integrity of the entity's management and those charged with governance. Nevertheless, a belief that management and those charged with governance are honest and have integrity does not relieve the practitioner of the need to maintain professional skepticism or allow the practitioner to be satisfied with evidence that is inadequate for the purpose of the review engagement.

 ©2017, AICPA

Engagement Level Quality Control in a Review Engagement

1.17 In a review engagement performed in accordance with SSARSs, the engagement partner is required to possess the competence and capabilities to perform the engagement and competence in financial reporting, appropriate to the engagement circumstances.

1.18 In a review engagement performed in accordance with SSARSs, the engagement partner is required to take responsibility for the following:

a. The overall quality of the engagement

b. The direction, supervision, planning, and performance of the engagement in compliance with professional standards and applicable legal and regulatory requirements

c. The accountant's report being appropriate in the circumstances

d. The engagement being performed in accordance with the firm's quality control policies and procedures, including the following:

   i. Being satisfied that appropriate procedures regarding the acceptance and continuance of client relationships and engagements have been followed, and that conclusions reached are appropriate, including considering whether there is information that would lead the engagement partner to conclude that management lacks integrity

   ii. Being satisfied that the engagement team collectively has the appropriate competence and capabilities to perform the engagement and expertise in financial reporting to

      (1) perform the engagement in accordance with professional standards and applicable legal and regulatory requirements and

      (2) enable a report that is appropriate in the circumstances to be issued, if applicable

   iii. Taking responsibility for appropriate engagement documentation being maintained

1.19 If the engagement partner obtains information that would have caused the firm to decline the engagement had that information been available earlier, the engagement partner is required to communicate that information promptly to the firm, so that the firm and the engagement partner can take the necessary action.

1.20 Throughout the engagement, the engagement partner is required to remain alert, through observation and making inquiries as necessary, for evidence of noncompliance with relevant ethical requirements by members of the engagement team. If matters come to the engagement partner's attention through the firm's system of quality control or otherwise that indicate that members of the engagement team have not complied with relevant ethical requirements, the engagement partner, in consultation with others in the firm, is required to determine the appropriate action.

1.21 An effective system of quality control for a firm includes a monitoring process designed to provide the firm with reasonable assurance that the firm's policies and procedures relating to the system of quality control are relevant, adequate, and operating effectively. The engagement partner is required to consider the results of the firm's monitoring process as evidenced in the latest information circulated by the firm and, if applicable, other network firms and whether deficiencies noted in that information may affect the engagement.

Independence

1.22 The accountant must be independent of the entity when performing a review of financial statements in accordance with SSARSs. If, during the performance of the review engagement, the accountant determines that the accountant's independence is impaired, the accountant should withdraw from the review engagement. The interpretations of the "Independence Rule" (AICPA, *Professional Standards*, ET sec. 1.200.001) of the AICPA Code of Professional Conduct provide authoritative guidance with respect to independence. In the absence of an interpretation of the "Independence Rule" that addresses a particular relationship or circumstance, a member should apply the "Conceptual Framework for Independence" interpretation (AICPA, *Professional Standards*, ET sec. 1.210.010).

1.23 Although an accountant can prepare the financial statements that are the subject of the review engagement, the preparation of financial statements (in whole or in part) is a nonattest service separate from the review engagement. The preparation of financial statements is subject to the requirements of the "Nonattest Services" subtopic (AICPA, *Professional Standards*, ET sec. 1.295) of the "Independence Rule." When an accountant prepares financial statements for an attest client, threats to compliance with the "Independence Rule" may exist. Pursuant to paragraph .01 of the "General Requirements for Performing Nonattest Services" subtopic (AICPA, *Professional Standards*, ET sec. 1.295.040) of the "Independence Rule," these threats would be at an acceptable level and independence would not be impaired when all of the following safeguards are met:

- Management agrees to
  - — assume all management responsibilities as described in the "Management Responsibilities" interpretation (AICPA, *Professional Standards*, ET sec. 1.295.030).
  - — oversee the service by designating an individual (preferably within senior management) who possesses suitable skill, knowledge, or experience (or all of these traits). The member should assess and be satisfied that such an individual understands the services to be performed sufficiently to oversee them. However, the individual is not required to possess the expertise to perform or re-perform the services.
  - — evaluate the adequacy and results of the nonattest services performed.
  - — accept responsibility for the results of the services.
- The accountant does not assume management responsibilities when providing nonattest services and is satisfied that the entity and management will
  - — be able to meet all of the criteria listed in the aforementioned "management agrees to" section;

 ©2017, AICPA

- make an informed judgment on the results of the accountant's nonattest services; and
- accept responsibility for making the significant judgments and decisions that are the proper responsibility of management.

If management is unable or unwilling to assume these responsibilities (for example, management cannot oversee the nonattest services provided or is unwilling to carry out such responsibilities due to lack of time or desire), the accountant's performance of nonattest services would impair independence.

- Before performing nonattest services, the accountant establishes and documents in writing his or her understanding with management regarding
  - objectives of the engagement,
  - services to be performed,
  - the client's acceptance of its responsibilities,
  - accountant's responsibilities, and
  - any limitations of the engagement.

1.24 Nothing prohibits an accountant who is unable to complete a review engagement due to a determination that the accountant's independence is impaired from performing a compilation engagement on those financial statements.

Preconditions for Accepting a Review Engagement

1.25 In accordance with paragraph .25 of AR-C section 60 and paragraph .08 of AR-C section 90, the accountant is precluded from accepting a review engagement if

a. the accountant has reason to believe that relevant ethical requirements will not be satisfied;

b. the accountant's preliminary understanding of the engagement circumstances indicates that information needed to perform the engagement is likely to be unavailable or unreliable;

c. the accountant has cause to doubt management's integrity such that it is likely to affect the performance of the engagement; or

d. management or those charged with governance impose a limitation on the scope of the accountant's work in terms of a proposed review engagement such that the accountant believes the limitation will result in the accountant being unable to perform review procedures to provide an adequate basis for issuing a review report.

1.26 An example of when the accountant may determine that information needed to perform the review engagement is likely to be unavailable or unreliable is when financial statements or accounting records necessary to perform the review are suspected to be substantially inaccurate and incomplete.

1.27 As a precondition for accepting a review engagement to be performed in accordance with SSARSs, certain items are to be considered. In accordance with paragraph .26 of AR-C section 60 and paragraph .09 of AR-C section 90, the accountant is required to do the following:

a. Determine whether preliminary knowledge of the engagement circumstances indicate that ethical requirements regarding professional competence will be satisfied.

b. Determine whether the financial reporting framework selected by management to be applied in the preparation of the financial statements is acceptable.

Application to a Review of a Single Financial Statement or a Specified Element, Account, or Item of a Financial Statement

In a review of a single financial statement or a specific element, account, or item of a financial statement, the accountant's determination about whether the financial reporting framework selected by management to be applied in the preparation of the single financial statement, account, or item of a financial statement includes consideration of whether the application of the financial reporting framework will result in a presentation that provides adequate disclosure to enable the intended users to understand the information conveyed in the financial statement or the specific element and the effect of material transactions and events on the information conveyed in the financial statement or the specific element.

1.28 Accounting principles generally accepted in the United States of America (GAAP) and International Financial Reporting Standards (IFRS) are general purpose frameworks and are presumed to be acceptable. In determining whether the financial reporting framework selected by management to be applied in the preparation of the financial statements is acceptable, the accountant may consider whether the financial reporting framework exhibits the characteristics of suitable criteria. Suitable criteria exhibit all of the following characteristics:

- *Relevance*. Criteria are relevant to the subject matter.
- *Objectivity*. Criteria are free from bias.
- *Measurability*. Criteria permit reasonably consistent measurements, qualitative or quantitative, of subject matter.
- *Completeness*. Criteria are complete when subject matter prepared in accordance with them does not omit relevant factors that could reasonably be expected to affect decisions of the intended users made on the basis of that subject matter.

The relative importance of each characteristic to a particular engagement is a matter of professional judgment. For example, even though a financial reporting framework designed for a special purpose may not result in the preparation of financial statements that is free from bias, that financial reporting framework may be acceptable in the circumstances.

1.29 Additionally, the accountant's determination of the acceptability for the financial reporting framework to be applied in the preparation of financial statements would include a consideration of the nature of the entity and the intended purpose and users of the financial statements. Financial statements prepared in accordance with a special purpose framework may not be suitable for general purposes, as the users may not understand the financial reporting framework.

 ©2017, AICPA

1.30 Additionally, as a precondition for accepting a review engagement, in accordance with paragraph .25*c* of AR-C section 60, the accountant is required to obtain the agreement of management that it acknowledges and understands its responsibility

a. for the selection of the financial reporting framework to be applied in the preparation of financial statements.

b. for the preparation and fair presentation of financial statements in accordance with the applicable financial reporting framework and the inclusion of all informative disclosures that are appropriate for the applicable financial reporting framework used to prepare the entity's financial statements. If the financial statements are prepared in accordance with a special purpose framework, this includes

   i. a description of the special purpose framework, including a summary of significant accounting policies, and how the framework differs from GAAP, the effect of which need not be quantified, and informative disclosures similar to those required by GAAP, in the case of special purpose financial statements that contain items that are the same as, or similar to, those in financial statements prepared in accordance with GAAP,

   ii. a description of any significant interpretations of the contract on which the special purpose financial statements are prepared, in the case of financial statements prepared in accordance with a contractual-basis of accounting, and

   iii. additional disclosures beyond those specifically required by the framework that may be necessary for the special purpose framework to achieve fair presentation.

c. for the design, implementation, and maintenance of internal control relevant to the preparation and fair presentation of the financial statements that are free from material misstatement, whether due to fraud or error, unless the accountant decides to accept responsibility for such internal control.

Practice Reminder

AR-C section 60 acknowledges that an accountant may decide to accept responsibility for the design, implementation, and maintenance of internal control relevant to the preparation and fair presentation of the financial statements that are free from material misstatement, whether due to fraud or error. However, in such instances, the accountant is precluded from performing a review in those circumstances because the accountant's independence would be impaired.

d. for preventing and detecting fraud.

e. for ensuring that the entity complies with laws and regulations applicable to its activities.

f. for the accuracy and completeness of the records, documents, explanations, and other information, including significant judgments provided by management for the preparation of financial statements.

g. to provide the accountant

   i. with access to all information of which management is aware that is relevant to the preparation and fair presentation of the financial statements, such as records, documentation, and other matters.

   ii. with additional information that the accountant may request from management for the purpose of the engagement.

   iii. with unrestricted access to persons within the entity of whom the accountant determines it necessary to make inquiries.

   iv. at the conclusion of the engagement, with a letter that confirms certain representations made during the review.

h. to include the accountant's review report in any document containing financial statements that indicates that such financial statements have been reviewed by the entity's accountant, unless a different understanding is reached.

Communications With Predecessor Accountants

1.31 SSARSs do not require a successor accountant to communicate with a predecessor accountant in connection with acceptance of a review engagement, but he or she may believe it is beneficial to obtain information that will assist in determining whether to accept the engagement. The successor accountant may consider making inquiries of the predecessor accountant when circumstances such as the following exist:

a. The information obtained about the prospective client and its management and principals is limited or appears to require special attention.

b. The change in accountants takes place substantially after the end of the accounting period for which statements are to be reviewed.

c. There have been frequent changes in accountants.

The predecessor accountant and the prospective client may have disagreed about accounting principles, procedures applied by the predecessor accountant, or similarly significant matters.

1.32 Except as permitted by the AICPA Code of Professional Conduct, an accountant is precluded from disclosing any confidential information obtained in the course of an engagement unless the client specifically consents. Accordingly, if the successor accountant decides to communicate with the predecessor, it is important that the successor accountant request the client to (*a*) permit the successor accountant to make inquiries of the predecessor accountant and (*b*) authorize the predecessor accountant to respond fully to those inquiries. If the prospective client refuses to permit the predecessor accountant to respond or limits the response, the successor accountant may want to inquire about the reasons and consider the implications of that refusal in connection with acceptance of the engagement.

1.33 When the successor accountant decides to communicate with the predecessor accountant, the inquiries may be oral or written. The inquiries are

 ©2017, AICPA

most useful if they are specific and reasonable regarding matters that will assist the successor accountant in determining whether to accept the engagement. Matters subject to inquiry would include (*a*) information that might bear on the integrity of management (owners), (*b*) disagreements with management (owners) about accounting principles or the necessity for the performance of certain procedures or similarly significant matters, (*c*) the cooperation of management (owners) in providing additional or revised information, if necessary, (*d*) the predecessor's knowledge of any fraud or illegal acts perpetrated within the client, and (*e*) the predecessor's understanding of the reason for the change of accountants.

1.34 It is considered good practice for the predecessor accountant to respond promptly and fully to the inquiries, on the basis of known facts. However, the predecessor accountant may decide, due to unusual circumstances such as impending, threatened, or potential litigation; disciplinary proceedings; or other unusual circumstances, to not respond fully to the inquiries and instead indicate that the response is limited. A limited response may have implications in connection with acceptance of the engagement.

Agreement on Engagement Terms

1.35 Paragraph .11 of AR-C section 90 states that the accountant should agree upon the terms of the engagement with management or those charged with governance, as appropriate. The agreed-upon terms of the engagement should be documented in an engagement letter or other suitable form of written agreement between the parties that is signed by both the accountant or the accountant's firm and management or those charged with governance as appropriate.

1.36 Such an understanding reduces the risk that the accountant or the client may misinterpret the needs or expectations of the other party. For example, it reduces the risk that management may inappropriately rely on the accountant to protect the entity against certain risks or to perform certain functions that are management's responsibility.

1.37 The accountant should ensure that the engagement letter includes the objectives of the engagement, management's responsibilities as set forth in paragraph 1.30, the accountant's responsibilities, the limitations of the review engagement, identification of the applicable financial reporting framework for the preparation of the financial statements, and the expected form and content of the accountant's review report and a statement that there may be circumstances in which the report may differ from its expected form and content.

Observations and Suggestions

Obtaining an engagement letter at least annually is considered a best practice. The engagement letter can cover multiple services and address both nonattest and attest services (for example, an engagement to prepare monthly financial statements and review the annual financial statements for an entity).

1.38 Illustrations of engagement letters for review engagements are included in paragraph 1.235.

Understanding of the Industry

1.39 According to paragraph .14 of AR-C section 90, to perform the review engagement, the accountant should possess or obtain an understanding of the industry in which the entity operates, including the accounting principles and practices generally used in the industry, sufficient to enable the accountant to review financial statements that are appropriate for an entity operating in that industry. Review procedures can be performed effectively only if the accountant is familiar with the industry-specific accounting principles used by the entity. For example, if the entity is a real estate developer, the accountant should be aware of the existence and application of specialized accounting methods for real estate developers. For many review engagements, the entity does not use specialized or unique accounting practices. In this case, the knowledge the accountant obtains related to accounting principles generally applicable to all entities is sufficient background to successfully execute a review.

Knowledge of the Entity

1.40 Pursuant to paragraph .15 of AR-C section 90, the accountant is required to obtain knowledge about the entity sufficient to identify areas in the financial statements where there is a greater likelihood that material misstatements may arise and to be able to design procedures to address those areas. The knowledge should include an understanding of (*a*) the entity's business and (*b*) the accounting principles and practices used by the entity.

1.41 However, when the entity operates in an industry characterized by specialized accounting principles, the accountant should be familiar with that industry's specialized accounting principles, practices, and methods. If the accountant is not already knowledgeable about the industry-specific principles, he or she may obtain an understanding of such principles by referring to appropriate material. For example, the accountant may

- review relevant AICPA Audit and Accounting Guides;
- review industry publications;
- review financial statements of other entities in the same industry;
- consult with other individuals familiar with accounting practices in the industry;
- read periodicals, textbooks, and other publications that discuss financial accounting and reporting practices;
- attend seminars conducted by accounting and industry groups; and
- take continuing professional education courses on the subject matter.

1.42 The accountant should understand the accounting principles and practices used by the entity in measuring, recognizing, recording, and disclosing all significant accounts and disclosures in the financial statements. The accountant may obtain an understanding of the accounting policies and procedures used by management through inquiry, the review of entity prepared documents, or experience with the entity.

1.43 The accountant's understanding may include, for example, the entity's policies and procedures related to the following:

- Inventory valuation

©2017, AICPA

- Fixed asset depreciation
- Revenue recognition, including whether the entity has a unique revenue recognition policy
- Estimates
- Asset impairment

1.44 The accountant's understanding also may include matters such as changes in accounting practices and principles and differences in the entity's business model as compared with normal practices within the industry. The accountant's review procedures will be affected if unusual accounting policies and procedures come to the accountant's attention.

1.45 According to paragraph .A32 of AR-C section 90, the accountant's understanding of the entity's business encompasses a general understanding of the entity's organization; its operating characteristics; and the nature of its assets, liabilities, revenues, and expenses. The accountant's understanding of the entity's business is fundamental to a successful review.

1.46 Factors to consider in understanding the organization include the form of business organization, the entity's history, and the management structure.

1.47 A general understanding of the entity's organization is part of the accountant's knowledge of the entity's business. Some of the factors the accountant might consider include the following:

- Form of business organization
- Principals involved in the organization
- Organizational chart
- Related party transactions

Form of Business Organization

1.48 The business may be set up as a corporation, a partnership, a sole proprietorship, or some other business form allowed by the state in which the organization is located. Knowledge of the form of business allows the accountant to anticipate how transactions, especially capital transactions, should be recorded and classified. For example, property or cash distributions may be treated as a dividend or withdrawal, depending on whether the organization is a corporation or sole proprietorship. In addition, the business form dictates the form of the equity section of the financial statements.

1.49 In a similar fashion, whether the organization is a taxpaying entity or simply files tax returns for informational purposes may affect the financial statements. For example, for a taxpaying entity, certain transactions are required to be presented net of tax effects, but an entity that does not pay taxes (such as a partnership) would not present those transactions net of tax.

1.50 The legal form and tax status of an entity also are important when the entity is one of several entities owned by a single investor or the same group of investors. If the accountant is reviewing the financial statements of one of several commonly owned entities, it is imperative that the concept of an accounting entity be clearly identified before financial statements are prepared. For example, the reporting entity may include all businesses owned by the same group of investors, and even though there is no equity interest among the entities, many of the practices used in accounting for consolidating entities must nonetheless be used.

Principals and Key Personnel

1.51 For some engagements, the principals involved and the key personnel may be the same. Knowledge of the principals and key personnel of the organization allows the accountant to assess the level of sophistication those people have with respect to financial reporting. This information also enables the accountant to be alert to related party transactions or conflicts of interest that may affect the financial statements.

Related Party Transactions

1.52 Understanding an entity's organization helps the accountant identify any related party transactions. Related party transactions occur when one party to a transaction can impose on the other party contract terms that would not have been acceptable in an arm's length transaction.

1.53 Factors that may assist the accountant in identifying potential related party transactions include, but are not limited to, the following:

- Major sources of financing
- Significant vendors and customers
- Relationships (if any) of key employees to the entity
- Relationships (if any) of the entity to affiliated companies (through equity investments, common ownership, family ties, and so on)

Understanding the Entity's Operating Characteristics

1.54 The accountant's knowledge of the entity's business includes a general understanding of the entity's operating characteristics. This understanding may include the following:

- Understanding the entity's products and services
- Identifying the entity's operating locations
- Understanding the entity's production methods
- Understanding the entity's distribution system
- Understanding the entity's compensation methods

1.55 An understanding of an entity's operating characteristics can be obtained by making inquiries of the entity's principals and key personnel and by observing the entity's operations.

Products and Services

1.56 The accountant may want to obtain a list of products sold or services provided and develop knowledge of special accounting or disclosure problems related to the entity's products or services.

1.57 For example, some products may be sensitive to technological or style changes and would require the entity to consider periodic write-downs based on the lower of cost or market test. Other products may be sold with warranty commitments that require the entity to estimate the amount of liability to be

 ©2017, AICPA

recorded. If the entity custom builds products for its customers and the products require an extended period of time to complete, then revenue recognition methods specific to long-term contracts (that is, contract accounting) may apply.

Operating Locations

1.58 The accountant may want to request a list of business locations and the business activity that occurs at each location (the accountant would be interested in the accounting related to the activities conducted at each location).

1.59 With respect to physical assets, such as fixed assets and inventories, the entity should have adequate controls to reasonably ensure the existence and valuation of such assets. If transactions are authorized or executed (or both) at a location, accounting controls should be in place to record the transactions on a timely basis.

Production Methods

1.60 If the entity is a manufacturer, knowledge of production methods is an important part of the accountant's development of an understanding of the entity's business. Familiarity with the production process might help the accountant identify factors affecting the financial statements, such as a high level of spoiled goods, the use of returnable containers, the need to estimate the percentage of completion of unfinished goods, and the accounting for by-products. Each of these factors has accounting implications that might be considered in determining whether the entity has the capabilities to prepare financial statements that conform to the applicable financial reporting framework.

Distribution System

1.61 A general understanding of the entity's distribution system allows the accountant to consider whether there are inventory control problems. For example, the entity could be in an industry characterized by consignment contracts. Whether the entity is the consignor or the consignee, its accounting system generally should be capable of identifying inventory ownership. On the other hand, if the entity has multiple outlets and warehouses, the inventory system generally should be capable of identifying goods in transit at the end of the year in order to execute a proper cutoff.

1.62 In addition, understanding the distribution system gives the accountant insight regarding the location of property, plant, and equipment and accrual procedures for various sales transactions that occur during the period.

Compensation Methods

1.63 Employees may be compensated in a variety of ways other than simple periodic cash payments. For example, key employees may receive stock options or direct distributions of stock. Additionally, some or all employees may be involved in qualified or nonqualified pension plans. Knowledge of the compensation methods the entity uses would provide a basis for the accountant to raise questions about whether the entity has properly valued and disclosed its compensation methods and, when appropriate, satisfied tax regulations and filed appropriate tax forms.

Understanding the Entity's Assets, Liabilities, Revenues, and Expenses

1.64 Developing an understanding of the accounting principles used in the entity's industry and a general understanding of the entity's business (entity's organization and operating characteristics) provides a basis for understanding the nature of the entity's assets, liabilities, revenues, and expenses. For example, if the entity is in an industry characterized by significant sales returns, the accountant would expect to see not only a sales return and allowance account but also supporting control procedures and methodology that suggest a reasonable estimate of the year-end sales returns the entity expects to make after the balance sheet date.

Assets

1.65 Routine accounting procedures are used to properly record and measure an entity's assets and, if appropriate, allocate the cost of certain assets to the income statement. For example, routine cash procedures include the preparation of bank reconciliations on a timely basis and the surprise counting (by entity personnel) of cash funds on-hand. Also, less routine procedures would have to be adopted if cosignees hold a considerable amount of the entity's inventory.

Liabilities

1.66 Routine procedures for accounting for liabilities might include using a voucher system to control cash disbursements and record liabilities on a timely basis. Less routine procedures may include an assessment of contract liabilities, such as threatened litigation or accounting for finance (capital) leases.

Revenues

1.67 Routine accounting procedures would be expected to record sales when the basis of revenue recognition is the delivery date for the goods or services. However, if the entity is involved in the construction of buildings, equipment, and similar assets that require a long construction period, the entity would have to consider whether the percentage-of-completion method is more appropriate than the completed-contract method for revenue recognition. If it is, the entity would need to implement estimation procedures to institute this revenue recognition method successfully.

Expenses

1.68 Generally, routine accounting procedures are in place to recognize personnel costs, cost of sales, and other operating expenses. However, other transactions—such as defined benefit pension plans and stock compensation plans—require a level of accounting sophistication that cannot be characterized as routine, that is, requiring complex accounting procedures.

Designing and Performing Review Procedures

1.69 According to paragraph .17 of AR-C section 90, based on the accountant's understanding of the industry, his or her knowledge of the entity, and his or her awareness of the risks that the accountant may unknowingly fail to modify the accountant's review report on financial statements that are materially misstated, the accountant should design and perform analytical procedures and make inquiries and perform other procedures, as appropriate, to obtain limited assurance as a basis for reporting whether the accountant is aware of any material modifications that should be made to the financial statements in order for the statements to be in accordance with the applicable financial reporting framework.

 ©2017, AICPA

1.70 Although evidence obtained through the performance of analytical procedures and inquiry will ordinarily provide the accountant with a reasonable basis for obtaining limited assurance, the practitioner may find it necessary to design and perform additional procedures if the accountant believes that the performance of analytical procedures and inquiries by themselves do not provide a basis for obtaining limited assurance. Keeping in mind that analytical procedures and inquiries are required in all review engagements, the accountant may choose a combination of additional procedures to obtain limited assurance. The following procedures, for example, may be performed:

- Inspection
- Observation
- Confirmation
- Recalculation
- Reperformance

1.71 Understanding the industry and knowledge of the entity usually includes having an awareness of (*a*) broad economic conditions, (*b*) industry-specific conditions, and (*c*) entity-specific conditions. For example, if the accountant is aware that the entity has built or purchased additional warehouse facilities during the current year, the accountant would expect that depreciation expense would likely increase.

1.72 The accountant should focus analytical procedures and inquiries in those areas where the accountant believes there are increased risks of material misstatements.

Observations and Suggestions

If the accountant performs procedures in addition to analytical procedures and inquiries, the engagement remains a review, and the accountant is not required to perform an audit of the financial statements.

Analytical Procedures

1.73 Analytical procedures involve the study, comparison, and evaluation of relationships among financial and nonfinancial data at a point in time and the trend in those relationships over a period of time. A basic premise underlying analytical procedures is that plausible relationships among data may reasonably be expected to exist in the absence of known conditions to the contrary. Particular conditions that can cause variations in these relationships include, for example, specific unusual transactions or events, accounting changes, business changes, or misstatements.

1.74 Understanding financial and nonfinancial relationships is essential in planning and evaluating the results of analytical procedures and, generally, requires knowledge of the entity and the industry in which the entity operates. An understanding of the purposes of analytical procedures and the limitations of those procedures also is important. Accordingly, the identification of the relationships and types of data used, as well as conclusions reached when recorded amounts are compared with expectations, requires judgment.

1.75 Analytical procedures involve comparisons of recorded amounts, or ratios developed from recorded amounts, with expectations the accountant develops. *Expectations* are the accountant's predictions of recorded amounts or ratios developed from recorded amounts. In performing analytical procedures, the accountant develops expectations in such a way that material differences between the expectations and the recorded amounts or ratios developed from those recorded amounts may be indicative of possible misstatements, and therefore, the accountant should obtain explanations for the differences (for example, an unusual event occurred). Expectations are developed by identifying plausible relationships (for example, store square footage and retail sales) that are reasonably expected to exist based on the accountant's understanding of the entity and the industry in which the entity operates. A variety of data sources exist from which the accountant can form expectations. For example, the accountant may use prior period information (adjusted for expected changes), management's budgets or forecasts, industry data, or nonfinancial data.

1.76 The accountant develops expectations by identifying and using plausible relationships that are reasonably expected to exist based on the accountant's understanding of the industry in which the entity operates and knowledge of the entity's business. Following are examples of information sources for developing expectations:

- *a.* Financial information for comparable prior period(s), giving consideration to known changes
- *b.* Anticipated results (for example, budgets or forecasts, including extrapolations from interim or annual data)
- *c.* Relationships among elements of financial information within the period
- *d.* Information regarding the industry in which the entity operates (for example, gross margin information)
- *e.* Relationships of financial information with relevant nonfinancial information (for example, payroll costs to number of employees)

1.77 The accountant cannot, under any circumstances, perform effective analytical procedures without first developing expectations related to the results of those analytical procedures. Expectations the accountant develops in performing analytical procedures in connection with a review of financial statements ordinarily are less encompassing than those developed in an audit.

1.78 The accountant should apply analytical procedures to the financial statements to identify and provide a basis for inquiry about the relationships and individual items that appear to be unusual and may indicate a material misstatement. Such analytical procedures should include the following:

- *a.* Comparing the financial statements with comparable information for the prior period, giving consideration to knowledge about changes in the entity's business and specific transactions
- *b.* Considering plausible relationships among both financial and, when relevant, nonfinancial information
- *c.* Comparing recorded amounts or ratios developed from recorded amounts to expectations developed by the accountant through identifying and using relationships that are reasonably expected to exist, based on the accountant's understanding of the entity and the industry in which the entity operates
- *d.* Comparing disaggregated revenue data, as applicable. The following are examples of how data may be disaggregated:

 ©2017, AICPA

i. By period (for example, financial statement items disaggregated into quarterly, monthly, or weekly amounts)
ii. By product line or operating segment
iii. By location (for example, subsidiary, division, or branch)

1.79 When designing and performing analytical procedures, the accountant should

a. determine the suitability of particular analytical procedures;

b. consider the reliability of data from which the accountant's expectation of recorded amounts or ratios is developed—taking into account the source, comparability, and nature and relevance of information available;

c. develop an expectation of recorded amounts or ratios and evaluate whether the expectation is sufficiently precise to provide the accountant with limited assurance that a misstatement will be identified that, either individually or when aggregated with other misstatements, may cause the financial statements to be materially misstated; and

d. determine the amount of any difference of recorded amounts from expected values that is acceptable without further investigation as required by paragraph .21 of AR-C section 90 and compare the recorded amounts, or ratios developed from recorded amounts, with the expectations.

1.80 Examples of analytical procedures the accountant may consider performing in a review of financial statements include, but are not limited to, the following:

- Comparing financial statements with statements for comparable prior period(s)
- Comparing current financial information with anticipated results, such as budgets or forecasts (for example, comparing tax balances and the relationship between the provision for income taxes and pretax income in the current financial information with corresponding information in budgets, using expected rates, and financial information for prior periods).
- Comparing current financial information with relevant nonfinancial information
- Comparing ratios and indicators for the current period with expectations based on prior periods (for example, performing gross profit analysis by product line and operating segment using elements of the current financial information and comparing the results with corresponding information for prior periods)
- Comparing ratios and indicators for the current period with those of entities in the same industry
- Comparing relationships among elements in the current financial information with corresponding relationships in the financial information of prior periods (for example, expense by type as a percentage of sales, assets by type as a percentage of total assets, and percentage of change in sales to percentage of change in receivables)

1.81 Analytical procedures may include such statistical techniques as trend analysis or regression analysis and may be performed manually or with the use of computer-assisted techniques.

1.82 Analytical procedures often will provide a basis for additional inquiries because the procedures may identify other significant matters affecting the financial statements that might otherwise not have been apparent.

Types of Analytical Procedures

1.83 The accountant can use various types of analytical procedures to evaluate the reasonableness of the financial information, ranging from simple comparisons to complex models involving many relationships and elements of data. The following are the three broad types of analytical procedures commonly used by accountants:

1. *Trend analysis*. The comparison of a recorded amount to the prior year balance or to a trend of balances from two or more periods. A common example is comparing monthly totals for sales for the current and preceding year.
2. *Ratio analysis*. The comparison of a ratio calculated for the current period to a related or similar ratio for a prior period, an industry standard, or a budget. Financial and operating ratios commonly are classified into four major categories: liquidity, profitability, leverage, and activity ratios.
3. *Model-based procedures (reasonableness tests)*. The use of entity operating data and the relevant external data (industry information and general economic information) to develop an expectation for the recorded amount. These procedures typically use operating and external data, in addition to financial data, to perform reasonableness tests. For example, the number of employees can be used to determine average wages or vacation pay per employee.

1.84 In practice, a specific analytical procedure may take on characteristics of all three types of procedures (trend analysis, ratio analysis, and reasonableness tests). For example, the results of computing the current ratio (ratio analysis) are compared with current ratios of previous years (trend analysis) and evaluated based on the accountant's understanding of current factors affecting the entity's working capital accounts (test of reasonableness).

Comparison of Current Financial Data to Prior Periods

1.85 The method most commonly used in practice is comparison with amounts from prior periods. This involves using financial information for the comparable prior period(s) (giving consideration to known changes) to develop expected amounts and comparing these expected amounts with current-year recorded amounts.

1.86 A variety of techniques are used to facilitate comparisons, including trend analysis and ratio analysis. Common examples include the following:

- Compare the current year's account balance with that of a prior year.
- Compare the detail of the current year's account balance with that of a prior year.
- Compare current year ratios with those of the prior year.

 ©2017, AICPA

- Compare current year percentage relationships with previous years.

Comparison of Current Financial Data to Budgets and Forecasts

1.87 Although many small businesses do not prepare meaningful budgets or forecasts, comparison with carefully prepared budgets and forecasts may be very effective. Even when financial budgets or forecasts are not prepared, some companies maintain manufacturing or production budgets that may be very effective for certain analytical purposes.

> **Observations and Suggestions**
>
> Keep in mind that management may be motivated to manipulate financial results to meet budgets or forecasts and that budgets or forecasts may be used more for motivational purposes than as realistic expectations.

Comparisons to Industry Data

1.88 Published industry data can provide a rich source of information for analytical procedures. A number of industry trade organizations publish industry data. If the entity is a member of an industry trade organization, data may be available directly from the organization. However, if an entity differs from the other firms in the industry with respect to such characteristics as ownership or financial structure, product diversity, age of assets, or customer mix, then the industry ratios may not be meaningful or may need to be adjusted..

Comparisons Using Nonfinancial Information

1.89 An entity may generate a variety of nonfinancial data that may be used to make comparisons with recorded amounts. Examples of this data are as follows:

- Production in units
- Direct labor hours
- Number of sales calls
- Size of sales staff
- Square feet of selling space

1.90 Because nonfinancial operating data often are generated and maintained outside of the accounting department, comparisons involving such data can offer an independent check on the reasonableness of related financial information. Tests involving nonfinancial data are sometimes referred to as reasonableness tests because nonfinancial data are used to determine the reasonableness of amounts recorded in the financial information. The accountant would consider the accuracy and completeness of the nonfinancial data.

Limitations of Analytical Procedures

1.91 Analytical procedures can provide a useful insight into the evaluation of an entity's financial statements in a review engagement; however, like any tool, they have limitations.

Relationship of the Past to the Future

1.92 Analytical procedures, especially those related to trend analysis, are based on past events. Results from prior periods are not always an indication of what should occur in the current period. The historical ratios and trend analyses can provide some insight into the future but only if they are evaluated in the context of current factors. Analyzing what has happened in the past is necessary and useful in performing analytical procedures, but it is certain that the future environment in which a business will operate will be, to some extent, different from the environment in which it operated in the past.

It Is Still Judgmental

1.93 The performance of analytical procedures obviously results in numbers. The accountant may, for example, compute the current ratio or the debt-to-equity ratio. Though those statistics are verifiable, a tendency exists for the numbers to hide the judgment involved in the process. The purpose of the analysis is not to compute innumerable statistics—that is, only a means to an end. The purpose of the analysis is to provide insight into the financial statements. That assessment, although based on quantitative information (the various ratios) and qualitative information (for example, the general economic conditions), is in the final analysis based on the accountant's informed and overall judgment.

Diversified Businesses

1.94 The computation of analytical procedures previously described assumes that the business operates in one industry. This assumption allows the accountant to compare a business's ratios with those experienced by the industry in which it operates. The assumption makes it easier to evaluate the results of the financial statement analysis in the context of the economics and governmental regulation of a single industry. In reality, many businesses operate in diversified industries. Although diversification is a characteristic of large publicly held companies, closely held companies and other private enterprises also can be involved in disparate business activities.

1.95 When the resources (balance sheets) and activities (income statements) of a diversified business are combined, segments that are performing poorly are combined with highly successful units, and the overall financial information may be misinterpreted. In order to resolve this potential distortion, financial statement information may be reported and then analyzed on a disaggregated basis. Ideally, financial statements are presented for each significant segment of the diversified business. Financial reporting standards require that public companies present information on a segment basis in a note to the financial statements. For a closely held company, the accountant may want to request that the financial information be segregated into business segments, product lines, or some other classification scheme that provides a basis for meaningful analysis.

Practical Guidelines

1.96 The nature, timing, and extent of the analytical procedures are a matter of judgment. In determining the appropriate analytical procedures, the accountant may consider: (*a*) the nature and materiality of the items reflected in the financial statements, (*b*) the likelihood of a misstatement in the financial statements, (*c*) knowledge obtained during current and previous engagements,

 ©2017, AICPA

(*d*) the stated qualifications of the entity's accounting personnel, (*e*) the extent to which a particular item is affected by management's judgment, and (*f*) inadequacies in the entity's underlying financial data. Although professional judgment should be used in the selection of analytical procedures, the accountant might consider the preceding practical guidelines in making the selection.

Level of Detail

1.97 Information gathered from applying analytical procedures is quite broad. For this reason, analytical procedures are most useful when they are applied to disaggregated data. For example, it is generally more useful to compute the gross profit margin for a single product line than for the company as a whole. Of course, the level of detail at which the accountant will apply analytical procedures to the financial information depends on the entity's practices for collecting, processing, and storing data. Analytical procedures may be performed at the financial statement level or the detailed account level.

Estimates

1.98 Accounting estimates lack the precision of financial information that is derived from specific transactions. Ranges of acceptable amounts will be larger for balances based on estimates than for balances based on actual transactions. For example, the amount of revenue a retailer recognizes should be based on the summation of all individual sales made during the period; however, the balance in an estimated warranty liability account will be based on the entity's judgment for such factors as rate of product return and estimated cost of future repair work. Generally, an acceptable deviation from the financial statement amount is going to be somewhat larger for the estimated liability than for actual sales.

Developing Expectations

1.99 The development of expectations about an entity is highly judgmental. The following fundamental categories of information may assist the accountant in developing expectations about an entity:

- Broad economic conditions
- Industry-specific conditions
- Entity-specific conditions

Broad Economic Conditions

1.100 Broad economic conditions establish the background for developing expectations concerning an entity. Different phases of the regional and national business cycle can have a significant effect on the entity and, ultimately, the entity's financial statements. For example, if interest rates are on an upward trend, the accountant would expect the entity's interest costs (assuming the amount of debt outstanding is relatively stable and its maturity is short-term) to increase compared with the previous year's results.

1.101 Generally, broad economic conditions are not documented in the review documentation; rather, the accountant's awareness of the conditions provides a framework in which more specific information is evaluated. For example, changes in the level of interest rates may be an important factor for an entity with significant short-term debt. Conversely, for an entity with little or no debt or with debt with fixed interest rates, changes in the level of interest rates would not be important in forming expectations about the entity's financial statements.

Industry-Specific Conditions

1.102 The conditions that characterize the entity's industry provide information that allows the accountant to formulate more detailed expectations about the entity. These conditions include the economic cycle of the industry, the maturity of the industry, the pace of technological change within the industry, and relevant governmental regulations. For example, if the entity's industry is in the trough of the business cycle, the accountant would expect excess operating capacity to create significant volume variances that would affect the gross profit margin and the entity's overall profitability.

1.103 Industry-specific conditions generally are not documented in a review engagement because, like broad economic conditions, they provide the background information for developing expectations about the entity. Some of the factors may be relevant to one engagement, but other factors may be relevant to another engagement. Once a specific condition related to the industry is considered to be relevant to developing an understanding of an entity, however, the accountant should determine its relevance to developing expectations in the analytical procedures. For example, if there has been a changed level of competition in the industry since the previous review engagement, the accountant may expect the gross profit margin of the entity to change.

Entity-Specific Conditions

1.104 Generally, awareness of factors unique to an entity is obtained through inquiry or prior knowledge of the entity. The accountant may have developed knowledge of an entity's production methods, distribution system, and products and services as a result of having performed prior review engagements and other services for the entity. For example, on the basis of prior reviews of an entity's financial statements, the accountant might be aware that the entity usually makes costing errors when pricing certain raw materials.

Investigating Actual Results and Expectations

1.105 If analytical procedures performed identify fluctuations or relationships that are inconsistent with other relevant information or that differ from expected values by a significant amount, the accountant should investigate these differences by inquiring of management and performing other review procedures if considered necessary in the circumstances. Review evidence relevant to management's responses may be obtained by evaluating those responses, taking into account the accountant's understanding of the entity and its environment, along with other review evidence obtained during the course of the review. Although the accountant is not required to corroborate management's responses with other evidence, the accountant may need to perform other procedures when, for example, management is unable to provide an explanation or the explanation, together with review evidence obtained relevant to management's response, is not considered adequate.

1.106 Comparing actual results to expectations consists of the accountant developing guidelines on what defines a significant deviation. For example, an entity's gross profit percentage might be 47 percent this year compared with 45 percent last year, and the accountant has the expectation that, in general, there is no reason to expect a change in the gross profit percentage. In this case,

 ©2017, AICPA

the 2 percentage-point difference may or may not be considered significant, depending on the level of precision of the analysis.

1.107 In determining whether a difference between an actual result and an expectation is significant, the accountant relates the item being analyzed to materiality thresholds established for the engagement. For example, in the case of the gross profit percentage difference of 2 percentage points, the accountant may have determined that an item is potentially material if operating income could be misstated by 7 percent or current assets could be misstated by 10 percent. Initially, the 2 percentage point difference may or may not be treated as an error. If it is determined to be an error, the accountant converts it to a dollar amount and relates it to (*a*) operating income (cost of goods sold understated and tax expense understated) and (*b*) current assets (ending inventories overstated).

1.108 The materiality analysis is preliminary and is performed to provide the accountant with some direction. If the assumed error is clearly immaterial, the accountant generally would not investigate the matter further. If the assumed error is material or approaches the materiality threshold, the accountant should investigate such differences, as discussed in paragraph 1.105. In the preceding example of the unexpected increase in the gross profit percentage, the accountant may decide to inquire further about the entity's inventory count procedures or perform further analytics on the costing for the inventory summarization.

1.109 The identification of significant differences to be investigated based on the application of analytical procedures concentrates on comparing actual results and expectations, not simply on comparing actual results from comparative years. For example, in computing gross profit percentages, the accountant may discover that the percentage is essentially the same for each year. This does not necessarily mean that the results do not require additional investigation. In the current engagement, the accountant may discover that the gross profit for a line of products is expected to decrease because a competitor began to sell a similar product during the current year. The lack of change in gross profit percentages may indicate a misstatement that could have a material effect on the financial statements.

1.110 The evaluation of the results of applying analytical procedures depends on the materiality of the accounts and transactions being analyzed. Thus, the accountant should utilize professional judgment in selecting analytical procedures for each individual engagement. In other words, usually, no reason exists to apply analytical procedures to items that clearly could not have a material effect on the financial statements. In addition, for those items that have been reviewed by applying other procedures, analytical procedures may not be necessary.

Engagement Efficiency

1.111 In a review engagement, the following steps may help improve efficiency related to analytical procedures:

- Omit or limit comparisons of current-year financial data to budgets or forecasts if prior experience with the entity has shown that the budgets and forecasts are unreasonable, unrealistic, or do not represent management's best estimate.

- Before spending any amount of time performing analytical procedures involving comparisons with industry data, evaluate if the entity's line of business is the same as that on which the industry standards are based and whether there is significant variation in the data reported and the structure of the companies.
- When planning analytical procedures, determine the extent and availability of entity-prepared financial and operating data and become familiar with such information. Most entities develop a vast amount of information to help management analyze operations and make business decisions. Before spending the time to accumulate and analyze such information, try to obtain any internally prepared management reports and analyses that would serve the same purpose.

1.112 Sometimes, accountants tend to perform an excessive number of analytical procedures and ratios, regardless of their relevance to the engagement. Before performing an analytical procedure or ratio, ask what type of useful evidence this relationship provides.

1.113 In applying analytical procedures in a review engagement, both effectiveness and efficiency may be achieved by using the following approach:

1. Identify account balances or classes of transactions to which other accounting services (for example, bookkeeping or payroll services) have been applied. Consider the evidence already obtained and whether any material errors are likely to remain. If current and relevant review evidence for those account balances has been obtained from other services to provide limited assurance that they are not materially misstated, do not apply analytical procedures to them.
2. For the remaining account balances, develop expectations for them (for example, using historical trends adjusted for known changes). The precision of analytical procedures will vary, based on the accountant's risk awareness and professional judgment. For larger balances in which the accountant believes there may be higher risks of material misstatement, the accountant may want to design and perform analytical procedures that are more precise in order to obtain review evidence that the account is not materially misstated. For smaller balances or when the risks of material misstatement are lower, the accountant may design and perform analytical procedures that are less precise.
3. Identify immaterial account balances or classes of transactions. Apply no analytical procedures to them.
4. Consider how close the existing account balance or class of transaction comes to the expectation developed in item (2). If the differences are within an acceptable range, based on professional judgment, then no additional evidence is needed.
5. If the differences are large, material errors could exist. As a result, inquire about valid business reasons for the difference. If the results of inquiry are plausible and agree with other evidence, then the accountant may conclude that no additional evidence is necessary in the circumstance.

 ©2017, AICPA

6. If additional evidence is needed, the accountant should apply other review procedures to obtain suitable evidence as necessary in the circumstances.

Illustrative Analytics

1.114 The purpose of the documentation guidance presented here is to illustrate how the accountant might document expectations in a review engagement. The examples are presented for illustrative purposes only and are not intended to represent either minimum or maximum documentation requirements.

Example 1—Expected Increase in Revenue

1.115 The accountant is engaged to review the financial statements of a company that manufactures components that are utilized by other companies in customizing video gaming equipment. Because of recent legislation in several states that legalized slot machine gambling, the accountant reasonably expects sales to increase. Using his or her knowledge of the entity, the entity's business, and the industry in which the entity operates, the accountant expects a 10 percent to 15 percent increase in sales. Further, the accountant concludes that receivables should increase and that loans payable and interest expense also would increase because the entity would need to borrow money to fund the additional production.

Sample documentation

Teemickmag Gaming Company

Analytical Procedures

For the year ended December 31, 20X2

Expectations

The following are factors that should affect the relationship between current and prior year amounts:

- Increase in demand for video gaming equipment due to recent legislation in several states that legalized slot machine gambling should result in an increase in sales. Expected increase is between 10 percent and 15 percent. The accountant expects a similar increase in accounts receivable and days sales in receivables.
- Because of an increase in the production of video gaming equipment, the company had to borrow additional funds. Therefore, expected increase in loans payable and interest expense is between 10 percent and 15 percent.
- No significant change in either days sales in inventory or inventory turnover is expected. Although a build-up in inventory is expected, that build-up is not expected to correspond with the increase in sales because the video gaming equipment is expected to be sold near the date of completion. Any change greater than 5 percent will be subjected to additional inquiries.

Balance sheets and income statements are available for the current year and the two years prior to the current year.

	Trend Analysis			
	Current Year	*Prior Year*	*Change*	*% Change*
Sales	$2,500,000	$2,175,000	$325,000	14.94%
Cost of goods sold	1,780,000	1,566,000	214,000	13.67%
Gross margin	720,000	609,000		
Gross margin as a % of sales	28.80%	28.00%		
Selling expenses	230,000	184,000	46,000	25.00%
Interest expense	48,000	42,000	6,000	14.29%

	Balance Sheet Ratio Analysis		
	Current Year	*Prior Year*	*Two Years Prior*
Accounts receivable, net	$1,100,000	$843,000	$703,000
Inventory	1,000,000	832,000	694,000
Loans payable	498,000	437,000	418,000

<u>Days sales in receivables</u>

Days sales in receivables = Accounts receivable, net at end of period ÷ (Net sales ÷ 365)

Current year days sales in receivables = $1,100,000 ÷ ($2,500,000 ÷ 365) = 161 days

Prior year days sales in receivables = $843,000 ÷ ($2,175,000 ÷ 365) = 141 days

The increase of 20 days sales in receivables (161 days – 141 days) represents a 14 percent increase. Because this increase is within the expected range, no further inquiry is necessary.

<u>Days sales in inventory</u>

Days sales in inventory = Inventory at the end of period ÷ (Total cost of goods sold ÷ 365)

Current year days sales in inventory = $1,000,000 ÷ ($1,780,000 ÷ 365) = 205 days

Prior year days sales in inventory = $832,000 ÷ ($1,566,000 ÷ 365) = 194 days

The increase of 11 days sales in inventory (205 days – 194 days) represents a 6 percent increase. Because this increase is greater than expected, the accountant should inquire of the entity and document the reason for the unexpected increase.

<u>Inventory turnover</u>

Inventory turnover = Cost of goods sold ÷ Average inventory

Current year inventory turnover = $1,780,000 ÷ (($1,000,000 + 832,000) ÷ 2) = 1.94 times

Prior year inventory turnover = $1,566,000 ÷ (($832,000 + 694,000) ÷ 2) = 2.05 times

©2017, AICPA

The inventory turnover decreased 11 percent; therefore, because this decrease is greater than expected, the accountant should inquire of the entity and document the reason for the unexpected decrease.

The preceding documentation would be adequate. Further, after performing the trend analysis, the accountant concludes that sales, costs of goods sold, and interest expense are all reasonable, given the expectations associated with these amounts. In addition, with respect to balance sheet accounts, the increase in loans payable also is reasonable (14 percent increase) when considered with the corresponding increase in interest expense and the expectation associated with the loan payable account; however, because selling expenses increased by 25 percent, the accountant should inquire of the entity and document the reason for that unexpected increase (actual increase does not correspond to expected increase).

Example 2—Expected Decrease in Revenue

1.116 The accountant is engaged to review the financial statements of an entity that owns and manages a shopping mall. Due to a poor economy, the mall lost tenants during the year; as such, the accountant reasonably expects revenue to decrease. Using his or her knowledge of the entity, the entity's business, and the industry in which the entity operates, the accountant expects a 5 percent to 10 percent decrease in revenue during the year. Further, the accountant expects that general and administrative expenses should increase due to an increase in leasing and sales expenses and that management fees should decrease due to a decrease in tenants in the building.

<u>Sample documentation</u>

Pearl River Mall

Analytical Procedures

For the year ended December 31, 20X2

<u>Expectations</u>

The following are factors that should affect the relationship between current and prior year amounts:

- Loss of tenants due to poor economy should result in a decrease in revenue. Expected decrease is between 5 percent and 10 percent.
- Because of the increased number of vacancies, general and administrative expenses are expected to increase because of an increase in leasing and sales expenses. Expected increase is between 5 percent and 10 percent (corresponds with the decrease in revenue).
- Because of the decrease in the number of tenants in the building, management fees are expected to decrease between 5 percent and 10 percent (corresponds with decrease in revenue).

Balance sheets and income statements are available for the current year and the two years prior to the current year.

	Trend Analysis			
	Current Year	*Prior Year*	*Change*	*% Change*
Total revenue	$7,223,000	$8,603,000	$(1,380,000)	(16.04)%
Costs and expenses: management fees	339,000	387,000	(48,000)	(12.40)%
General and administrative	583,000	511,000	72,000	14.09%

Similar balance sheet analytics would be performed as those performed in the preceding example 1.

The preceding documentation would be adequate; however, the results of the analytical procedures do not agree with the documented expectations associated with those procedures. Therefore, the accountant should inquire and document why the decrease in tenant revenue, the decrease in management fees, and the increase in general and administrative expenses exceeded expectations.

Example 3—No Significant Change in Revenue or Expenses Expected

1.117 The accountant is engaged to review the financial statements of a small, privately held entity in the candy store business. The accountant has performed a review of the financial statements of the candy store for each of the past five years with no significant change in revenue or expenses in any of those years. The accountant expects that trend to continue.

Sample documentation

Mom and Pop Candy Store

Analytical Procedures

For the year ended December 31, 20X2

Expectations

- Based on discussions with the owner-manager, no significant changes from prior year amounts are expected.
- All increases and decreases greater than 5 percent will be subjected to additional inquiries.

	Trend Analysis			
	Current Year	*Prior Year*	*Change*	*% Change*
Sales	$44,000	$39,000	$5,000	12.82%
Cost of goods sold	32,500	31,000	1,500	4.84%
Gross margin	11,500	8,000		
Gross margin as a % of sales	26.14%	20.51%		
Operating expenses	5,200	4,500	700	15.56%
Net income	6,300	3,500		

Similar balance sheet analytics would be performed as those performed in the preceding example 1.

 ©2017, AICPA

The preceding documentation would be adequate; however, the results of the analytical procedures do not agree with the documented expectations associated with those procedures. Therefore, the accountant may deem it appropriate to inquire and document why sales increased by an amount greater than expected. In addition, the accountant should inquire about why there was not a comparable increase in cost of goods sold. Also, the accountant should discuss with the owner-manager why there is a greater than expected increase in operating expenses and document the results of the discussion.

Example 4—Expected Changes in Construction Contracts

1.118 The accountant is engaged to review the financial statements of a general construction contractor primarily engaged in the construction of commercial office buildings. The accountant has performed the review of this company's financial statements for several years and expects that the current project in process should yield a 5 percent gross profit margin, consistent with similar projects in the past and in accordance with the initial project estimate.

Sample documentation

Charlton, Donnelly, and Oates Construction Contractors

Analytical Procedures

For the Year Ended December 31, 20X2

Expectations

- Based upon discussions with the project manager, it is believed that the gross margin will be consistent with the 5 percent margin achieved in the past and in accordance with the initial project estimate.
- Any deviation in the margin greater than 1 percent will be subjected to additional inquiries.

	Trend Analysis			
Building Contract	*Current Year*	*Prior Year*	*$ Change*	*% Change*
Contract value	$5,000,000	$5,000,000		
Estimated costs at completion	4,900,000	4,750,000	$150,000	3.16%
Planned profit	100,000	250,000	(150,000)	60.00%
Costs incurred	2,500,000	1,000,000		
Profit recognized contract to date	50,000	50,000		

1.119 The preceding documentation indicates that the profit margin on the contract has slipped from 5 percent to 2 percent. Additionally, in accordance with the cost-to-cost method of percentage of completion accounting, it now appears that all of the contract profit was recognized in year one. This may indicate a potential error in the original estimate or a project that is quickly running over budget. The result may be a reversal of profits recognized in earlier periods under the percentage of completion method of contract revenue recognition or a potential loss contract. Further inquiry of management should be considered to discuss potential project issues that will negatively affect profit recognition in the financial statements.

Inquiries and Other Review Procedures

1.120 Inquiry is a fundamental technique used in a review engagement to collect evidence relevant to the financial statements. Although the process of inquiry is simple, successful use of the technique depends on the individual who makes the inquiries. Specifically, the inquiry procedures are most effective when the accountant considers what questions to ask and pursues a significant line of aggressive questioning. The quality of the review engagement is reduced if the accountant performs inquiry in a mechanical fashion and accepts responses from entity personnel without being appropriately skeptical.

1.121 A variety of similar questions apply to almost all review engagements. Most of these standard questions are asked in a somewhat formal manner, interviewing appropriate entity personnel and recording their responses directly in the review documentation.

1.122 Inquiry certainly is not limited to the formal process previously described. As the accountant becomes aware of a circumstance, fact, or relationship, the accountant will logically see a number of questions that can be asked. On the basis of responses given by the entity's personnel, the direction of the questioning may change or it may stop because the accountant is satisfied with the answer. In a review engagement, the inquiry process is an ongoing activity, reflecting the accountant's inquisitive nature and professional judgment.

1.123 The review engagement does not contain a specific place where inquiry should begin or end. The effectiveness of the review engagement is improved when the accountant remains inquisitive throughout the review engagement, raising appropriate questions and carefully evaluating the responses in the context of the specific engagement. In addition, it is not possible to script the inquiries that should be made in a review engagement. Each engagement is unique, and each practitioner is unique. Nonetheless, effective inquiries are focused and relevant. Asking irrelevant questions results in an inefficient review engagement and can damage entity confidence.

1.124 Although SSARSs state that the accountant should inquire of members of management who have responsibility for financial and accounting matters, the accountant may also direct inquiries to others within the entity and those charged with governance, if appropriate.

1.125 Because of the nature of the inquiry technique previously described, no complete list exists of the inquiries that should be made in a review engagement; however, SSARSs specifically identify the following as areas of interest that should be explored with management.

Inquiries Concerning Whether the Financial Statements Have Been Prepared and Fairly Presented

1.126 According to paragraph .22*a* of AR-C section 90, the accountant should make inquiries regarding whether the financial statements have been prepared and fairly presented in accordance with the applicable financial reporting framework consistently applied. As part of this inquiry, the accountant would consider whether there have been changes in the application of accounting principles. If such changes have occurred, follow-up inquiries would assist the accountant in concluding whether the changes are appropriate and, if so,

 ©2017, AICPA

whether the changes have been accounted for and disclosed in a manner consistent with the applicable financial reporting framework.

1.127 As discussed earlier, the accountant's understanding of the entity should include an understanding of the procedures and accounting principles that the entity uses. The entity's procedures and accounting principles should be adequate to record, classify, and summarize transactions and accumulate information for disclosure in the financial statements in accordance with the applicable financial reporting framework. The understanding of the nature of the entity's accounts provides the accountant with background to determine whether the procedures and accounting principles used are appropriate for the entity's industry.

1.128 Inquiries relative to the recording of transactions are focused on how individual transactions are authorized and documented and how those transactions are recorded in a book of original entry. Inquiries that relate to the classification of transactions provide evidence about how transactions are coded and to what extent supporting accounting manuals and descriptions are available that describe what transactions should be processed through a particular account. Inquiries concerning the summarization of transactions address the issue of how books of original entry are used to update the general ledger. Finally, the accountant may also make inquiries about how information is accumulated to provide a basis for disclosures in the financial statements.

Inquiries Concerning Unusual or Complex Situations That May Have an Effect on the Financial Statements

1.129 Paragraph .22 of AR-C section 90 also requires the accountant to inquire about unusual or complex situations that may have an effect on the financial statements. The following are examples of situations that may have an effect on the financial statements about which the accountant would ordinarily inquire:

- Business combinations
- New or complex revenue recognition methods
- Impairment of assets
- Disposal of a business segment
- Use of derivative instruments and hedging activities
- Sales and transfers that may call into question the classification of investments in securities, including management's intent and ability with respect to the remaining securities classified as held to maturity
- Adoption of new stock compensation plans or changes to existing plans
- Restructuring charges taken in the current and prior periods
- Significant, unusual, or infrequently occurring transactions
- Changes in litigation or contingencies
- Changes in major contracts with customers or suppliers
- Application of new accounting principles
- Changes in accounting principles or the methods of applying them

©2017, AICPA

- Trends and developments affecting accounting estimates, such as allowance for bad debts and excess or obsolete inventories, provisions for warranties and employee benefits, and realization of unearned income and deferred charges
- Compliance with debt covenants
- Changes in related parties or significant new related party transactions
- Material off-balance-sheet transactions, special-purpose entities, and other equity investments
- Unique terms for debt or capital stock that could affect classification.

Inquiries Concerning Significant Transactions Occurring or Recognized During the Period

1.130 Paragraph .22 of AR-C section 90 requires the accountant to inquire about significant transactions occurring or recognized during the period, particularly those in the last several days of the period.

Inquiries Concerning the Status of Uncorrected Misstatements Identified During the Previous Review

1.131 Paragraph .22 of AR-C section 90 requires the accountant to inquire about the status of uncorrected misstatements identified during the previous review. That is, whether adjustments had been recorded subsequent to the periods covered by the prior review and, if so, the amounts recorded and period in which such adjustments were recorded.

Inquiries Concerning Matters About Which Questions Have Arisen

1.132 Paragraph .22 of AR-C section 90 requires the accountant to inquire about matters about which questions have arisen in the course of applying the review procedures.

Inquiries Concerning Events Subsequent to the Date of the Financial Statements

1.133 Paragraph .22 of AR-C section 90 requires the accountant to inquire about events subsequent to the date of the financial statements that could have a material effect on the financial statements. When evidence or information that subsequent events that require adjustment of, or disclosure in, the financial statements comes to an accountant's attention during a review engagement, the accountant should request that management consider whether each such event is appropriately reflected in the financial statements in accordance with the applicable financial reporting framework.

Inquiries Concerning Fraud or Suspected Fraud Affecting the Entity

1.134 Paragraph .22 of AR-C section 90 requires the accountant to inquire about management's (who has responsibility for financial or accounting matters) knowledge of any fraud or suspected fraud affecting the entity involving (*a*) management, (*b*) employees who have significant roles in internal control, or (*c*) others when the fraud could have a material effect on the financial statements.

 ©2017, AICPA

1.135 The accountant is also required to inquire whether management is aware of any fraud or suspected fraud affecting the entity communicated by employees, former employees, regulators, or others.

Inquiries Concerning Known Instances of Noncompliance or Suspected Noncompliance With Laws and Regulations

1.136 Paragraph .22 of AR-C section 90 requires the accountant to inquire whether management has disclosed to the accountant all known instances of noncompliance with laws and regulations whose effects should be considered when preparing financial statements.

Inquiries Concerning Significant Journal Entries

1.137 Paragraph .22 of AR-C section 90 requires the accountant to inquire about any significant journal entries and other adjustments.

Inquiries Concerning Communications From Regulatory Agencies

1.138 Paragraph .22 of AR-C section 90 requires the accountant to inquire about communications from regulatory agencies, if applicable.

Inquiries Concerning Related Parties and Significant New Related Party Transactions

1.139 Paragraph .22 of AR-C section 90 requires the accountant to inquire about related parties and significant new related party transactions.

Inquiries Concerning Any Litigation, Claims, and Assessments

1.140 Paragraph .22 of AR-C section 90 requires the accountant to inquire about any litigation, claims, and assessments that existed at the date of the balance sheet being reported on and during the period from the balance sheet date to the date of management's response to the accountant's inquiry.

Inquiries Concerning Significant Assumptions

1.141 Paragraph .22 of AR-C section 90 requires the accountant to inquire whether management believes that significant assumptions used by it in making accounting estimates are reasonable.

Inquiries Concerning Actions Taken at Meetings of Stockholders, the Board of Directors, Committees of the Board of Directors, or Comparable Meetings

1.142 Paragraph .22 of AR-C section 90 requires the accountant to inquire about actions taken at meetings of stockholders, the board of directors, committees of the board of directors, or comparable meetings that may affect the financial statements. Relevant matters include the following:

- Approval of key employee stock option plans
- Approval of officer compensation
- Approval of loan agreements
- Approval of disposition of specific assets or segments of the business
- Declaration of stock, cash, or other dividends

©2017, AICPA

Inquiries Concerning Any Other Matters That the Accountant May Consider Necessary

1.143 Paragraph .22 of AR-C section 90 requires the accountant to inquire about any other matters that the accountant may consider necessary.

Illustrative Inquiries

1.144 The following list of inquiries is for illustrative purposes only. These inquiries will not necessarily be applicable in every review engagement, nor are these inquiries meant to be all-inclusive. These illustrative inquiries are not intended to serve as a program or checklist to be utilized in performing a review engagement; rather, they address general areas where inquiries might be made in a review engagement. Also, the accountant may feel that it is necessary to make several inquiries in an effort to answer questions related to the issues addressed in these illustrative inquiries. The specific inquiries to be made are ultimately determined by the accountant's professional judgment:

- General
  - — Have there been any changes in the entity's business activities?
  - — Have there been any changes in the entity's personnel in the accounting or governance functions?
  - — In what type of industry (industries) does the business operate?
  - — Does the entity follow any industry-specific AICPA guide or industry publication?
  - — Are there any existing, new, or proposed regulatory policies or practices applicable to the entity?
  - — Were there any communications from regulatory agencies?
  - — Are there any unusual or complex situations that may have an effect on the financial statements (for example, business combinations, restructuring plans, or litigation)?
  - — What procedures are in place related to recording, classifying, and summarizing transactions and accumulating information related to financial statement disclosures?
  - — Have the financial statements been prepared in accordance with accounting principles generally accepted in the United States of America (or other applicable financial reporting framework, for example the cash-basis or the tax-basis of accounting)? Have there been any changes in accounting principles and the methods of applying those principles? Have voluntary changes in accounting principles been reflected in the financial statements through retrospective application of the new principle in comparative financial statements?
  - — Have there been any instances, allegations, or suspicions that fraud or illegal acts might have occurred or might be occurring within the entity? If so, where and how?

 ©2017, AICPA

- — Are any entities, other than the reporting entity, commonly controlled by the owners? If so, has an evaluation been performed to determine whether those other entities should be consolidated into the financial statements of the reporting entity?
- — Are there any entities, other than the reporting entity, in which the owners have significant investments (for example, variable interest entities)? If so, has an evaluation been performed to determine whether the reporting entity is the primary beneficiary related to the activities of these other entities?
- — Is the reporting entity a general partner in a limited partnership arrangement? If so, has an evaluation been performed to determine whether the limited partnership should be consolidated into the financial statements of the reporting entity?
- — Is the reporting entity a controlling partner in a general partnership arrangement? If so, has an evaluation been performed to determine whether the partnership should be consolidated into the financial statements of the controlling partner?
- — Have any significant transactions occurred or been recognized near the end of the reporting period?
- — Have events occurred subsequent to the balance sheet date that would require adjustment to, or disclosure in, the financial statements? Such inquiries may include, but not be limited to, pending or new litigations, claims, and assessments, losses on assets, noncompliance with laws or regulations, changes in entity, or changes in operations.

- Cash and Cash Equivalents
    - — Is the entity's policy regarding the composition of cash and cash equivalents in accordance with FASB *Accounting Standards Codification* (ASC) 230, *Statement of Cash Flows*? Has the policy been applied on a consistent basis? Have there been any changes to withdrawal restrictions related to short-term investments that could affect the description and classification of cash equivalents?
    - — Are all cash and cash equivalents[1] accounts reconciled on a timely basis?
    - — Have old or unusual reconciling items between bank balances and book balances been reviewed and adjustments made, when necessary?
    - — Has there been a proper cutoff of cash receipts and disbursements?

---

[1] Cash and cash equivalents include all cash and highly liquid investments that are both (*a*) readily convertible to cash, and (*b*) so near to maturity that they present insignificant risk of changes in value because of changes in interest rates, in accordance with the requirements in FASB ASC 230, *Statement of Cash Flows*.

- Has a reconciliation of intercompany transfers been prepared?
- Have checks that have been written, but not mailed as of the financial statement date, been properly reclassified into the liability section of the balance sheet?
- Have material bank overdrafts been properly reclassified into the liability section of the balance sheet?
- Are there compensating balances or other restrictions on the availability of cash and cash equivalents balances? If so, has consideration been given to reclassifying these amounts as noncurrent assets?
- Have cash funds been counted and reconciled with control accounts?

- Receivables
  - Has an adequate allowance for doubtful accounts been properly reflected in the financial statements?
  - Have uncollectible receivables been written-off through a charge against the allowance account or earnings? Are there any customer bankruptcy or liquidity issues that would have a material effect on the financial statements?
  - Has interest earned on receivables been properly reflected in the financial statements?
  - Has there been a proper cutoff of sales transactions?
  - Have there been any changes in major contracts with customers that may affect the classification or valuation of receivables?
  - Are there receivables from employees or other related parties? Have receivables from owners been evaluated to determine if they should be reflected in the equity section (rather than the asset section) of the balance sheet?
  - Are any receivables pledged, discounted, or factored? Are recourse provisions properly reflected in the financial statements?
  - Have receivables been properly classified between current and noncurrent?
  - Are there significant credit balances which should be considered for reclassification into the liability section of the balance sheet?
  - Have there been significant numbers of sales returns or credit memoranda issued subsequent to the balance sheet date?
  - Is the accounts receivable subsidiary ledger reconciled to the general ledger account balance on a regular basis?
- Inventory
  - Are physical inventory counts performed on a regular basis, including at the end of the reporting period? Are the count procedures adequate to ensure an appropriate

 ©2017, AICPA

count? If not, how have amounts related to inventories been determined for purposes of financial statement presentation? If so, what procedures were used to take the latest physical inventory and what date was that inventory taken?

- — Have general ledger control accounts been adjusted to agree with the physical inventory count? If so, were the adjustments significant?
- — If the physical inventory counts were taken at a date other than the balance sheet date, what procedures were used to determine changes in inventory between the date of the physical inventory counts and the balance sheet date?
- — Were consignments in or out considered in taking physical inventories?
- — Is any inventory held at other locations or held for others?
- — What is the basis of valuing inventory for purposes of financial statement presentation?
- — Does inventory cost include material, labor, and overhead, when applicable?
- — Has inventory been reviewed for obsolescence or cost in excess of net realizable value? If so, how are these costs reflected in the financial statements?
- — What methods are used to value slow-moving or obsolete items?
- — Have proper cutoffs of purchases, goods in transit, and returned goods been made?
- — Are there any inventory encumbrances?
- — Is scrap inventoried and controlled?
- — Have abnormal costs related to inventory been expensed as incurred?

- Prepaid Expenses
  - — What is the nature of the amounts included in prepaid expenses?
  - — How are these amounts being amortized?
- Investments
  - — What is the basis of accounting for investments reported in the financial statements (for example, securities, joint ventures, or closely held businesses)?
  - — Are derivative instruments properly measured and disclosed in the financial statements? If those derivatives are utilized in hedge transactions, have the documentation or assessment requirements related to hedge accounting been met?
  - — Are investments in marketable debt and equity securities properly classified as trading, available-for-sale, and held-to-maturity?

- — Has appropriate consideration been given to the classification of investments between current and noncurrent?
- — How were fair values of the reported investments determined? Have unrealized gains and losses been properly reported in the financial statements?
- — If the fair values of marketable debt and equity securities are less than cost, have the declines in value been evaluated to determine whether the declines are other than temporary?
- — For any debt securities classified as held to maturity, does management have the positive ability and intent to hold the securities until they mature? If so, have those debt securities been properly measured?
- — Have gains and losses related to disposal of investments been properly reflected in the financial statements?
- — How was investment income determined? Is investment income properly reflected in the financial statements?
- — For investments made by the reporting entity, have consolidation, equity, or cost method accounting requirements been considered?
- — Are any investments encumbered?

- Property and Equipment
  - — Are property and equipment items properly stated at depreciated cost or other proper value?
  - — When was the last time a physical inventory of property and equipment was taken?
  - — Are all items reflected in property and equipment held for use? If not, have items that are held for sale been properly reclassified from property and equipment?
  - — Have gains or losses on disposal of property and equipment been properly reflected in the financial statements?
  - — What are the criteria for capitalization of property and equipment? Have the criteria been consistently and appropriately applied?
  - — Are repairs and maintenance costs properly reflected as an expense in the income statement?
  - — What depreciation methods and rates are utilized in the financial statements? Are these methods and rates appropriate and applied on a consistent basis?
  - — Are there any unrecorded additions, retirements, abandonments, sales, or trade-ins?
  - — Are all fully depreciated assets still in service?
  - — Does the entity have any material lease agreements? If so, have those agreements been properly evaluated for financial statement presentation purposes?

©2017, AICPA

- Are there any asset retirement obligations associated with tangible long-lived assets? If so, has the recorded amount of the related asset been increased because of the obligation, and is the liability properly reflected in the liability section of the balance sheet?
- Has the entity constructed any of its property and equipment items? If so, have all components of cost been reflected in measuring these items for purposes of financial statement presentation including, but not limited to, capitalized interest?
- Has there been any significant impairment in value of property and equipment items? If so, has any impairment loss been properly reflected in the financial statements?
- Are any property and equipment items mortgaged or otherwise encumbered? If so, are these mortgages and encumbrances properly disclosed in the financial statements?

- Intangibles and Other Assets
  - Are intangible assets with finite lives being appropriately amortized?
  - Are the costs associated with computer software properly reflected as intangible assets (rather than property and equipment) in the financial statements?
  - Has there been any significant impairment in value of these assets? If so, has any impairment loss been properly reflected in the financial statements?
  - Are goodwill and general intangibles other than goodwill properly reflected as intangible assets in the financial statements?
  - Is goodwill aggregated and presented as a separate line item in the statement of financial position?
  - Are general intangible assets other than goodwill aggregated and presented as a separate line item in the statement of financial position?
  - What is the nature of the amounts included in other assets?
  - Do these assets represent costs that will benefit future periods? What is the amortization policy related to these assets? Is this policy appropriate?
  - Have other assets been properly classified between current and noncurrent?
  - Are any of these assets mortgaged or otherwise encumbered?

- Accounts and Short-Term Notes Payable and Accrued Liabilities
  - Have significant payables been reflected in the financial statements?

- Are loans from financial institutions and other short-term liabilities properly classified in the financial statements? Are any covenants related to these liabilities properly disclosed in the financial statements?
- Have there been any changes in major contracts with suppliers that may affect the classification or valuation of payables?
- Have significant accruals (for example, payroll, interest, provisions for pension and profit sharing plans, or other postretirement benefit obligations) been properly reflected in the financial statements?
- Has a liability for employees' compensation for future absences been properly accrued and disclosed in the financial statements?
- Are any liabilities collateralized or subordinated? If so, are those liabilities disclosed in the financial statements?
- Are there any payables to employees and related parties? If so, are they properly disclosed in financial statements?

- Long-Term Liabilities
  - Are the terms and other provisions of long-term liability agreements properly disclosed in the financial statements?
  - Have liabilities been properly classified between current and noncurrent?
  - Has interest expense been properly accrued and reflected in the financial statements?
  - Is the company in compliance with loan covenants and agreements? Are loan covenants and agreements properly disclosed in the financial statements?
  - Are any long-term liabilities collateralized or subordinated? If so, are these facts disclosed in the financial statements?
  - Are there any obligations that, by their terms, are due on demand within one year from the balance sheet date? If so, have these obligations been properly reclassified into the current liability section of the balance sheet?
  - Are there any noncash financing activities where loan proceeds were paid directly to a vendor or other third party?

- Income and Other Taxes
  - Do the financial statements reflect an appropriate provision for current and prior year income taxes payable?
  - Have any assessments or reassessments been received? Are there tax authority examinations in process?
  - Are there any temporary differences between book and tax amounts? If so, have deferred taxes on these differences been properly reflected in the financial statements?

©2017, AICPA

- Do the financial statements reflect an appropriate provision for taxes other than income taxes (for example, franchise, sales, and so on)?
- Have all required tax payments been made on a timely basis?
- Has the entity assessed uncertain tax positions and related disclosures in accordance with FASB ASC 740, *Income Taxes*?

• Other Liabilities, Contingencies, and Commitments

- What is the nature of the amounts included in other liabilities?
- Have other liabilities been properly classified between current and noncurrent?
- Are there any guarantees, whether written or oral, whereby the entity must stand ready to perform or is contingently liable related to the guarantee? If so, are these guarantees properly reflected in the financial statements?
- Are there any contingent liabilities (for example, discounted notes, drafts, endorsements, warranties, litigation, and unsettled asserted claims)? Are there any potential unasserted claims? Are these contingent liabilities, claims, and assessments properly measured and disclosed in the financial statements?
- Are there any material contractual obligations for construction or purchase of property and equipment or any commitments or options to purchase or sell company securities? If so, are these facts clearly disclosed in the financial statements?
- Is the entity responsible for any environmental remediation liability? If so, is this liability properly measured and disclosed in the financial statements?
- Does the entity have any agreement to repurchase items that previously were sold? If so, have the repurchase agreements been taken into account in determining the appropriate measurements and disclosures in the financial statements?
- Are there purchase commitments for quantities in excess of requirements or at prices in excess of market?
- Does the entity have any sales commitments at prices expected to result in a loss at the consummation of the sale? If so, are these commitments properly reflected in the financial statements?
- Are there any violations or possible violations of laws or regulations, the effects of which should be considered for financial statement accrual or disclosure?
- Does the entity have any multi-employer pension plans? If so, have these plans been appropriately accounted for

and do the financial statements include proper disclosure?

- Equity
  - What is the nature of any changes in equity accounts during each reporting period?
  - What classes of stock (other ownership interests) have been authorized?
  - What is the par or stated value of the various classes of stock (other ownership interests)?
  - Do amounts of outstanding shares of stock (other ownership interests) agree with subsidiary records?
  - Have pertinent rights and privileges of ownership interests been properly disclosed in the financial statements?
  - Does the entity have any mandatorily redeemable ownership interests? If so, have these ownership interests been evaluated so that a proper determination has been made related to whether these ownership interests should be measured and reclassified to the liability section of the balance sheet? Are redemption features associated with ownership interests clearly disclosed in the financial statements?
  - Have dividend (distribution) and liquidation preferences related to ownership interests been properly disclosed in the financial statements?
  - Do disclosures related to ownership interests include any applicable call provisions (prices and dates), conversion provisions (prices and rates), unusual voting rights, significant terms of contracts to issue additional ownership interests, or any other unusual features associated with the ownership interests?
  - Are syndication fees properly reflected in the financial statements as a reduction of equity (rather than an asset)?
  - Have any stock options or other stock compensation awards been granted to employees or others? If so, are these options or awards properly measured and disclosed in the financial statements?
  - Has the entity made any acquisitions of its own stock? If so, are the amounts associated with these reacquired shares properly reflected in the financial statements as a reduction in equity? Is the presentation in accordance with applicable state laws?
  - Are there any restrictions or appropriations on retained earnings or other capital accounts? If so, are these restrictions or appropriations properly reflected in the financial statements?

 ©2017, AICPA

- Revenue and Expenses
  - — What is the entity's revenue recognition policy? Has the policy been consistently applied and appropriately disclosed?
  - — Are revenues from sales of products and rendering of services recognized in the appropriate reporting period (that is, when the products have been delivered and when the services have been performed)?
  - — Were any sales recorded under a "bill and hold" arrangement? If yes, have the criteria been met to record the transaction as a sale?
  - — Are purchases and expenses recognized in the appropriate reporting period (that is, matched against revenue) and properly classified in the financial statements?
  - — Do the financial statements include discontinued operations? If so, are amounts associated with discontinued operations properly displayed in the income statement?
  - — Does the entity have any gains or losses that would necessitate the display of comprehensive income (for example, gains or losses on available-for-sale securities or cash flow hedge derivatives)? If so, have these items been properly displayed within comprehensive income (rather than included in the determination of net income)?
- Other
  - — Has the entity considered whether declines in market values subsequent to the balance sheet date may be permanent or caused the entity to no longer be in compliance with its loan covenants, or both?
  - — Have actions taken at meetings of stockholders, directors, committees of directors, or comparable meetings that affect the financial statements been reflected in the financial statements?
  - — Are significant estimates and material concentrations (for example, customers or suppliers) properly disclosed in the financial statements?
  - — Are there plans or intentions that may materially affect the carrying amounts or classification of assets and liabilities reflected in the financial statements?
  - — Have there been any material transactions between or among related parties (for example, sales, purchases, loans, or leasing arrangements)? If so, are these transactions properly disclosed in the financial statements?
  - — Are there uncertainties that could have a material effect on the financial statements? Is there any change in the status of previously disclosed material uncertainties? Are all uncertainties that could have a material effect on the financial statements properly disclosed in the financial statements?

- — Has management performed an evaluation of the entity's ability to continue as a going concern? If so, has management identified conditions or events that raise substantial doubt about the entity's ability to continue as a going concern for a reasonable period of time and, if so, what are management's plans to address them? If not, do conditions or events exist that raise substantial doubt about the entity's ability to continue as a going concern for a reasonable period of time? Is management aware of conditions or events beyond the period of management's evaluation that may have an effect on the entity's ability to continue as a going concern?
- — Have barter or other nonmonetary transactions been properly recorded and disclosed? Have nonmonetary asset exchanges involving commercial substance been reflected in the financial statements at fair value? Have nonmonetary asset exchanges not involving commercial substance been reflected in the financial statements at carrying value?
- — Have all misstatements identified during the engagement been presented to management for correction in the entity's accounting system?

Consideration of Management's Responses

1.145 The accountant is required to consider the reasonableness and consistency of management's responses in light of the results of other review procedures and the accountant's knowledge of the entity's business. The accountant is not required to corroborate management's responses with other evidence.

Reading the Financial Statements

1.146 The accountant is required to read the financial statements and consider whether any information has come to the accountant's attention to indicate that such financial statements do not conform to the applicable financial reporting framework. The accountant's experience and professional judgment assists in assimilating the information obtained.

1.147 Although there is no set process to follow in determining whether financial statements are in accordance with the applicable financial reporting framework, the following steps illustrate one possible approach. The following decision process does not preclude the simultaneous performance of inquiries, analytical procedures, or other procedures that the accountant considers appropriate:

- Does it appear that the entity has consistently applied accounting principles used by the industry in preparing its financial statements?
- Does it appear that the entity's business transactions are consistent with the industry transactions?
- Are unique industry accounting principles adequately described in the summary of significant accounting policies?
- Does it appear that the entity has properly applied other accounting principles in preparing the financial statements?

 ©2017, AICPA

- If accounting principles were not applied on a consistent basis, do the financial statements appear to reflect the appropriate disclosures and adjustments?
- Do the entity's accounts on the financial statements appear consistent with the entity's operating characteristics?
- Do the accounting procedures for recording, classifying, and summarizing transactions appear to provide a basis for the actual accounts and disclosures contained in the financial statements?
- Have changes in the entity's business activities had an effect on the accounting system, and does it appear that the resulting changes in transactions and accounts have been properly reflected in the financial statements?
- Do the financial statements appear to properly reflect actions taken by the stockholders, board of directors, and other committees?
- Do the financial statements appear to properly reflect events and transactions that occurred after the end of the accounting period but before the completion of the review engagement?

1.148 Additionally, although there is no complete list of the questions that could be raised during a technical reading of the financial statements, the following are examples of the type of questions that might be raised as part of the process:

- Are headings on the financial statements appropriate?
- Are major sections of the financial statements properly captioned (such as the use of "Current" and "Noncurrent" captions on a classified balance sheet)?
- Are accounts grouped in appropriate captions (such as land held for investment classified as "Other Assets")?
- On the basis of titles of transactions, are such transactions properly classified?
- Are there arithmetical errors in the financial statements (such as the total of the amounts for items listed under the "Current Assets" category are equal to the total current assets on the balance sheet)?
- Are there clerical mistakes in the financial statements (such as typographical errors)?
- Are there mistakes in the application of accounting principles (such as the reporting of property, plant, and equipment at cost with no accumulated depreciation computed)?
- Are financial statement disclosures omitted (such as the omission of the method used to account for inventories)?

Reconciling the Financial Statements to the Underlying Accounting Records

1.149 Paragraph .26 of AR-C section 90 states that the accountant should obtain evidence that the financial statements agree or reconcile with the accounting records. The most common way used by many practitioners to obtain this evidence is to compare the financial statements to the entity's general ledger or trial balance.

Evaluating Evidence Obtained From the Procedures Performed

1.150 The accountant is required to accumulate misstatements, including inadequate disclosure, identified by the accountant in performing the review procedures or brought to the accountant's attention during the performance of the review. The accountant is further required to evaluate, individually and in the aggregate, misstatements, including inadequate disclosure, to determine whether material modification should be made to the financial statements for them to be in accordance with the applicable financial reporting framework.

1.151 If, during performance of review procedures, the accountant becomes aware that information coming to the accountant's attention is incorrect, incomplete, or otherwise unsatisfactory, the accountant should request that management consider the effect of these matters on the financial statements and communicate the results of its consideration to the accountant. Additionally, the accountant should consider the results communicated by management and whether such results indicate that the financial statements may be materially misstated.

1.152 If the accountant believes that the financial statements may be materially misstated, the accountant is required to perform additional procedures deemed necessary to obtain limited assurance that there are no material modifications that should be made to the financial statements in order for the statements to be in accordance with the applicable financial reporting framework. For example, through inquiry of revenue cutoff procedures and analytical review procedures applied to gross profit percentages and sales to receivable trends, the accountant comes to believe that revenues may be overstated. As a result of believing that a material misstatement may exist, the accountant requests management to investigate and analyze whether subsequent year sales (or perhaps fictitious sales) have been erroneously recorded in the current year. Depending on the information management provides the accountant in response to his or her request, the accountant should use professional judgment to either accept this information as a plausible explanation and then document that as such—or, if management's explanation and analysis are not plausible or incomplete, the accountant should perform yet more review procedures. For example, the accountant may decide to review close to year-end and subsequent year sales journals or other entity records to determine whether a cutoff misstatement occurred.

1.153 The accountant is required to evaluate whether sufficient appropriate review evidence has been obtained from the procedures performed. If the accountant determines that he or she has not accumulated sufficient review evidence to provide a reasonable basis that he or she has obtained limited assurance that the financial statements are in accordance with the applicable financial reporting framework, then the accountant should perform other procedures judged by the accountant to be necessary in the circumstances to be able to form a conclusion on the financial statements.

Written Representations

1.154 Written representations are necessary information that the accountant requires in connection with a review of the entity's financial statements. Accordingly, similar to responses to inquiries, written representations are review evidence.

©2017, AICPA

1.155 The accountant is required to request written representations from members of management who have appropriate responsibilities for the financial statements and knowledge of the matters concerned. Normally, the representation letter is signed by the CEO and CFO or those with equivalent responsibilities. For owner-managed entities, the owner-manager generally would be the person who signs the representation letter.

1.156 According to paragraph .34 of AR-C section 90, for all financial statements presented and all periods covered by the review, the accountant should request management to provide written representations that are dated as of the date of the accountant's review report. For example, if comparative financial statements are reported on, the representations obtained at the completion of the most recent review should address all periods being reported on. If the client's current management was not in place during the previous year(s) reported, the accountant is nonetheless required to obtain representations from the current management on all periods covered by the review report. The written representations should be in the form of a representation letter addressed to the accountant. The representation letter should include, at a minimum, the following statements:

- Management has fulfilled its responsibility for the preparation and fair presentation of the financial statements in accordance with the applicable financial reporting framework, as set out in the terms of the engagement.
- Management acknowledges its responsibility for designing, implementing, and maintaining internal control relevant to the preparation and fair presentation of financial statements, including its responsibility to prevent and detect fraud.
- Management has provided the accountant with all relevant information and access, as agreed upon in the terms of the engagement.
- Management has responded fully and truthfully to all of the accountant's inquiries.
- All transactions have been recorded and are reflected in the financial statements.
- Management has disclosed to the accountant its knowledge of fraud or suspected fraud affecting the entity involving
  - — management,
  - — employees who have significant roles in internal control, or
  - — others when the fraud could have a material effect on the financial statements.
- Management has disclosed to the accountant its knowledge of any allegations of fraud or suspected fraud affecting the entity's financial statements communicated by employees, former employees, regulators, or others.
- Management has disclosed to the accountant all known instances of noncompliance or suspected noncompliance with laws and regulations whose effects should be considered when preparing financial statements.

- Whether management believes that the effects of uncorrected misstatements are immaterial, individually and in the aggregate, to the financial statements as a whole. A summary of such items should be included in, or attached to, the written representation.
- Management has disclosed to the accountant all known actual or possible litigation and claims whose effects should be considered when preparing the financial statements, and it has appropriately accounted for and disclosed such litigation and claims in accordance with the applicable financial reporting framework.
- Whether management believes that significant assumptions used by it in making accounting estimates are reasonable.
- Management has disclosed to the accountant the identity of the entity's related parties and all of the related-party relationships and transactions of which it is aware, and it has appropriately accounted for and disclosed such relationships and transactions.
- All events occurring subsequent to the date of the financial statements and for which the applicable financial reporting framework requires adjustment or disclosure have been adjusted or disclosed.

1.157 If, in addition to the required representations, the accountant determines that it is necessary to obtain one or more written representations to support other review evidence relevant to the financial statements, the accountant is required to request such other written representations.

1.158 The accountant need not be in physical receipt of the management representation letter as of the date of the review report, provided that management has reviewed the final representation letter and will sign the representation letter without modification as of the date of the accountant's review report. Possession of the signed management representation letter prior to the release of the accountant's review report is necessary.

Observations and Suggestions

Because the representations are evidence, the representations set forth in the representation letter should be made as of the date of the accountant's review report. The dating of the representations is made in the body of the letter and is not intended to coincide with the date on the top of the letter (which is the date that management actually signs the letter).

The applicable paragraph in the representation letter that includes the dating of the representations reads as follows:

We represent that [*to the best of our knowledge and belief, having made such inquiries as we considered necessary for the purpose of appropriately informing ourselves*] [*as of (insert date of accountant's review report)*]:

1.159 The specific written representations obtained will depend on the circumstances of the engagement and the nature and basis of presentation of the financial statements. The following are examples of conditions (and the resultant representation) of which the accountant may become aware during the review engagement:

 ©2017, AICPA

General	
Condition	***Illustrative Examples***
The effect of a new accounting principle is not known.	We have not completed the process of evaluating the impact that will result from adopting FASB Accounting Standards Update (ASU) No. [*20X1-XX*], as discussed in note X. The company is therefore unable to disclose the impact that adopting FASB ASU No. [*20X1-XX*] will have on its financial position and the results of operations when such statement is adopted.
Justification exists for a change in accounting principles.	We believe that [describe the newly adopted accounting principle] is preferable to [describe the former accounting principle] because [describe management's justification for the change in accounting principles].
The accountant believes that substantial doubt exists about the entity's ability to continue as a going concern for a reasonable period of time.	We have appropriately disclosed a description of management's plans that are intended to mitigate the adverse effects of conditions or events that indicate there is substantial doubt about the entity's ability to continue as a going concern for a reasonable period of time and the probability that those plans will be adequately implemented. Note X to the financial statements discloses all of the matters of which we are aware that are relevant to the company's ability to continue as a going concern for a reasonable period of time, including principal conditions or events and management's plans.
The possibility exists that the value of specific significant long-lived assets or certain identifiable intangibles may be impaired.	We have reviewed long-lived assets and certain identifiable intangibles to be held and used for impairment whenever events or changes in circumstances have indicated that the carrying amount of its assets might not be recoverable and have appropriately recorded the adjustment.
The entity has a variable interest in another entity.	Variable interest entities (VIEs) and potential VIEs and transactions with VIEs and potential VIEs have been properly recorded and disclosed in the financial statements in accordance with accounting principles generally accepted in the United States of America. We have considered both implicit and explicit variable interests in (*a*) determining whether potential VIEs should be considered VIEs, (*b*) calculating expected losses and residual returns, and (*c*) determining which party, if any, is the primary beneficiary.

(*continued*)

General	
Condition	***Illustrative Examples***
	We have provided you with lists of all identified variable interests in (*a*) VIEs, (*b*) potential VIEs that we considered but judged not to be VIEs, and (*c*) entities that were afforded the scope exceptions of FASB *Accounting Standards Codification* (ASC) 810, *Consolidation*. We have advised you of all transactions with identified VIEs, potential VIEs, or entities afforded the scope exceptions of FASB ASC 810. We have made available all relevant information about financial interests and contractual arrangements with related parties, de facto agents, and other entities, including but not limited to, their governing documents, equity and debt instruments, contracts, leases, guarantee arrangements, and other financial contracts and arrangements. The information we provided about financial interests and contractual arrangements with related parties, de facto agents, and other entities includes information about all transactions, unwritten understandings, agreement modifications, and written and oral side agreements. Our computations of expected losses and expected residual returns of entities that are VIEs and potential VIEs are based on the best information available and include all reasonably possible outcomes. Regarding entities in which the company has variable interests (implicit and explicit), we have provided all information about events and changes in circumstances that could potentially cause reconsideration about whether the entities are VIEs or whether the company is the primary beneficiary or has a significant variable interest in the entity. We have made and continue to make exhaustive efforts to obtain information about entities in which the company has an implicit or explicit interest, but that were excluded from complete analysis under FASB ASC 810 due to lack of essential information to determine one or more of the following: • Whether the entity is a VIE. • Whether the company is the primary beneficiary. • The accounting required to consolidate the entity.

©2017, AICPA

General	
Condition	***Illustrative Examples***
The work of a specialist has been used by the entity.	We agree with the findings of specialists in evaluating the [describe assertion] and have adequately considered the qualifications of the specialist in determining the amounts and disclosures used in the financial statements and underlying accounting records. We did not give or cause any instructions to be given to specialists with respect to the values or amounts derived in an attempt to bias their work, and we are not otherwise aware of any matters that have had an impact on the independence or objectivity of the specialists.
Supplementary information is required.	We are responsible for the fair presentation of the additional information [supplemental schedules] accompanying the basic [consolidated] financial statements that is [are] presented for the purpose of additional analysis of the basic [consolidated] financial statements.
Management has used accounting conventions.	We have disclosed to you the accounting conventions used when preparing our financial statements. The effect of applying these accounting conventions and the use of such applications is immaterial to the financial statements.
Financial statement misstatements in the current period relate to the prior period[*s*].	We believe the effects of the uncorrected financial statement misstatements detected in the current [*specify period; for example,* year] that relate to the prior [*specify period; for example,* year] presented, when combined with those misstatements aggregated by you during the prior-[*specify period; for example,* year] review engagement and pertaining to the prior [*specify period; for example,* year] presented, are immaterial, both individually and in the aggregate, to the financial statements for the [*specify period(s); for example,* the year ended [*date*]] taken as a whole.

Assets	
Condition	***Illustrative Examples***
Cash	
Disclosure is required of compensating balances or other arrangements involving restrictions on cash balances, lines of credit, or similar arrangements.	Arrangements with financial institutions involving compensating balances or other arrangements involving restrictions on cash balances, lines of credit, or similar arrangements have been properly disclosed.
Financial Instruments	
Management intends to and has the ability to hold to maturity debt securities classified as held to maturity.	Debt securities that have been classified as held to maturity have been so classified due to the company's intent to hold such securities to maturity and the company's ability to do so. All other debt securities have been classified as available for sale or trading.
Management considers the decline in value of debt or equity securities to be temporary.	We consider the decline in value of debt or equity securities classified as either available for sale or held to maturity to be temporary.
Management has determined the fair value of significant financial instruments that do not have readily determinable market values.	The methods and significant assumptions used to determine fair values of financial instruments are as follows: [*describe methods and significant assumptions used to determine fair values of financial instruments*]. The methods and significant assumptions used result in a measure of fair value appropriate for financial statement measurement and disclosure purposes.
Financial instruments with off-balance-sheet risk and financial instruments with concentrations of credit risk exist.	The following information about financial instruments with off-balance-sheet risk and financial instruments with concentrations of credit risk has been properly disclosed in the financial statements: 1. The extent, nature, and terms of financial instruments with off-balance-sheet risk 2. The amount of credit risk of financial instruments with off-balance-sheet risk and information about the collateral supporting such financial instruments 3. Significant concentrations of credit risk arising from all financial instruments and information about the collateral supporting such financial instruments

©2017, AICPA

Assets	
Condition	***Illustrative Examples***
Receivables	
Receivables have been recorded in the financial statements.	Receivables recorded in the financial statements represent valid claims against debtors for sales or other charges arising on or before the balance sheet date and have been appropriately reduced to their estimated net realizable value.
Inventories	
Excess or obsolete inventories exist.	Provision has been made to reduce excess or obsolete inventories to their estimated net realizable value.
Investments	
Unusual considerations are involved in determining the application of equity accounting.	[For investments in common stock that are either nonmarketable or of which the entity has a 20 percent or greater ownership interest, select the appropriate representation from the following:] • The equity method is used to account for the company's investment in the common stock of [investee] because the company has the ability to exercise significant influence over the investee's operating and financial policies. • The cost method is used to account for the company's investment in the common stock of [investee] because the company does not have the ability to exercise significant influence over the investee's operating and financial policies.
Deferred Charges	
Material expenditures have been deferred.	We believe that all material expenditures that have been deferred to future periods will be recoverable.

Liabilities	
Condition	***Illustrative Examples***
Debt	
Short-term debt could be refinanced on a long-term basis and management intends to do so.	The company has excluded short-term obligations totaling $[amount] from current liabilities because it intends to refinance the obligations on a long-term basis. [Complete with appropriate wording detailing how amounts will be refinanced as follows:] The company has issued a long-term obligation [debt security] after the date of the balance sheet but prior to the issuance of the financial statements for the purpose of refinancing the short term obligations on a long term basis. The company has the ability to consummate the refinancing, by using the financing agreement referred to in note [X] to the financial statements.
Tax-exempt bonds have been issued.	Tax exempt bonds issued have retained their tax-exempt status.
Taxes	
Management intends to reinvest undistributed earnings of a foreign subsidiary.	We intend to reinvest the undistributed earnings of [name of foreign subsidiary].
Special tax status exists under Subchapter S.	The Company has claimed a special tax status under Subchapter S of the Internal Revenue Code. The Company has met all of the eligibility requirements, and the election remained in effect through [*the end of the review period*].
A deferred tax asset exists at the balance sheet date.	The valuation allowance has been determined pursuant to the provisions of FASB ASC 740, including the company's estimation of future taxable income, if necessary, and is adequate to reduce the total deferred tax asset to an amount that will more likely than not be realized. [Complete with appropriate wording detailing how the entity determined the valuation allowance against the deferred tax asset.] or A valuation allowance against deferred tax assets at the balance sheet date is not considered necessary because it is more likely than not that the deferred tax asset will be fully realized.

 ©2017, AICPA

Liabilities	
Condition	*Illustrative Examples*
The entity does not have income tax contingencies.	We do not have (*a*) asserted and unsettled income tax contingencies or (*b*) unasserted income tax contingencies caused by uncertain tax positions taken in our income tax returns filed with the Internal Revenue Service and state, [and] local [, and foreign] tax authorities that are probable of assertion by such tax authorities under the provisions of FASB ASC 450, *Contingencies*. Furthermore, we have not received either written or oral tax opinions that are contrary to our assessment.
Contingencies	
Estimates and disclosures have been made of environmental remediation liabilities and related loss contingencies.	Provision has been made for any material loss that is probable from environmental remediation liabilities associated with [name of site]. We believe that such estimate is reasonable based on available information and that the liabilities and related loss contingencies and the expected outcome of uncertainties have been adequately described in the company's financial statements.
Agreements may exist to repurchase assets previously sold.	Agreements to repurchase assets previously sold have been properly disclosed.
Pension and Post-retirement Benefits	
An actuary has been used to measure pension liabilities and costs.	We believe that the actuarial assumptions and methods used to measure pension liabilities and costs for financial accounting purposes are appropriate in the circumstances.
Involvement with a multi-employer plan exists.	We are unable to determine the possibility of a withdrawal liability in a multi-employer benefit plan. or We have determined that there is the possibility of a withdrawal liability in a multi-employer plan in the amount of $[XX].
Post-retirement benefits have been eliminated.	We do not intend to compensate for the elimination of post-retirement benefits by granting an increase in pension benefits. or We plan to compensate for the elimination of post-retirement benefits by granting an increase in pension benefits in the amount of $[XX].

(*continued*)

Liabilities	
Condition	***Illustrative Examples***
Employee layoffs that would otherwise lead to a curtailment of a benefit plan are intended to be temporary.	Current employee layoffs are intended to be temporary.
Management intends to either continue to make or not make frequent amendments to its pension or other post-retirement benefit plans, which may affect the amortization period of prior service cost, or has expressed a substantive commitment to increase benefit obligations.	We plan to continue to make frequent amendments to pension or other post-retirement benefit plans, which may affect the amortization period of prior service cost. or We do not plan to make frequent amendments to pension or other post-retirement benefit plans.

Equity	
Condition	***Illustrative Example***
Capital stock repurchase options or agreements or capital stock reserved for options, warrants, conversions, or other requirements exist.	Capital stock repurchase options or agreements or capital stock reserved for options, warrants, conversions, or other requirements have been properly disclosed.

Income Statement	
Condition	***Illustrative Example***
There may be a loss from sales commitments.	Provisions have been made for losses to be sustained in the fulfillment of or from inability to fulfill any sales commitments.
Nature of the product or industry indicates the possibility of undisclosed sales terms.	We have fully disclosed to you all sales terms, including all rights of return or price adjustments and all warranty provisions.

1.160 In accordance with paragraph .37 of AR-C section 90, if management does not provide the written representations, or the accountant concludes that there is cause to doubt management's integrity such that the written representations provided are not reliable, the accountant should discuss the matter with management and those charged with governance, as appropriate. If management does not provide the required representations or the accountant

 ©2017, AICPA

continues to doubt management's integrity such that the written representations provided may not be reliable, the accountant should withdraw from the engagement.

Communicating to Management and Others Regarding Fraud or Noncompliance With Laws and Regulations

1.161 Paragraph .13 of AR-C section 90 states that the accountant should communicate with management or those charged with governance, as appropriate, on a timely basis during the course of the review engagement, all matters concerning the review engagement that, in the accountant's professional judgment, are of significant importance to merit the attention of management or those charged with governance, as appropriate.

1.162 Although the accountant performing the review engagement is not required to assess the risk of fraud or plan and perform review procedures specifically to discover fraud, paragraph .22*g* of AR-C section 90 does require the accountant to inquire of members of management who have responsibility for financial and accounting matters about its knowledge of any fraud or suspected fraud affecting the entity involving management, employees who have significant roles in internal control, or others, when fraud could have a material effect on the financial statements. Further, paragraph .22*h* of AR-C section 90 requires the accountant to inquire of members of management who have responsibility for financial and accounting matters about whether management is aware of any allegations of fraud or suspected fraud affecting the entity communicated by employees, former employees, regulators, or others. The accountant is also required by paragraph .34 of AR-C section 90 to request that management provide written representations acknowledging its responsibility to prevent and detect fraud; that it has disclosed to the accountant its knowledge of fraud or suspected fraud affecting the entity involving management, employees who have significant roles in internal control, or others, when the fraud could have a material effect on the financial statements; and that it has disclosed to the accountant its knowledge of any allegations of fraud or suspected fraud affecting the entity's financial statements communicated by employees, regulators, or others.

1.163 Typically, the accountant describes his or her responsibility with respect to fraud and illegal acts in the engagement letter. The following illustration shows how the accountant may describe his or her responsibilities with respect to fraud and illegal acts in the engagement letter:

> Our engagement cannot be relied upon to identify or disclose any financial statement misstatements, including those caused by error or fraud, or to identify or disclose any wrongdoing within the entity or noncompliance with laws and regulations. However, we will inform the appropriate level of management of any material errors and any evidence or information that comes to our attention during the performance of our review procedures that indicates fraud may have occurred. In addition, we will report to you any evidence or information that comes to our attention during the performance of our review procedures regarding noncompliance with laws and regulations that may have occurred, unless they are clearly inconsequential.

1.164 Additionally, paragraph .56 of AR-C section 90 requires the accountant to consider whether modification of the standard accountant's review report is adequate to disclose a departure from the applicable financial reporting framework, when the accountant becomes aware of such departure. A material departure from the applicable financial reporting framework may be due to error or fraud.

1.165 Communication is required when the accountant becomes aware of a potential fraud or noncompliance with laws and regulations. Fraud is a broad legal concept, and accountants do not make determinations whether an act is, in fact fraudulent. If the accountant becomes aware, through the inquiries performed in accordance with paragraph .22 of AR-C section 90 or otherwise during the course of the review engagement, that fraud (including misappropriation of assets) may have occurred, the accountant is required to communicate the matter as soon as practicable to the appropriate level of management (at a level above those involved with the suspected fraud, if possible). If the accountant becomes aware of matters involving identified or suspected noncompliance with laws and regulations whose effects should be considered when preparing financial statements, the accountant should communicate the matters to management, other than when matters are clearly inconsequential. If the fraud or noncompliance with laws or regulations involves senior management or results in a material misstatement of the financial statements, the accountant should communicate the matter directly to those charged with governance. If management or, as appropriate, those charged with governance do not provide sufficient information that supports that (*a*) the financial statements are not materially misstated due to fraud, or (*b*) the entity is in compliance with laws and regulations, and the effect of the suspected noncompliance may be material to the financial statements in the accountant's professional judgment, then the accountant should consider the need to obtain legal advice and take appropriate action, including potential withdrawal.

1.166 Although the communication may be written or oral, in accordance with paragraph .92 of AR-C section 90, the accountant is required to document communications to management and others regarding fraud or noncompliance with laws and regulations.

1.167 If matters regarding fraud or noncompliance with laws and regulations involve an owner of the business, the accountant may consider whether withdrawal from the review engagement is necessary. The accountant may perform this consideration in consultation with his or her counsel and insurance provider.

1.168 The disclosure of any evidence or information that comes to the accountant's attention during the performance of review procedures that fraud or noncompliance with laws or regulations may have occurred to parties other than the entity's senior management (or those charged with governance, if applicable) ordinarily is not part of the accountant's responsibility and, ordinarily, would be precluded by the accountant's ethical or legal obligations of confidentiality. However, a duty to disclose to parties outside of the entity may exist in the following circumstances:

- To comply with certain legal and regulatory requirements
- To a successor accountant when management has given permission for communication between the predecessor accountant and the successor accountant
- In response to a subpoena

In such circumstances, the accountant may consider it appropriate to consult with legal counsel.

 ©2017, AICPA

Observations and Suggestions

Summary of Accountant's Actions With Respect to Fraud and Noncompliance With Laws and Regulations

- In the engagement letter (which is required for all review engagements), include an acknowledgment by management that it is responsible for the prevention and detection of fraud and to ensure that the entity complies with all laws and regulations applicable to its activities. Additionally, include a statement that the accountant cannot be relied upon to identify any financial statement misstatements caused by fraud or to identify any wrongdoing within the entity or noncompliance with laws and regulations.
- Inquire of management who has responsibility for financial and accounting matters about fraud or suspected fraud.
- Obtain written representations regarding fraud and noncompliance with laws and regulations.
- Communicate all matters involving fraud, suspected fraud, or noncompliance with laws and regulations on a timely basis to management or those charged with governance, as appropriate and consider consultation with the accountant's legal counsel and insurance provider.
- Document all communications regarding fraud or noncompliance with laws and regulations.

Reporting on the Financial Statements—General

1.169 When the accountant performs a review of financial statements, the financial statements should be accompanied by a report. The accountant's review report should be in writing and include

a. a title that includes the word "independent" to clearly indicate that it is the report of an independent accountant.

b. an addressee, as appropriate for the circumstances of the engagement.

c. an introductory paragraph that

   i. identifies the entity whose financial statements have been reviewed,

   ii. states that the financial statements identified in the report were reviewed,

   iii. identifies the financial statements,

   iv. specifies the date or period covered by each financial statement,

   v. includes a statement that a review includes primarily applying analytical procedures to management's (owner's) financial data and making inquiries of company management (owners), and

   vi. includes a statement that a review is substantially less in scope than an audit, the objective of which is the expression of an opinion regarding the financial statements as a whole, and that, accordingly, the accountant does not express such an opinion.

d. a section with the heading "Management's Responsibility for the Financial Statements" that includes an explanation that management is responsible for the preparation and fair presentation of the financial statements in accordance with the applicable financial reporting framework; this responsibility includes the design, implementation, and maintenance of internal control sufficient to provide a reasonable basis for the preparation and fair presentation of financial statements in accordance with the applicable financial reporting framework.

e. a section with the heading "Accountant's Responsibility" that includes the following statements:

i. The accountant's responsibility is to conduct the review engagement in accordance with SSARSs promulgated by the Accounting and Review Services Committee of the AICPA. The accountant's review report should also explain that those standards require that the accountant perform the procedures to obtain limited assurance as a basis for reporting whether the accountant is aware of any material modifications that should be made to the financial statements for them to be in accordance with the applicable financial reporting framework.

ii. The accountant believes that the review evidence the accountant has obtained is sufficient and appropriate to provide a basis for the accountant's conclusion.

f. a concluding section with an appropriate heading that includes a statement about whether the accountant is aware of any material modifications that should be made to the accompanying financial statements for them to be in accordance with the applicable financial reporting framework and that identifies the country of origin of those accounting principles, if applicable.

g. the signature of the accountant or the accountant's firm.

h. the city and state where the accountant practices.

i. the date of the review report.

1.170 The review report should be dated no earlier than the date on which the accountant completed procedures sufficient to obtain limited assurance as a basis for reporting whether the accountant is aware of any material modifications that should be made to the financial statements for them to be in accordance with the applicable financial reporting framework, including evidence that

a. all the statements that the financial statements comprise, including the related notes, have been prepared and

b. management has asserted that they have taken responsibility for those financial statements.

 ©2017, AICPA

Observations and Suggestions

Management's assertion that it has taken responsibility for the financial statements, including the related notes, is generally made in the representation letter. Paragraph .34 of AR-C section 90 requires that the accountant request management to provide written representations that are dated as of the date of the accountant's review report.

Observations and Suggestions

When the accountant is reporting on comparative financial statements and the service performed on the statements is different (for example, the financial statements for the current year are reviewed and the statements for the prior year were subjected to a compilation engagement), the report title may be generic to the level of service (for example, the report could be titled "Independent Accountant's Report"). Illustrative accountant's reports on comparative financial statements are provided at the end of this chapter.

Observations and Suggestions

When reporting on financial statements prepared in accordance with GAAP, FASB ASC 855, *Subsequent Events*, requires disclosure by nongovernmental entities of the date through which subsequent events have been evaluated. Because the review report should not be dated earlier than the date on which the accountant has accumulated review evidence sufficient to provide a reasonable basis for concluding that he or she has obtained limited assurance, the review report date can never be earlier than management's subsequent event note date. In most cases, the date that management discloses as the date through which it has evaluated subsequent events (in the notes to the financial statements and in the management representation letter) is the same date as the accountant's review report. In order to coordinate that these dates (the note date, the representation letter date, and the accountant's review report date) are the same, the accountant may want to discuss these dating requirements with management in advance of beginning the review engagement. The accountant may also include, in the terms of the engagement (engagement letter), that management will not date the subsequent event note earlier than the date of management's representations and the date of the accountant's review report.

Reporting on Financial Statements Prepared in Accordance With a Special Purpose Framework

1.171 When the reviewed financial statements are prepared in accordance with a special purpose framework, such as the cash- or tax-basis of accounting or the AICPA's Financial Reporting Framework for Small- and Medium-Sized Entities, the accountant's review report should

a. make reference to management's responsibility for determining that the applicable financial reporting framework is acceptable in the circumstances when management has a choice of financial reporting frameworks in the preparation of such financial statements and

b. describe the purpose for which the financial statements are prepared or refer to a note in the financial statements that contains that information when the financial statements are prepared in accordance with a regulatory- or contractual-basis of accounting.

1.172 The accountant's review report on financial statements prepared in accordance with a special purpose framework should include an emphasis-of-matter paragraph, under an appropriate heading that

a. indicates that the financial statements are prepared in accordance with the applicable special purpose framework,

b. refers to the note to the financial statements that describes the framework, and

c. states that the special purpose framework is a basis of accounting other than GAAP.

1.173 The accountant's review report on special purpose financial statements should include an other-matter paragraph, under an appropriate heading, that restricts the use of the accountant's review report when the special purpose financial statements are prepared in accordance with

a. a contractual-basis of accounting;

b. a regulatory-basis of accounting; or

c. an other-basis of accounting when

  i. measurement or disclosure criteria are determined by the accountant to be suitable only for a limited number of users that can be presumed to have an adequate understanding of the criteria, or

  ii. measurement or disclosure criteria is available only to the specified parties.

1.174 The accountant should modify the review report when the accountant becomes aware that the financial statements do not include

a. a description of the special purpose framework.

b. a summary of significant accounting policies.

c. an adequate description about how the special purpose framework differs from GAAP. The effects of these differences need not be quantified.

d. informative disclosures similar to those required by GAAP when the financial statements contain items that are the same as, or similar to, those in financial statements prepared in accordance with GAAP.

1.175 In the case of financial statements prepared in accordance with a contractual-basis of accounting, the accountant should modify the review report if the financial statements do not adequately describe any significant interpretations of the contract on which the financial statements are based.

Reporting on Comparative Financial Statements

1.176 When comparative financial statements are presented, the accountant's report should refer to each period for which financial statements are presented.

 ©2017, AICPA

1.177 When reporting on all periods presented, a continuing accountant should update the report on one or more prior periods presented on a comparative basis with those of the current period. When issuing an updated report, the continuing accountant should consider information that the accountant has become aware of during the review of the current period financial statements. If circumstances or events come to the accountant's attention during the current engagement that may affect the prior-period financial statements presented, the accountant should consider the effects on the review report.

1.178 The accountant's report on comparative financial statements should not be dated earlier than the date that the accountant completed procedures sufficient to obtain limited assurance as a basis for reporting whether the accountant is aware of any material modifications that should be made to the financial statements for them to be in accordance with the applicable financial reporting framework with respect to the current period.

1.179 A predecessor may reissue his or her report on prior period financial statements at the client's request. However, a predecessor is not required to reissue his or her report on the financial statements of a prior period. When the financial statements of a prior period have been subject to a compilation engagement or reviewed by a predecessor whose report is not presented and the successor has not reviewed those financial statements, the successor is not required to make reference to the compilation or review report on the prior period financial statements. However, the successor is not precluded from making reference in an other-matter paragraph(s) of his or her report on the current-period financial statements to the predecessor's report on the prior-period financial statements. Ordinarily, this reference would include the following matters:

a. A statement that the financial statements of the prior period were subjected to a compilation engagement or reviewed by another accountant (other accountants)[2]

b. The date of his or her (their) report

c. If the financial statements of the prior period were subjected to a compilation engagement, a statement that the other accountant(s) did not audit or review the financial statements and, accordingly, did not express an opinion or provide any assurance about whether the financial statements are in accordance with the applicable financial reporting framework

d. If the financial statements of the prior period were reviewed, a statement that, based on his or her review, the other accountant(s) are not aware of any material modifications that should be made to the financial statements in order for them to be in accordance with the applicable financial reporting framework other than those modifications, if any, indicated in the report

e. A description or a quotation of any modifications of the standard report and of any emphasis-of-matter paragraphs

1.180 When the accountant's report on the financial statements of the prior period contains a changed reference to a departure from the applicable

[2] The successor accountant would not name the predecessor accountant in his or her report unless the predecessor accountant's practice was acquired by, or merged with, that of the successor accountant.

financial reporting framework, the accountant's review report should include an other-matter paragraph indicating

a. the date of the accountant's previous review report;

b. the circumstances or events that caused the reference to be changed; and

c. when applicable, that the financial statements of the prior period have been changed.

1.181 When the prior period financial statements were audited and the auditor's report on the prior period financial statements is not reissued, the review report on the current-period financial statements should include an other-matter paragraph indicating

a. that the financial statements of the prior period were previously audited;

b. the date of the auditor's report on the prior period financial statements;

c. the type of opinion issued on the prior period financial statements;

d. if the opinion was modified, the substantive reasons for the modification; and

e. that no auditing procedures were performed after the date of the previous report.

1.182 When prior-period financial statements have been restated and the predecessor does not to reissue his or her report, the successor accountant may be engaged to report on the financial statements for the prior year. If the predecessor accountant does not reissue his or her report and the successor accountant is not engaged to report on the prior year financial statements, the successor accountant would indicate in an other-matter paragraph of the accountant's review report that a predecessor accountant reported on the financial statements of the prior period before restatement. In addition, if the successor accountant is engaged to perform a review of the restatement adjustment(s), the accountant may also indicate in the accountant's review report that the accountant reviewed the adjustment(s) that was (were) applied to restate prior-year financial statements. An example review report for this situation is included in paragraph 1.239.

Reporting on Known Departures From the Applicable Financial Reporting Framework

1.183 In the course of performing a review on the client's financial statements, the accountant may become aware of a departure from the applicable financial reporting framework (including inadequate disclosure) that is material to the financial statements.

1.184 If the financial statements are not revised, the accountant should consider whether modification of the standard report is adequate to disclose the departure. If the accountant concludes that modification of the standard report is adequate, the departure should be disclosed in a separate paragraph of the report under the heading "Known Departures From the [*identify the applicable financial reporting framework*]," including disclosure of the effects of the departure on the financial statements if such effects have been determined by management or are known to the accountant as the result of the accountant's procedures. The accountant is not required to determine the effects of a

 ©2017, AICPA

departure if management has not done so or if the effects are not known to the accountant as a result of the accountant's procedures. In such circumstances, the accountant is required to state in the report that such determination has not been made.

1.185 If the accountant believes that modification of the standard report is not adequate to indicate the deficiencies in the financial statements as a whole, the accountant should withdraw from the review engagement. The accountant may wish to consult with his or her legal counsel in those circumstances.

1.186 The accountant should not modify the standard report to include a statement that the financial statements are not in accordance with the applicable financial reporting framework. However, the accountant may wish to state the limitations of the financial statements in a separate paragraph in the accountant's review report, depending on the accountant's assessment of the possible dollar magnitude of the effects of the departures, the significance of the affected items to the entity, the pervasiveness and overall impact of the misstatements, and whether disclosure has been made of the effect of the departures. The following is an illustration of such a separate paragraph with respect to an accountant's review report on financial statements prepared in accordance GAAP:

> ***Limitations of the financial statements***
>
> Because the significance and pervasiveness of the matters described in the Known Departures From Accounting Principles Generally Accepted in the United States of America paragraphs makes it difficult to assess their impact on the financial statements, users of the accompanying financial statements should recognize that they might reach different conclusions about the company's financial position, results of operations, and cash flows if they had access to revised financial statements prepared in accordance with accounting principles generally accepted in the United States of America.

1.187 Inclusion of such a separate paragraph in the accountant's review report is not a substitute for disclosure of the specific departures or the effects of such departures when they have been determined by management or are known as a result of the accountant's procedures.

1.188 When faced with a situation in which financial statements contain a departure from promulgated accounting principles that prevents the financial statements from being misleading, the accountant would turn to the "Accounting Principles Rule" (AICPA, *Professional Standards*, ET sec. 1.320.001), which states that a member shall not (1) express an opinion or state affirmatively that the financial statements or other financial data of any entity are presented in conformity with generally accepted accounting principles, or (2) state that he or she is not aware of any material modifications that should be made to such statements or data in order for them to be in conformity with generally accepted accounting principles if such statements or data contain any departure from an accounting principle promulgated by bodies designated by Council to establish such principles that have a material effect on the statements or data taken as a whole. If, however, the statements or data contain such a departure and the member can demonstrate that due to unusual circumstances the financial statements or data would otherwise have been misleading, the member can comply with the rule by describing the departure, its approximate effects (if practicable), and the reasons why compliance with the principle would result in a misleading statement. In this situation, in accordance with paragraph .56 of AR-C section 90, the accountant's review report should include, in a separate paragraph or paragraphs, the information required by the "Accounting Principles Rule," as described previously. In such a case, the accountant would not modify the standard review report, except for the addition of the separate paragraph(s) that contains the information required by the "Accounting Principles Rule," unless there are other reasons to do so that are not associated with the departure from a promulgated principle.

Emphasis-of-Matter and Other-Matter Paragraphs in the Accountant's Review Report

1.189 If the accountant considers it necessary to draw users' attention to a matter appropriately presented or disclosed in the financial statements that, in the accountant's professional judgment, is of such importance that it is fundamental to users' understanding of the financial statements, the accountant should include an emphasis-of-matter paragraph in the accountant's review report, provided that the accountant does not believe that the financial statements may be materially misstated. Such a paragraph should refer only to information presented or disclosed in the financial statements.

1.190 When the accountant includes an emphasis-of-matter paragraph in the accountant's review report, the accountant should

a. include it immediately after the accountant's conclusion paragraph in the accountant's review report,

b. use the heading "Emphasis of a Matter" or other appropriate heading,

c. include in the paragraph a clear reference to the matter being emphasized and to where relevant disclosures that fully describe the matter can be found in the financial statements, and

d. indicate that the accountant's conclusion is not modified with respect to the matter emphasized.

1.191 If the accountant considers it necessary to communicate a matter other than those that are presented or disclosed in the financial statements that (in the accountant's professional judgment) is relevant to the users' understanding of the review, the accountant's responsibilities, or the accountant's review report, the accountant should do so in a paragraph in the accountant's review report with the heading "Other Matter" or other appropriate heading. The accountant should include this paragraph immediately after the accountant's conclusion paragraph and any emphasis-of-matter paragraph.

1.192 If the accountant expects to include an emphasis-of-matter or other-matter paragraph in the accountant's review report, the accountant should communicate with management regarding this expectation and the proposed wording of this paragraph.

1.193 If the accountant concludes that management's disclosure of a material uncertainty is in accordance with the applicable financial reporting framework but further decides to include an emphasis-of-matter paragraph with respect to the uncertainty in the accountant's review report, he or she may use the following language (the following is assuming that the financial statements were prepared in accordance with GAAP):

 ©2017, AICPA

Emphasis of Matter

As discussed in Note X, the Company is currently named in a legal action. The Company has determined that it is not possible to predict the eventual outcome of the legal action but has determined that the resolution of the action will not result in an adverse judgment that would materially affect the financial statements. Accordingly, the accompanying financial statements do not include any adjustments related to the legal action under FASB ASC 450, *Contingencies*.

Alert That Restricts the Use of the Accountant's Review Report

1.194 An accountant's review report should include an alert, in a separate paragraph, that restricts its use when the subject matter of the accountant's review report is based on

a. measurement or disclosure criteria that are determined by the accountant to be suitable only for a limited number of users who can be presumed to have an adequate understanding of the criteria, or

b. measurement or disclosure criteria that are available only to the specified parties.

The alert that restricts the use of the accountant's review report should

a. state that the accountant's review report is intended solely for the information and use of the specified parties.

b. identify the specified parties for whom use is intended.

c. state that the accountant's review report is not intended to be, and should not be, used by anyone other than the specified parties.

1.195 When the accountant includes an alert that restricts the use of the accountant's review report to certain specified parties and the accountant is requested to add other parties as specified parties, the accountant should determine whether to agree to add the other parties as specified parties.

1.196 If the other parties are added after the release of the accountant's review report, the accountant should either:

a. Amend the accountant's review report to add the other parties and, in such circumstances, not change the original date of the accountant's review report.

b. Provide a written acknowledgment to management and the other parties that such parties have been added as specified parties and state in the acknowledgment that no procedures were performed subsequent to the original date of the accountant's review report.

1.197 An accountant's review report for general-use may be included in a document that also includes a separate restricted-use report. For example, the review report on financial statements may be included in a document that also includes an agreed-upon procedures report. The inclusion of the separate restricted-use report does not affect the intended use of the general-use report nor does the inclusion of the general-use report affect the intended use of the restricted-use report. The restricted-use report remains restricted as to use, and the general-use report continues to be for general use.

Reporting on Financial Statements Prepared in Accordance With a Financial Reporting Framework Generally Accepted in Another Country

1.198 An accountant may be engaged to review financial statements that have been prepared in accordance with a financial reporting framework generally accepted in another country (including financial statements prepared in accordance with a jurisdictional variation of IFRSs such that the entity's financial statements do not contain an explicit and unreserved statement of compliance with IFRSs as issued by the International Accounting Standards Board [IASB]). In such instances, the accountant should report in accordance with SSARSs modified as appropriate to identify the applicable financial reporting framework. The accountant may report using the standard review report form and content of the other country if all of the required reporting elements of SSARSs are present.

1.199 The standard review report used in another country, even when it appears similar to that used in the United States of America, may convey a different meaning and entail a different responsibility on the part of the accountant due to custom or culture. Issuing a standard review report of another country may require an understanding of local laws. When issuing the accountant's standard review report of another country, the accountant would obtain an understanding of applicable legal responsibilities, in addition to the review standards and accounting principles generally accepted in the other country. Therefore, depending on the nature and extent of the accountant's knowledge and experience, the accountant may wish to consult with persons having expertise in the reporting practices of the other country and associated legal responsibilities to obtain the understanding needed to issue that country's standard review report.

1.200 A need for restriction on the use of the report may result from a number of circumstances, including, but not limited to, the purpose of the report and the potential for the report to be misunderstood when taken out of context in which it was intended to be used. Because of the nature of the basis of presentation of the financial statements, there is a presumption that the report would be misunderstood or taken out of context in which it was intended to be used. An example review report for this situation is included in this chapter as illustration 12, "An Accountant's Review Report on Comparative Financial Statements Prepared in Accordance With a Financial Reporting Framework Generally Accepted in Another Country."

1.201 Nothing precludes the accountant from issuing two reports—a report to be used only outside of the United States of America and another report to be used in the United States of America—as long as both reports include all of the reporting elements required by SSARSs.

The Accountant's Consideration of an Entity's Ability to Continue as a Going Concern

1.202 FASB issued Accounting Standards Update (ASU) No. 2014-15, *Presentation of Financial Statements—Going Concern (Subtopic 205-40): Disclosure of Uncertainties about an Entity's Ability to Continue as a Going Concern*, in August 2014. The ASU establishes management's responsibility to evaluate whether there is substantial doubt about the entity's ability to continue as a going concern and to make certain related disclosures in the notes to the

 ©2017, AICPA

financial statements. Previously, such guidance did not exist in U.S. GAAP issued by FASB. In summary, FASB ASC 205-40 provides the following new guidance as a result of the issuance of FASB ASU No. 2014-15:

a. Defines the term *substantial doubt about an entity's ability to continue as a going concern* (substantial doubt) as follows:

> Substantial doubt about an entity's ability to continue as a going concern exists when conditions and events, considered in the aggregate, indicate that it is probable that the entity will be unable to meet its obligations as they become due within one year after the date that the financial statements are issued (or within one year after the date that the financial statements are available to be issued when applicable). The term *probable* is used consistently with its use in Topic 450 on contingencies.

b. Requires an evaluation every reporting period, including interim periods.

c. Provides that the mitigating effect of management's plans should be considered only to the extent it is probable the plans will be effectively implemented and mitigate the conditions or events giving rise to substantial doubt.

d. Requires certain disclosures when substantial doubt is alleviated as a result of consideration of management's plans.

e. Requires an explicit statement in the notes to the financial statements that there is substantial doubt and other disclosures when substantial doubt is not alleviated.

f. Requires an evaluation for a period of one year after the date that the financial statements are issued (or available to be issued).

FASB ASC 205-40 applies to all entities required to comply with standards issued by FASB and becomes effective for annual periods ending after December 15, 2016, and for interim periods thereafter. Early application is permitted.

1.203 Going concern responsibilities for preparers of financial statements for state and local governments were incorporated into GASB's standards in 2009 with the issuance of GASB Statement No. 56, *Codification of Accounting and Financial Reporting Guidance Contained in the AICPA Statements on Auditing Standards*, and is currently effective. Although GASB Statement No. 56 generally adopted the guidance included in AU-C section 570A, *The Auditor's Consideration of an Entity's Ability to Continue as a Going Concern* (AICPA, *Professional Standards*), including providing indicators related to when there may be substantial doubt about a governmental entity's ability to continue as a going concern, GASB made certain modifications to require that financial statement preparers evaluate whether there is substantial doubt about a governmental entity's ability to continue as a going concern for 12 months beyond the financial statement date. GASB Statement No. 56 further requires that if information is currently known to the governmental entity that may raise substantial doubt shortly thereafter (for example, within an additional three months), such information also should be considered. Additionally, GASB Statement No. 56 establishes disclosure requirements when a governmental entity determines that there is substantial doubt.

1.204 Paragraph .65 of AR-C section 90 requires the accountant to consider whether, during the performance of review procedures, evidence or information came to the accountant's attention indicating that there could be an uncertainty about the entity's ability to continue as a going concern for a reasonable period of time. Although the term *substantial doubt about an entity's ability to continue as a going concern* is not used in SSARSs, when the applicable financial reporting framework uses the term *substantial doubt about an entity's ability to continue as a going concern*, the accountant performing the review engagement would consider that term as part of the consideration about whether an uncertainty about the entity's ability to continue as a going concern for a reasonable period of time exists. For example, if an entity is required to comply with FASB ASC 205-40, the accountant would consider whether *substantial doubt about an entity's ability to continue as a going concern* as set out in FASB ASC 205-40 exists as part of the accountant's consideration about whether an uncertainty about the entity's ability to continue as a going concern for a reasonable period of time exists.

1.205 Paragraph .65 of AR-C section 90 states that a reasonable period of time is the same period of time required of management to assess going concern when specified by the applicable financial reporting framework. For example, if an entity is required to comply with FASB ASC 205-40, the accountant's consideration about whether, during the performance of review procedures, evidence or information came to the accountant's attention indicating that there could be an uncertainty about the entity's ability to continue as a going concern would need to be for the same period of time as required by FASB ASC 205-40 that management is required to evaluate going concern (that is, one year after the date that the financial statements are issued or available to be issued). If the applicable financial reporting framework does not specify a period of time for management, a reasonable period is one year from the date of the financial statements being reviewed (hereinafter referred to as a *reasonable period of time*).

1.206 Paragraph .17 of AR-C section 90 requires the accountant to design and perform analytical procedures and make inquiries and perform other procedures, as appropriate, to obtain limited assurance as a basis for reporting whether the accountant is aware of any material modifications that should be made to the financial statements in order for the statements to be in accordance with the applicable financial reporting framework. Included would be the design and performance of review procedures related to management's evaluation of the entity's ability to continue as a going concern and the adequacy of the related disclosures in financial statements prepared in accordance with an applicable financial reporting framework that contains explicit requirements concerning management's responsibilities related to evaluating an entity's ability to continue as a going concern when preparing financial statements in accordance with that framework.

1.207 If the accountant concludes that the financial statements are not in accordance with the applicable financial reporting framework, including inadequate disclosure, the accountant should consider whether modification of the standard report is adequate to disclose the departure from the applicable financial reporting framework.

Subsequent Events and Subsequently Discovered Facts

1.208 When evidence or information that subsequent events that require adjustment of, or disclosure in, the financial statements comes to the accountant's attention, the accountant should request that management consider

 ©2017, AICPA

whether each such event is appropriately reflected in the financial statements in accordance with the applicable financial reporting framework.

1.209 The accountant is not required to perform any review procedures regarding the financial statements after the date of the accountant's review report. However, if a subsequently discovered fact becomes known to the accountant before the report release date, the accountant should

a. discuss the matter with management and, when appropriate, those charged with governance and

b. determine whether the financial statements need revision and, if so, inquire how management intends to address the matter in the financial statements.

1.210 If management revises the financial statements, the accountant should perform the review procedures necessary in the circumstances on the revision. The accountant also should either

a. date the accountant's review report as of a later date or

b. include an additional date in the accountant's review report on the revised financial statements that is limited to the revision (that is, dual-date the accountant's review report for that revision), thereby indicating that the accountant's review procedures subsequent to the original date of the accountant's review report are limited solely to the revision of the financial statements described in the relevant note to the financial statements.

1.211 If management does not revise the financial statements in circumstances when the accountant believes they need to be revised, the accountant should modify the accountant's review report, as appropriate.

1.212 If a subsequently discovered fact becomes known to the accountant after the report release date, the accountant should

a. discuss the matter with management and, when appropriate, those charged with governance and

b. determine whether the financial statements need revision and, if so, inquire how management intends to address the matter in the financial statements.

1.213 If management revises the financial statements, the accountant should

a. perform the review procedures necessary in the circumstances on the revision and either

   i. date the accountant's review report as of a later date or

   ii. include an additional date in the accountant's review report on the revised financial statements that is limited to the revision (that is, dual-date the accountant's review report for that revision), thereby indicating that the accountant's review procedures subsequent to the original date of the accountant's review report are limited solely to the revision of the financial statements described in the relevant note to the financial statements.

b. if the reviewed financial statements (before revision) have been made available to third parties, assess whether the steps taken by management are timely and appropriate to ensure that anyone in receipt of those financial statements is informed of the situation, including that the reviewed financial statements are not to be used.

c. if the accountant's conclusion on the revised financial statements differs from the accountant's conclusion on the original financial statements, disclose in an emphasis-of-matter paragraph

   i. the date of the accountant's previous report,

   ii. a description of the revisions, and

   iii. the substantive reasons for the revisions.

1.214 If management does not revise the financial statements in circumstances when the accountant believes they need to be revised, then

a. if the reviewed financial statements have not been made available to third parties, the accountant should notify management and those charged with governance, unless all of those charged with governance are involved in managing the entity, not to make the reviewed financial statements available to third parties before the necessary revisions have been made and a new accountant's review report on the revised financial statements has been provided. If the reviewed financial statements are, nevertheless, subsequently made available to third parties without the necessary revisions, the accountant should assess whether the steps taken by management are timely and appropriate to ensure that anyone in receipt of those financial statements is informed of the situation, including that the reviewed financial statements are not to be used.

b. if the reviewed financial statements have been made available to third parties, the accountant should assess whether the steps taken by management are timely and appropriate to ensure that anyone in receipt of the reviewed financial statements is informed of the situation, including that the reviewed financial statements are not to be used. If management does not take the necessary steps, the accountant should notify management and those charged with governance (unless all of those charged with governance are involved in managing the entity) that the accountant will seek to prevent future use of the accountant's review report. If, despite such notification, management or those charged with governance do not take the necessary steps, the accountant should take appropriate action to seek to prevent use of the accountant's review report. The accountant's course of action depends upon the accountant's legal and ethical rights and obligations. Consequently, the accountant may consider it appropriate to seek legal advice.

Initial Review Engagements—Opening Balances

1.215 An accountant may be engaged to perform an initial review engagement in which either

a. the financial statements for the prior period were not audited or reviewed or

b. the financial statements for the prior period were audited or reviewed by a predecessor practitioner.

1.216 Paragraph .17 of AR-C section 90 requires the accountant to design and perform analytical procedures and make inquiries and perform other procedures, as appropriate, to obtain limited assurance as a basis for reporting

 ©2017, AICPA

whether the accountant is aware of any material modifications that should be made to the financial statements in order for the financial statements to be in accordance with the applicable financial reporting framework. That requirement includes obtaining sufficient appropriate review evidence about whether the opening balances contain misstatements that materially affect the current period's financial statements.

1.217 When performing an initial review engagement, the opening balances may contain misstatements that materially affect the current period's financial statements. In obtaining sufficient appropriate review evidence about whether the opening balances contain misstatements that materially affect the current period's financial statements, the practitioner may consider

- determining whether the prior period's closing balances have been correctly brought forward to the current period or, when appropriate, have been restated.
- determining whether the opening balances reflect the consistent application of appropriate accounting policies.
- evaluating whether procedures performed in the current period provide evidence relevant to the opening balances.
- performing procedures to obtain sufficient appropriate review evidence about whether material modification should be made to the opening balances for them to be in accordance with the applicable financial reporting framework.

Reference to the Work of Other Accountants in an Accountant's Review Report

1.218 Paragraph .25 of AR-C section 90 states that if other accountants have issued a report on the financial statements of significant components, such as subsidiaries and investees, the accountant should obtain and read reports from such other accountants.

1.219 If other accountants audited or reviewed the financial statements of significant components, such as consolidated and unconsolidated subsidiaries and investees, and the accountant of the reporting entity decides not to assume responsibility for the audit or review performed by the other accountants, the accountant of the reporting entity should make reference to the review or audit of such other accountants in the accountant's review report. In that instance, the accountant should clearly indicate in the accountant's review report that the accountant used the work of other accountants and should include the magnitude of the portion of the financial statements audited or reviewed by the other accountants.

1.220 Regardless of whether the accountant of the reporting entity decides to make reference to the review or audit of other accountants, the accountant of the reporting entity should communicate with the other accountants and ascertain

a. that the other accountants are aware that the financial statements of the component that the other accountants have audited or reviewed are to be included in the financial statements on which the accountant of the reporting entity will report and that the other accountants' report thereon will be relied upon (and, where applicable, referred to) by the accountant of the reporting entity.

b. that the other accountants are familiar with the applicable financial reporting framework and with SSARSs or auditing standards generally accepted in the United States of America, as applicable, and will conduct the review or audit in accordance therewith.

c. that a review will be made of matters affecting elimination of intercompany transactions and accounts and, if appropriate in the circumstances, the uniformity of accounting practices among the components included in the financial statements.

Supplementary Information That Accompanies Reviewed Financial Statements

1.221 When supplementary information accompanies reviewed financial statements and the accountant's review report thereon, the accountant should clearly indicate the degree of responsibility, if any, the accountant is taking with respect to such information in either

a. an other-matter paragraph in the accountant's review report on the financial statements or

b. a separate report on the supplementary information.

1.222 When the accountant has subjected the supplementary information to the review procedures applied in the accountant's review of the basic financial statements, the other-matter paragraph in the accountant's review report on the financial statements or the separate report on the supplementary information should state that

a. the supplementary information is presented for purposes of additional analysis and is not a required part of the basic financial statements.

b. the supplementary information is the responsibility of management and was derived from, and relates directly to, the underlying accounting and other records used to prepare the financial statements.

c. the supplementary information has been subjected to the review procedures applied in the accountant's review of the basic financial statements, and whether the accountant is aware of any material modifications that should be made to the supplementary information.

d. the accountant has not audited the supplementary information and, accordingly, does not express an opinion on such information.

1.223 When the accountant has not subjected the supplementary information to the review procedures applied in the accountant's review of the basic financial statements, the other-matter paragraph in the accountant's review report on the financial statements or the separate report on the supplementary information should state that

a. the supplementary information is presented for purposes of additional analysis and is not a required part of the basic financial statements.

b. the supplementary information is the responsibility of management.

 ©2017, AICPA

c. the accountant has not audited or reviewed the supplementary information and, accordingly, does not express an opinion, a conclusion, nor provide any assurance on such information.

Required Supplementary Information

1.224 With respect to required supplementary information, the accountant should include an other-matter paragraph in the accountant's review report on the financial statements. The other matter-paragraph should include language to explain the following circumstances, as applicable:

a. The required supplementary information is included, and the accountant performed a compilation engagement on the required supplementary information.

b. The required supplementary information is included, and the accountant reviewed the required supplementary information.

c. The required supplementary information is included, and the accountant did not perform a compilation, review, or audit on the required supplementary information.

d. The required supplementary information is omitted.

e. Some required supplementary information is missing, and some is presented in accordance with the prescribed guidelines.

f. The accountant has identified departures from the prescribed guidelines.

g. The accountant has unresolved doubts about whether the required supplementary information is presented in accordance with prescribed guidelines.

1.225 If the entity has presented all or some of the required supplementary information and the accountant did not perform a compilation or review on the required supplementary information, the other-matter paragraph should include the following elements:

a. A statement that [*identify the applicable financial reporting framework (for example, accounting principles generally accepted in the United States of America)*] require that the [*identify the required supplementary information*] be presented to supplement the basic financial statements

b. A statement that such information, although not a part of the basic financial statements, is required by [*identify designated accounting standard setter*], who considers it to be an essential part of financial reporting for placing the basic financial statements in an appropriate operational, economic, or historical context

c. A statement that the accountant did not perform a compilation, review, or audit on the required supplementary information and does not express an opinion or provide any assurance on the information

d. If some of the required supplementary information is omitted

   i. a statement that management has omitted [*description of the missing required supplementary information*] that [*identify the applicable financial reporting framework (for example, accounting principles generally accepted in the United States of America)*] require to be presented to supplement the basic financial statements

ii. a statement that such missing information, although not a part of the basic financial statements, is required by [*identify designated accounting standards-setter*], who considers it to be an essential part of financial reporting for placing the basic financial statements in an appropriate operational, economic, or historical context

e. If the measurement or presentation of the required supplementary information departs materially from the prescribed guidelines, a statement that material departures from prescribed guidelines exist [*describe the material departures from the applicable financial reporting framework*]

f. If the accountant has unresolved doubts about whether the required supplementary information is measured or presented in accordance with prescribed guidelines, a statement that the accountant has doubts about whether material modifications should be made to the required supplementary information for it to be presented in accordance with guidelines established by [*identify designated accounting standard setter*]

1.226 If all the required supplementary information is omitted, the other-matter paragraph should include the following elements:

a. A statement that management has omitted [*description of the missing required supplementary information*] that [*identify the applicable financial reporting framework (for example, accounting principles generally accepted in the United States of America)*] require to be presented to supplement the basic financial statements

b. A statement that such missing information, although not a part of the basic financial statements, is required by [*identify designated accounting standard setter*], who considers it to be an essential part of financial reporting for placing the basic financial statements in an appropriate operational, economic, or historical context

Change in Engagement From Audit to Review

1.227 If the accountant, who was engaged to perform an audit engagement in accordance with generally accepted auditing standards, has been requested to change the engagement to a review engagement, the accountant should consider the following before deciding whether to agree to the change:

a. The reason given for the request, particularly the implications of a restriction on the scope of the audit engagement, whether imposed by management or by circumstances

b. The additional audit effort required to complete the audit engagement

c. The estimated additional cost to complete the audit engagement

1.228 In all circumstances, if the audit procedures are substantially complete or the cost to complete such procedures is relatively insignificant, the accountant should consider the propriety of accepting a change in the engagement.

1.229 If the accountant concludes, based upon the accountant's professional judgment, that reasonable justification exists to change the engagement,

 ©2017, AICPA

and if the accountant complies with the standards applicable to a review engagement, the accountant should issue an appropriate review report.

1.230 The report should not include reference to

a. the original engagement,

b. any audit procedures that may have been performed, or

c. scope limitations that resulted in the changed engagement.

1.231 When the accountant has been engaged to audit an entity's financial statements and management refuses to allow the accountant to correspond with the entity's legal counsel, the accountant, except in rare circumstances, is precluded from accepting an engagement to review those financial statements.

Review Documentation

1.232 Documentation provides the principal support for the representation in the review report that the accountant performed the review in accordance with SSARSs and the statement in the review report that, based upon the accountant's review, the accountant is not aware of any material modifications that should be made to the financial statements in order for them to be in accordance with the applicable financial reporting framework.

1.233 The accountant should prepare review documentation in connection with each review engagement in sufficient detail to enable an experienced accountant, having no previous connection to the review, to understand

a. the nature, timing, and extent of the review procedures performed to comply with SSARSs;

b. the results of the review procedures performed and the review evidence obtained; and

c. significant findings or issues arising during the review, the conclusions reached thereon, and significant professional judgments made in reaching those conclusions.

1.234 In addition to the requirements stated in paragraph 1.233, the review documentation should include the following:

a. The engagement letter or other suitable form of written documentation with management

b. Communications to management and others regarding fraud or noncompliance with laws and regulations

c. Communications with management regarding the accountant's expectation to include an emphasis-of-matter or other-matter paragraph in the accountant's review report

d. Communications with other accountants that have audited or reviewed the financial statements of significant components

e. The representation letter

f. A copy of the reviewed financial statements and the accountant's review report thereon

Observations and Suggestions

The accountant is not precluded from supporting the review report by other means, in addition to the review documentation. Such other means might include written documentation contained in other engagement files or quality control files (for example, consultation files) and, in limited situations, oral explanations.

Illustrative Engagement Letters

Notice to Readers

The illustrative engagement letters presented in this section are intended to show how the engagement letter can be presented assuming that the accountant has been engaged to perform a review engagement on the financial statements or financial information. The engagement letter will vary according to individual requirements and circumstances and may be modified to include other services that the accountant may be engaged to perform such as nonattest services. In those cases, the engagement letter may include management's acknowledgment of its responsibilities in accordance with the "Nonattest Services" subtopic of the "Independence Rule." The accountant may seek legal advice about whether the proposed letter is suitable.

1.235 The illustrative engagement letters in this paragraph are as follows:

Illustration 1—An Engagement Letter for a Review Engagement With Respect to Financial Statements Prepared in Accordance With Accounting Principles Generally Accepted in the United States of America

Illustration 2—An Engagement Letter for a Review Engagement With Respect to Financial Statements Prepared in Accordance With the Tax-Basis of Accounting

Illustration 3—Engagement Letter for an Engagement to Review One or More Specified Elements, Accounts, or Items of a Financial Statement

Illustration 1—An Engagement Letter for a Review Engagement With Respect to Financial Statements Prepared in Accordance With Accounting Principles Generally Accepted in the United States of America

Circumstances include the following:

- The accountant will prepare, as a nonattest service, the financial statements, including related notes, subject to the review engagement.
- The financial statements will be prepared in accordance with accounting principles generally accepted in the United States of America.

To the appropriate representative of management of ABC Company:[3]

[3] The addresses and references in the engagement letter would be those that are appropriate in the circumstances of the review engagement, including the relevant jurisdiction. It is important to refer to the appropriate persons. See paragraph .A15 of AR-C section 90, *Review of Financial Statements* (AICPA, *Professional Standards*).

 ©2017, AICPA

You[4] have requested that we prepare the financial statements of ABC Company (the Company), which comprise the balance sheet as of December 31, 20X2, and the related statements of income, changes in stockholders' equity, and cash flows for the year then ended, and the related notes to the financial statements and perform a review engagement with respect to those financial statements.[5] We are pleased to confirm our acceptance and understanding of this engagement by means of this letter.

Our Responsibilities

The objective of our engagement is to

a. prepare financial statements in accordance with accounting principles generally accepted in the United States of America based on information provided by you and

b. obtain limited assurance as a basis for reporting whether we are aware of any material modifications that should be made to the financial statements in order for the statements to be in accordance with accounting principles generally accepted in the United States of America.

We will conduct our engagement in accordance with Statements on Standards for Accounting and Review Services (SSARSs) promulgated by the Accounting and Review Services Committee of the AICPA and comply with the AICPA's Code of Professional Conduct, including ethical principles of integrity, objectivity, professional competence, and due care.

A review engagement includes primarily applying analytical procedures to your financial data and making inquiries of Company management. A review engagement is substantially less in scope than an audit engagement, the objective of which is the expression of an opinion regarding the financial statements as a whole. A review engagement does not contemplate obtaining an understanding of the Company's internal control; assessing fraud risk; testing accounting records by obtaining sufficient appropriate audit evidence through inspection, observation, confirmation, or the examination of source documents; or other procedures ordinarily performed in an audit engagement. Accordingly, we will not express an opinion regarding the financial statements.

Our engagement cannot be relied upon to identify or disclose any financial statement misstatements, including those caused by error or fraud, or to identify or disclose any wrongdoing within the Company or noncompliance with laws and regulations. However, we will inform the appropriate level of management of any material errors and any evidence or information that comes to our attention during the performance of our review procedures that indicates fraud may have occurred. In addition, we will report to you any evidence or information that comes to our attention during the performance of our review procedures regarding noncompliance with laws and regulations that may have occurred, unless they are clearly inconsequential.

Your Responsibilities

The engagement to be performed is conducted on the basis that you acknowledge and understand that our role is to prepare financial statements in accordance with accounting principles generally accepted in the United States of

---

[4] Throughout this engagement letter, references to *you*, *we*, *us*, *management*, and *accountant* would be used or amended as appropriate in the circumstances.

[5] The accountant may include other nonattest services to be performed as part of the engagement, such as income tax preparation and bookkeeping services.

America and to obtain limited assurance as a basis for reporting whether we are aware of any material modifications that should be made to the financial statements in order for the statements to be in accordance with accounting principles generally accepted in the United States of America. You have the following overall responsibilities that are fundamental to our undertaking the engagement in accordance with SSARSs:

a. The selection of accounting principles generally accepted in the United States of America as the financial reporting framework to be applied in the preparation of the financial statements

b. The preparation and fair presentation of the financial statements in accordance with accounting principles generally accepted in the United States of America and the inclusion of all informative disclosures that are appropriate for accounting principles generally accepted in the United States of America

c. The design, implementation, and maintenance of internal control relevant to the preparation and fair presentation of the financial statements

d. The prevention and detection of fraud

e. To ensure that the Company complies with the laws and regulations applicable to its activities

f. The accuracy and completeness of the records, documents, explanations, and other information, including significant judgments, you provide to us for the engagement

g. To provide us with:

   i. access to all information of which you are aware is relevant to the preparation and fair presentation of the financial statements, such as records, documentation, and other matters

   ii. additional information that we may request from you for the purpose of the review engagement

   iii. unrestricted access to persons within the Company of whom we determine it necessary to make inquiries

h. To provide us, at the conclusion of the engagement, with a letter that confirms certain representations made during the review

You are also responsible for all management decisions and responsibilities, and for designating an individual with suitable skills, knowledge, and experience to oversee our preparation of your financial statements. You are responsible for evaluating the adequacy and results of services performed and accepting responsibility for such services.

Our Report

[*Insert appropriate reference to the expected form and content of the accountant's review report. Example follows.*]

We will issue a written report upon completion of our review of the Company's financial statements. Our report will be addressed to the board of directors of the Company. We cannot provide assurance that an unmodified accountant's review report will be issued. Circumstances may arise in which it is necessary for us to report known departures from accounting principles generally accepted in the United States of America, add an emphasis-of-matter or other-matter

 ©2017, AICPA

paragraph(s), or withdraw from the engagement. If, for any reason, we are unable to complete the review of your financial statements, we will not issue a report on such statements as a result of this engagement.

You agree to include our accountant's review report in any document containing financial statements that indicates that such financial statements have been reviewed by us and, prior to inclusion of the report, to ask our permission to do so.

Other Relevant Information

Our fees for these services. . .

[*The accountant may include language, such as the following, regarding limitation of or other arrangements regarding the liability of the accountant or the entity, such as indemnification to the accountant for liability arising from knowing misrepresentations to the accountant by management (regulators may restrict or prohibit such liability limitation arrangements):*

You agree to hold us harmless and to release, indemnify, and defend us from any liability or costs, including attorney's fees, resulting from management's knowing misrepresentations to us or resulting from any actions against us by third parties relying on the financial statements described herein except for our own intentional wrongdoing.]

If you request us to perform additional services not contemplated or described in this engagement letter, we will provide you with a separate agreement describing those additional services and fees.

Please sign and return the attached copy of this letter to indicate your acknowledgment of, and agreement with, the arrangements for our engagement to prepare the financial statements described herein and to perform a review of those same financial statements and our respective responsibilities.

Sincerely yours,

____

[*Signature of accountant or accountant's firm*]

Acknowledged and agreed on behalf of ABC Company by:

____

[*Signed*]
[*Name and Title*]

____

[*Date*]

Illustration 2—An Engagement Letter for a Review Engagement With Respect to Financial Statements Prepared in Accordance With the Tax-Basis of Accounting

Circumstances include the following:

- The accountant will prepare, as a nonattest service, the financial statements, including related notes, subject to the review engagement.
- The financial statements will be prepared in accordance with the tax-basis of accounting.

To the appropriate representative of management of ABC Company:[6]

You[7] have requested that we prepare the financial statements of ABC Company (the Company), which comprise the statement of assets, liabilities, and equity—tax-basis as of December 31, 20X2, and the related statements of operations and retained earnings—tax-basis, and cash flows—tax-basis for the year then ended, and the related notes to the financial statements and to perform a review engagement with respect to those financial statements.[8] We are pleased to confirm our acceptance and our understanding of this engagement by means of this letter.

Our Responsibilities

The objective of our engagement is to

a. prepare financial statements in accordance with the tax-basis of accounting based on information provided by you and

b. obtain limited assurance as a basis for reporting whether we are aware of any material modifications that should be made to the financial statements in order for the statements to be in accordance with the tax-basis of accounting.

We will conduct our review engagement in accordance with Statements on Standards for Accounting and Review Services (SSARSs) promulgated by the Accounting and Review Services Committee of the AICPA and comply with the AICPA's Code of Professional Conduct, including ethical principles of integrity, objectivity, professional competence, and due care.

A review engagement includes primarily applying analytical procedures to your financial data and making inquiries of Company management. A review engagement is substantially less in scope than an audit engagement, the objective of which is the expression of an opinion regarding the financial statements as a whole. A review engagement does not contemplate obtaining an understanding of the Company's internal control; assessing fraud risk; testing accounting records by obtaining sufficient appropriate audit evidence through inspection, observation, confirmation, or the examination of source documents; or other procedures ordinarily performed in an audit engagement. Accordingly, we will not express an opinion regarding the financial statements.

Our engagement cannot be relied upon to identify or disclose any financial statement misstatements, including those caused by error or fraud, or to identify or disclose any wrongdoing within the Company or noncompliance with laws and regulations. However, we will inform the appropriate level of management of any material errors and any evidence or information that comes to our attention during the performance of our review procedures that indicates fraud may have occurred. In addition, we will report to you any evidence or information that comes to our attention during the performance of our review procedures regarding noncompliance with laws and regulations that may have occurred, unless they are clearly inconsequential.

Your Responsibilities

The engagement to be performed is conducted on the basis that you acknowledge and understand that our role is to prepare financial statements in accordance with the tax-basis of accounting and to obtain limited assurance as a

[6] See footnote 3.

[7] See footnote 4.

[8] See footnote 5.

©2017, AICPA

basis for reporting whether we are aware of any material modifications that should be made to the financial statements in order for the statements to be in accordance with the tax-basis of accounting. You have the following overall responsibilities that are fundamental to our undertaking the engagement in accordance with SSARSs:

a. The selection of the tax-basis of accounting as the financial reporting framework to be applied in the preparation of the financial statements

b. The preparation and fair presentation of the financial statements in accordance with the tax-basis of accounting and the inclusion of all informative disclosures that are appropriate for the tax-basis of accounting. This includes

   i. a description of the tax-basis of accounting, including a summary of significant accounting policies, and how the tax-basis of accounting differs from accounting principles generally accepted in the United States of America, the effects of which need not be qualified

   ii. informative disclosures similar to those required by accounting principles generally accepted in the United States of America

c. The design, implementation, and maintenance of internal control relevant to the preparation and fair presentation of the financial statements

d. The prevention and detection of fraud

e. To ensure that the Company complies with the laws and regulations applicable to its activities

f. The accuracy and completeness of the records, documents, explanations, and other information, including significant judgments, you provide to us for the engagement

g. To provide us with

   i. access to all information of which you are aware is relevant to the preparation and fair presentation of the financial statements, such as records, documentation, and other matters

   ii. additional information that we may request from you for the purpose of the review engagement

   iii. unrestricted access to persons within the Company of whom we determine it necessary to make inquiries

h. To provide us, at the conclusion of the engagement, with a letter that confirms certain representations made during the review

You are also responsible for all management decisions and responsibilities and for designating an individual with suitable skills, knowledge, and experience to oversee our preparation of your financial statements. You are responsible for evaluating the adequacy and results of the services performed and accepting responsibility for such services.

Our Report

[*Insert appropriate reference to the expected form and content of the accountant's review report. Example follows.*]

We will issue a written report upon completion of our review of the Company's financial statements. Our report will be addressed to the board of directors of the Company. We cannot provide assurance that an unmodified accountant's review report will be issued. Circumstances may arise in which it is necessary of us to report known departures from the tax-basis of accounting, add an emphasis-of-matter or other-matter paragraph(s), or withdraw from the engagement. If, for any reason, we are unable to complete the review of your financial statements, we will not issue a report on such statements as a result of this engagement.

Our report will state that the financial statements are prepared in accordance with the basis of accounting the Company uses for income tax purposes, which is a basis of accounting other than accounting principles generally accepted in the United States of America. Our conclusion will not be modified with respect to this matter.

You agree to include our accountant's review report in any document containing financial statements that indicates that such financial statements have been reviewed by us and, prior to inclusion of the report, to ask our permission to do so.

Other Relevant Information

Our fees for these services. . .

[*The accountant may include language, such as the following, regarding limitation of or other arrangements regarding the liability of the accountant or the entity, such as indemnification to the accountant for liability arising from knowing misrepresentations to the accountant by management (regulators may restrict or prohibit such liability limitation arrangements):*

You agree to hold us harmless and to release, indemnify, and defend us from any liability or costs, including attorney's fees, resulting from management's knowing misrepresentations to us or resulting from any actions against us by third parties relying on the financial statements described herein except for our own intentional wrongdoing.]

If you request us to perform additional services not contemplated or described in this engagement letter, we will provide you with a separate agreement describing those additional services and fees.

Please sign and return the attached copy of this letter to indicate your acknowledgment of, and agreement with, the arrangements for our engagement to prepare the financial statements described herein and to perform a review with respect to those same financial statements and our respective responsibilities.

Sincerely yours,

____

[*Signature of accountant or accountant's firm*]

Acknowledged and agreed on behalf of ABC Company by:

____

[*Signed*]
[*Name and Title*]

____

[*Date*]

 ©2017, AICPA

Illustration 3—An Engagement Letter for an Engagement to Review One or More Specified Elements, Accounts, or Items of a Financial Statement

Circumstances include the following:

- The accountant will prepare, as a nonattest service, the specified element(s), accounts(s), or item(s) of a financial statement subject to the review engagement.
- The specified element(s), account(s), or item(s) of a financial statement will be prepared in accordance with accounting principles generally accepted in the United States of America.

To the appropriate representative of management of ABC Company:[9]

You[10] have requested that we prepare the [*identify specified element(s), account(s), or item(s) of the financial statement, for example, schedule of accounts receivable, or schedule of depreciation*] of ABC Company (the Company) as of December 31, 20X2, and perform a review engagement with respect to the [*identify specified element(s), account(s), or item(s) of the financial statement, for example, schedule of accounts receivable, or schedule of depreciation*].[11] We are pleased to confirm our acceptance and understanding of this engagement by means of this letter.

Our Responsibilities

The objective of our engagement is to

a. prepare the [*identify specified element(s), account(s), or item(s) of the financial statement, for example, schedule of accounts receivable, or schedule of depreciation*] in accordance with accounting principles generally accepted in the United States of America based on information provided by you and

b. obtain limited assurance as a basis for reporting whether we are aware of any material modifications that should be made to the [*identify specified element(s), account(s), or item(s) of the financial statement, for example, schedule of accounts receivable, or schedule of depreciation*] in order for it to be in accordance with accounting principles generally accepted in the United States of America.

We will conduct our engagement in accordance with Statements on Standards for Accounting and Review Services (SSARSs) promulgated by the Accounting and Review Services Committee of the AICPA and comply with the AICPA's Code of Professional Conduct, including ethical principles of integrity, objectivity, professional competence, and due care.

A review engagement includes primarily applying analytical procedures to your financial data and making inquiries of Company management. A review engagement is substantially less in scope than an audit engagement, the objective of which is the expression of an opinion regarding the [*identify specified element(s), account(s), or item(s) of the financial statement, for example, schedule of accounts receivable, or schedule of depreciation*] as a whole. A review engagement does not contemplate obtaining an understanding of the Company's

[9] See footnote 3.

[10] See footnote 4.

[11] See footnote 5.

internal control; assessing fraud risk; testing accounting records by obtaining sufficient appropriate audit evidence through inspection, observation, confirmation, or the examination of source documents; or other procedures ordinarily performed in an audit engagement. Accordingly, we will not express an opinion regarding the [*identify specified element(s), account(s), or item(s) of the financial statement, for example, schedule of accounts receivable, or schedule of depreciation*].

Our engagement cannot be relied upon to identify or disclose any financial statement misstatements, including those caused by error or fraud, or to identify or disclose any wrongdoing within the Company or noncompliance with laws and regulations. However, we will inform the appropriate level of management of any material errors and any evidence or information that comes to our attention during the performance of our review procedures that indicates fraud may have occurred. In addition, we will report to you any evidence or information that comes to our attention during the performance of our review procedures regarding noncompliance with laws and regulations that may have occurred, unless they are clearly inconsequential.

Your Responsibilities

The engagement to be performed is conducted on the basis that you acknowledge and understand that our role is to prepare the [*identify specified element(s), account(s), or item(s) of the financial statement, for example, schedule of accounts receivable, or schedule of depreciation*] in accordance with accounting principles generally accepted in the United States of America and to obtain limited assurance as a basis for reporting whether we are aware of any material modifications that should be made to the [*identify specified element(s), account(s), or item(s) of the financial statement, for example, schedule of accounts receivable, or schedule of depreciation*] in order for it to be in accordance with accounting principles generally accepted in the United States of America. You have the following overall responsibilities that are fundamental to our undertaking the engagement in accordance with SSARSs:

a. The selection of accounting principles generally accepted in the United States of America as the financial reporting framework to be applied in the preparation of the [*identify specified element(s), account(s), or item(s) of the financial statement, for example, schedule of accounts receivable, or schedule of depreciation*]

b. The preparation and fair presentation of the [*identify specified element(s), account(s), or item(s) of the financial statement, for example, schedule of accounts receivable, or schedule of depreciation*] in accordance with accounting principles generally accepted in the United States of America and the inclusion of all informative disclosures that are appropriate for accounting principles generally accepted in the United States of America

c. The design, implementation, and maintenance of internal control relevant to the preparation and fair presentation of the [*identify specified element(s), account(s), or item(s) of the financial statement, for example, schedule of accounts receivable, or schedule of depreciation*]

d. The prevention and detection of fraud

e. To ensure that the Company complies with the laws and regulations applicable to its activities

 ©2017, AICPA

f. The accuracy and completeness of the records, documents, explanations, and other information, including significant judgments, you provide to us for the engagement

g. To provide us with:

i. access to all information of which you are aware is relevant to the preparation and fair presentation of the [*identify specified element(s), account(s), or item(s) of the financial statement, for example, schedule of accounts receivable, or schedule of depreciation*], such as records, documentation, and other matters

ii. additional information that we may request from you for the purpose of the review engagement

iii. unrestricted access to persons within the Company of whom we determine it necessary to make inquiries

h. To provide us, at the conclusion of the engagement, with a letter that confirms certain representations made during the review

You are also responsible for all management decisions and responsibilities, and for designating an individual with suitable skills, knowledge, and experience to oversee our preparation of your [*identify specified element(s), account(s), or item(s) of the financial statement, for example, schedule of accounts receivable, or schedule of depreciation*]. You are responsible for evaluating the adequacy and results of services performed and accepting responsibility for such services.

Our Report

[*Insert appropriate reference to the expected form and content of the accountant's review report. Example follows.*]

We will issue a written report upon completion of our review of the Company's [*identify specified element(s), account(s), or item(s) of the financial statement, for example, schedule of accounts receivable, or schedule of depreciation*]. Our report will be addressed to the board of directors of the Company. We cannot provide assurance that an unmodified accountant's review report will be issued. Circumstances may arise in which it is necessary for us to report known departures from accounting principles generally accepted in the United States of America, add an emphasis-of-matter or other-matter paragraph(s), or withdraw from the engagement. If, for any reason, we are unable to complete the review of your [*identify specified element(s), account(s), or item(s) of the financial statement, for example, schedule of accounts receivable, or schedule of depreciation*], we will not issue a report on such [*identify specified element, account(s), or item(s) of the financial statement, for example, schedule of accounts receivable, or schedule of depreciation*] as a result of this engagement.

You agree to include our accountant's review report in any document containing the [*identify specified element(s), account(s), or item(s) of the financial statement, for example, schedule of accounts receivable, or schedule of depreciation*] that indicates that such [*identify specified element(s), account(s), or item(s) of the financial statement, for example, schedule of accounts receivable, or schedule of depreciation*] has been reviewed by us and, prior to inclusion of the report, to ask our permission to do so.

Other Relevant Information

Our fees for these services. . .

[*The accountant may include language, such as the following, regarding limitation of or other arrangements regarding the liability of the accountant or the entity, such as indemnification to the accountant for liability arising from knowing misrepresentations to the accountant by management (regulators may restrict or prohibit such liability limitation arrangements):*

You agree to hold us harmless and to release, indemnify, and defend us from any liability or costs, including attorney's fees, resulting from management's knowing misrepresentations to us or resulting from any actions against us by third parties relying on the financial statements described herein except for our own intentional wrongdoing.]

If you request us to perform additional services not contemplated or described in this engagement letter, we will provide you with a separate agreement describing those additional services and fees.

Please sign and return the attached copy of this letter to indicate your acknowledgment of, and agreement with, the arrangements for our engagement to prepare the [*identify specified element(s), account(s), or item(s) of the financial statement, for example, schedule of accounts receivable, or schedule of depreciation*] described herein and to perform a review of that same [*identify specified element(s), account(s), or item(s) of the financial statement, for example, schedule of accounts receivable, or schedule of depreciation*] and our respective responsibilities.

Sincerely yours,

____

[*Signature of accountant or accountant's firm*]

Acknowledged and agreed on behalf of ABC Company by:

____

[*Signed*]
[*Name and Title*]

____

[*Date*]

Illustrative Representation Letter

1.236 The following illustrative letter is intended as an illustration that may be used to comply with the requirements of AR-C section 90. The representation letter will vary according to individual requirements and circumstances.

1.237 It is assumed in this illustration that the applicable financial reporting framework is accounting principles generally accepted in the United States of America, that no conditions or events exist that might be indicative of the entity's inability to continue as a going concern, and that no exceptions exist to the requested written representations. If circumstances differ from these assumptions, the representations would need to be modified to reflect the actual circumstances.

(Entity Letterhead)

(To Accountant)

(Date)

 ©2017, AICPA

This representation letter is provided in connection with your review of the financial statements of ABC Company (the Company), which comprise the balance sheets as of December 31, 20X2 and 20X1, and the related statements of income, changes in stockholders' equity and cash flows for the years then ended, and the related notes to the financial statements, for the purpose of obtaining limited assurance as a basis for reporting whether you are aware of any material modifications that should be made to the financial statements in order for the statements to be in accordance with accounting principles generally accepted in the United States of America.

Certain representations in this letter are described as being limited to matters that are material. Items are considered material, regardless of size, if they involve an omission or misstatement of accounting information that, in the light of surrounding circumstances, makes it probable that the judgment of a reasonable person relying on the information would be changed or influenced by the omission or misstatement.

We represent that [*to the best of our knowledge and belief, having made such inquiries as we considered necessary for the purpose of appropriately informing ourselves*] [*as of* (*date of accountant's review report*)]:

Financial Statements

- We acknowledge our responsibility and have fulfilled our responsibilities for the preparation and fair presentation of the financial statements in accordance with accounting principles generally accepted in the United States of America.
- We acknowledge our responsibility and have fulfilled our responsibilities for the design, implementation, and maintenance of internal control relevant to the preparation and fair presentation of financial statements that are free from material misstatement, whether due to fraud or error.
- We acknowledge our responsibility for the design, implementation, and maintenance of internal control to prevent and detect fraud.
- Significant assumptions used by us in making accounting estimates, including those measured at fair value, are reasonable.
- Related party relationships and transactions have been appropriately accounted for and disclosed in accordance with the requirements of accounting principles generally accepted in the United States of America.
- Guarantees, whether written or oral, under which the company is contingently liable have been properly accounted for and disclosed in accordance with the requirements of accounting principles generally accepted in the United States of America.
- Significant estimates and material concentrations known to management that are required to be disclosed in accordance with FASB *Accounting Standards Codification* (ASC) 275, *Risks and Uncertainties*, have been properly accounted for and disclosed in accordance with the requirements of accounting principles generally accepted in the United States of America. [Significant estimates *are estimates at the balance sheet date that could change materially within the next year.* Concentrations *refer to volumes of*

business, revenues, available sources of supply, or markets or geographic areas for which events could occur that would significantly disrupt normal finances within the next year.]

- All events subsequent to the date of the financial statements and for which accounting principles generally accepted in the United States of America requires adjustment or disclosure have been adjusted or disclosed.
- The effects of uncorrected misstatements are immaterial, both individually and in the aggregate, to the financial statements as a whole.
- The effects of all known actual or possible litigation and claims have been accounted for and disclosed in accordance with accounting principles generally accepted in the United States of America.

[*Any other matters that the accountant may consider appropriate.*]

Information Provided

- We have responded fully and truthfully to all inquiries made to us by you during your review.
- We have provided you with
  - — access to all information, of which we are aware, that is relevant to the preparation and fair presentation of the financial statements, such as records, documentation, and other matters;
  - — minutes of meetings of stockholders, directors, and committees of directors or summaries of actions of recent meetings for which minutes have not yet been prepared;
  - — additional information that you have requested from us for the purpose of the review; and
  - — unrestricted access to persons within the entity from whom you determined it necessary to obtain review evidence.
- All transactions have been recorded in the accounting records and are reflected in the financial statements.
- We have [*no knowledge of any*] [*disclosed to you all information that we are aware of regarding*] fraud or suspected fraud that affects the Company and involves
  - — management,
  - — employees who have significant roles in internal control, or
  - — others when the fraud could have a material effect on the financial statements.
- We have [*no knowledge of any*] [*disclosed to you all information that we are aware of regarding*] allegations of fraud, or suspected fraud, affecting the Company's financial statements as a whole communicated by employees, former employees, analysts, regulators, or others.
- We have no plans or intentions that may materially affect the carrying amounts or classification of assets and liabilities.

 ©2017, AICPA

- We have disclosed to you all known instances of noncompliance or suspected noncompliance with laws or regulations whose effects should be considered when preparing financial statements.
- We [*have disclosed to you all known actual or possible*] [*are not aware of any pending or threatened*] litigation and claims whose effects should be considered when preparing the financial statements [*and we have not consulted legal counsel concerning litigation or claims*]
- We have disclosed to you any other material liabilities or gain or loss contingencies that are required to be accrued or disclosed by FASB ASC 450, *Contingencies*.
- We have disclosed to you the identity of the Company's related parties and all the related party relationships and transactions of which we are aware.
- No material losses exist (such as from obsolete inventory or purchase or sale commitments) that have not been properly accrued or disclosed in the financial statements.
- The Company has satisfactory title to all owned assets, and no liens or encumbrances on such assets exist, nor has any asset been pledged as collateral, except as disclosed to you and reported in the financial statements.
- We have complied with all aspects of contractual agreements that would have a material effect on the financial statements in the event of noncompliance.
- We are in agreement with the adjusting journal entries that you have recommended, and they have been posted to the company's accounts (if applicable).

[*Any other matters that the accountant may consider necessary.*]

____

[*Name of Chief Executive Officer and Title*]

____

[*Name of Chief Financial Officer and Title*]

1.238 Representation letters ordinarily are tailored to include additional appropriate representations from management relating to matters specific to the entity's business or industry.

Illustrative Accountant's Review Reports on Financial Statements

1.239 The illustrative accountant's review reports in this section are intended as illustrations that may be used to comply with the requirements of AR-C section 90. The accountant's review report will vary according to individual requirements and circumstances.

Illustration 1—An Accountant's Review Report on Comparative Financial Statements Prepared in Accordance With Accounting Principles Generally Accepted in the United States of America When a Review Has Been Performed for Both Periods

©2017, AICPA

Illustration 2—An Accountant's Review Report on Single Year Financial Statements Prepared in Accordance With Accounting Principles Generally Accepted in the United States of America

Illustration 3—An Accountant's Review Report on Comparative Financial Statements Prepared in Accordance With the AICPA's Financial Reporting Framework for Small- and Medium Sized Entities

Illustration 4—An Accountant's Review Report on Single Year Financial Statements Prepared in Accordance With the Tax-Basis of Accounting

Illustration 5—An Accountant's Review Report on Single Year Financial Statements Prepared in Accordance With a Contractual Basis of Accounting

Illustration 6—An Accountant's Review Report on Interim Financial Statements Prepared in Accordance With Accounting Principles Generally Accepted in the United States of America

Illustration 7—An Accountant's Review Report on Comparative Financial Statements Disclosing a Departure From Accounting Principles Generally Accepted in the United States of America

Illustration 8—An Accountant's Review Report on Comparative Consolidated Financial Statements in Which the Accountant Makes Reference to the Work of Other Accountants Who Were Engaged to Review the Financial Statements of a Significant Component

Illustration 9—An Accountant's Review Report on Comparative Consolidated Financial Statements and all Required Supplementary Information Accompanies the Financial Statements and the Accountant Reviewed the Required Supplementary Information

Illustration 10—An Accountant's Review Report on Comparative Financial Statements Prepared in Accordance With Accounting Principles Generally Accepted in the United States of America and the Review Is Performed in Accordance With Statements on Standards for Accounting and Review Services and International Standard on Review Engagements 2400 (Revised) Issued by the International Auditing and Assurance Standards Board

Illustration 11—An Accountant's Review Report on Comparative Financial Statements Prepared in Accordance With International Financial Reporting Standards as Issued by the International Accounting Standards Board and the Review Is Performed in Accordance With Statements on Standards for Accounting and Review Services and International Standard on Review Engagements 2400 (Revised) Issued by the International Auditing and Assurance Standards Board

Illustration 12—An Accountant's Review Report on Comparative Financial Statements Prepared in Accordance With a Financial Reporting Framework Generally Accepted in Another Country

Illustration 13—An Accountant's Review Report on Comparative Financial Statements Prepared in Accordance With Accounting Principles Generally Accepted in the United States of America When the Financial Statements of the Prior Year Were Audited

 ©2017, AICPA

Illustration 14—An Accountant's Review Report on Comparative Financial Statements Prepared in Accordance With Accounting Principles Generally Accepted in the United States of America When the Accountant's Report on the Prior Period Includes a Changed Reference to a Departure From Accounting Principles Generally Accepted in the United States of America.

Illustration 15—An Accountant's Review Report on Comparative Financial Statements Prepared in Accordance With Accounting Principles Generally Accepted in the United States of America When the Prior Period Financial Statements Were Reviewed by a Predecessor Accountant and the Predecessor's Report Is Not Presented.

Illustration 16—An Accountant's Review Report on Comparative Financial Statements Prepared in Accordance With Accounting Principles Generally Accepted in the United States of America When the Prior Period Financial Statements Were Reviewed by a Predecessor Accountant, the Predecessor Accountant's Report Is Not Presented, and the Successor Accountant Is Engaged to Review the Restatement Adjustment(s).

Illustration 17—An Accountant's Review Report on Comparative Consolidated Financial Statements Prepared in Accordance With Accounting Principles Generally Accepted in the United States of America in Which the Accountant Makes Reference to the Review of the Financial Statements of a Significant Component Prepared Using the Same Financial Reporting Framework as That Used for the Financial Statements of the Reporting Entity and Performed by the Other Accountant in Accordance With Statements on Standards for Accounting and Review Services

Illustration 18—An Accountant's Review Report on Single Year Financial Statements Prepared in Accordance With Accounting Principles Generally Accepted in the United States of America and Supplementary Information Accompanies the Reviewed Financial Statements and the Accountant Subjected the Supplementary Information to the Review Procedures Applied in the Accountant's Review of the Basic Financial Statements

Illustration 19—An Accountant's Review Report on Single Year Financial Statements Prepared in Accordance With Accounting Principles Generally Accepted in the United States of America and Supplementary Information Accompanies the Reviewed Financial Statements and the Accountant Did Not Subject the Supplementary Information to the Review Procedures Applied in the Accountant's Review of the Basic Financial Statements

Illustration 20—An Accountant's Review Report on Single Year Financial Statements Prepared in Accordance With Accounting Principles Generally Accepted in the United States of America and Supplementary Information Is Presented on the Face of the Reviewed Financial Statements and the Accountant Did Not Subject the Supplementary Information to the Review Procedures Applied in the Accountant's Review of the Basic Financial Statements

Illustration 1—An Accountant's Review Report on Comparative Financial Statements Prepared in Accordance With Accounting Principles Generally Accepted in the United States of America When a Review Has Been Performed for Both Periods

Circumstances include the following:

- Review of a complete set of comparative financial statements.
- The financial statements are prepared in accordance with accounting principles generally accepted in the United States of America.

Independent Accountant's Review Report

[*Appropriate Addressee*]

I (We) have reviewed the accompanying financial statements of XYZ Company, which comprise the balance sheets as of December 31, 20X2 and 20X1, and the related statements of income, changes in stockholders' equity, and cash flows for the years then ended, and the related notes to the financial statements. A review includes primarily applying analytical procedures to management's (owners') financial data and making inquiries of company management (owners). A review is substantially less in scope than an audit, the objective of which is the expression of an opinion regarding the financial statements as a whole. Accordingly, I (we) do not express such an opinion.

Management's Responsibility for the Financial Statements

Management (Owners) is (are) responsible for the preparation and fair presentation of these financial statements in accordance with accounting principles generally accepted in the United States of America; this includes the design, implementation, and maintenance of internal control relevant to the preparation and fair presentation of financial statements that are free from material misstatement whether due to fraud or error.

Accountant's Responsibility

My (Our) responsibility is to conduct the review engagements in accordance with Statements on Standards for Accounting and Review Services promulgated by the Accounting and Review Services Committee of the AICPA. Those standards require me (us) to perform procedures to obtain limited assurance as a basis for reporting whether I am (we are) aware of any material modifications that should be made to the financial statements for them to be in accordance with accounting principles generally accepted in the United States of America. I (We) believe that the results of my (our) procedures provide a reasonable basis for my (our) conclusion.

Accountant's Conclusion

Based on my (our) reviews, I am (we are) not aware of any material modifications that should be made to the accompanying financial statements in order for them to be in accordance with accounting principles generally accepted in the United States of America.

[*Signature of accounting firm or accountant, as appropriate*]
[*Accountant's city and state*]
[*Date of the accountant's review report*]

 ©2017, AICPA

Illustration 2—An Accountant's Review Report on Single Year Financial Statements Prepared in Accordance With Accounting Principles Generally Accepted in the United States of America

Circumstances include the following:

- Review of a complete set of financial statements (single year).
- The financial statements are prepared in accordance with accounting principles generally accepted in the United States of America.

Independent Accountant's Review Report

[*Appropriate Addressee*]

I (We) have reviewed the accompanying financial statements of XYZ Company, which comprise the balance sheet as of December 31, 20X2, and the related statements of income, changes in stockholders' equity, and cash flows for the year then ended, and the related notes to the financial statements. A review includes primarily applying analytical procedures to management's (owners') financial data and making inquiries of company management (owners). A review is substantially less in scope than an audit, the objective of which is the expression of an opinion regarding the financial statements as a whole. Accordingly, I (we) do not express such an opinion.

Management's Responsibility for the Financial Statements

Management (Owners) is (are) responsible for the preparation and fair presentation of these financial statements in accordance with accounting principles generally accepted in the United States of America; this includes the design, implementation, and maintenance of internal control relevant to the preparation and fair presentation of financial statements that are free from material misstatement whether due to fraud or error.

Accountant's Responsibility

My (Our) responsibility is to conduct the review engagement in accordance with Statements on Standards for Accounting and Review Services promulgated by the Accounting and Review Services Committee of the AICPA. Those standards require me (us) to perform procedures to obtain limited assurance as a basis for reporting whether I am (we are) aware of any material modifications that should be made to the financial statements for them to be in accordance with accounting principles generally accepted in the United States of America. I (We) believe that the results of my (our) procedures provide a reasonable basis for my (our) conclusion.

Accountant's Conclusion

Based on my (our) review, I am (we are) not aware of any material modifications that should be made to the accompanying financial statements in order for them to be in accordance with accounting principles generally accepted in the United States of America.

[*Signature of accounting firm or accountant, as appropriate*]
[*Accountant's city and state*]
[*Date of the accountant's review report*]

Illustration 3—An Accountant's Review Report on Comparative Financial Statements Prepared in Accordance With the AICPA's Financial Reporting Framework for Small- and Medium-Sized Entities

Circumstances include the following:

- Review of a complete set of comparative financial statements.
- The financial statements are prepared in accordance with the AICPA's Financial Reporting Framework for Small- and Medium-Sized Entities (that is, a special purpose framework)
- Management has a choice of financial reporting frameworks.

Independent Accountant's Review Report

[*Appropriate Addressee*]

I (We) have reviewed the accompanying financial statements of XYZ Company, which comprise the statements of financial position as of December 31, 20X2 and 20X1 and the related statements of operations and cash flows for the years then ended, and the related notes to the financial statements. A review includes primarily applying analytical procedures to management's (owners') financial data and making inquiries of company management (owners). A review is substantially less in scope than an audit, the objective of which is the expression of an opinion regarding the financial statements as a whole. Accordingly, I (we) do not express such an opinion.

Management's Responsibility for the Financial Statements

Management (Owners) is (are) responsible for the preparation and fair presentation of these financial statements in accordance with the AICPA's Financial Reporting Framework for Small- and Medium-Sized Entities; this includes determining that the AICPA's Financial Reporting Framework for Small- and Medium-Sized Entities is an acceptable basis for the preparation of financial statements in the circumstances. Management (Owners) is (are) also responsible for the design, implementation, and maintenance of internal control relevant to the preparation and fair presentation of financial statements that are free from material misstatement whether due to fraud or error.

Accountant's Responsibility

My (Our) responsibility is to conduct the review engagements in accordance with Statements on Standards for Accounting and Review Services promulgated by the Accounting and Review Services Committee of the AICPA. Those standards require me (us) to perform procedures to obtain limited assurance as a basis for reporting whether I am (we are) aware of any material modifications that should be made to the financial statements for them to be in accordance with the AICPA's Financial Reporting Framework for Small- and Medium-Sized Entities. I (We) believe that the results of my (our) procedures provide a reasonable basis for my (our) conclusion.

Accountant's Conclusion

Based on my (our) reviews, I am (we are) not aware of any material modifications that should be made to the accompanying financial statements in order for them to be in accordance with the AICPA's Financial Reporting Framework for Small- and Medium-Sized Entities.

 ©2017, AICPA

Basis of Accounting

I (We) draw attention to Note X of the financial statements, which describes the basis of accounting. The financial statements are prepared in accordance with the AICPA's Financial Reporting Framework for Small- and Medium-Sized Entities, which is a basis of accounting other than accounting principles generally accepted in the United States of America. My (Our) conclusion is not modified with respect to this matter.

[*Signature of accounting firm or accountant, as appropriate*]
[*Accountant's city and state*]
[*Date of the accountant's review report*]

Illustration 4—An Accountant's Review Report on Single Year Financial Statements Prepared in Accordance With the Tax-Basis of Accounting

Circumstances include the following:

- Review of a complete set of financial statements (single year).
- The financial statements are of a partnership and prepared in accordance with the basis of accounting the partnership uses for income tax purposes (that is, a special purpose framework).
- Management has a choice of financial reporting frameworks.

Independent Accountant's Review Report

[*Appropriate Addressee*]

I (We) have reviewed the accompanying financial statements of XYZ Partnership, which comprise the statement of assets, liabilities, and partners' capital—tax-basis as of December 31, 20X2, and the related statements of revenue and expenses—tax-basis, and partners' capital—tax-basis for the year then ended, and the related notes to the financial statements. A review includes primarily applying analytical procedures to management's (partners') financial data and making inquiries of partnership management (owners). A review is substantially less in scope than an audit, the objective of which is the expression of an opinion regarding the financial statement as a whole. Accordingly, I (we) do not express such an opinion.

Management's Responsibility for the Financial Statements

Management (Partners) is (are) responsible for the preparation and fair presentation of these financial statements in accordance with the basis of accounting the partnership uses for income tax purposes; this includes determining that the basis of accounting the partnership uses for income tax purposes is an acceptable basis for the preparation of financial statements in the circumstances. Management (Partners) is (are) also responsible for the design, implementation, and maintenance of internal control relevant to the preparation and fair presentation of financial statements that are free from material misstatement, whether due to fraud or error.

Accountant's Responsibility

My (Our) responsibility is to conduct the review engagement in accordance with Statements on Standards for Accounting and Review Services promulgated by the Accounting and Review Services Committee of the AICPA. Those standards require me (us) to perform procedures to obtain limited assurance as a basis

©2017, AICPA

for reporting whether I am (we are) aware of any material modifications that should be made to the financial statements for them to be in accordance with the basis of accounting the partnership uses for income tax purposes. I (We) believe that the results of my (our) procedures provide a reasonable basis for my (our) conclusion.

Accountant's Conclusion

Based on my (our) review, I am (we are) not aware of any material modifications that should be made to the accompanying financial statements in order for them to be in accordance with the basis of accounting the partnership uses for income tax purposes.

Basis of Accounting

I (We) draw attention to Note X of the financial statements, which describes the basis of accounting. The financial statements are prepared in accordance with the basis of accounting the partnership uses for income tax purposes, which is a basis of accounting other than accounting principles generally accepted in the United States of America. My (Our) conclusion is not modified with respect to this matter.

[*Signature of accounting firm or accountant, as appropriate*]
[*Accountant's city and state*]
[*Date of the accountant's review report*]

Illustration 5—An Accountant's Review Report on Single Year Financial Statements Prepared in Accordance With a Contractual Basis of Accounting

Circumstances include the following:

- Review of a complete set of financial statements (single year).
- The financial statements are prepared in accordance with a contractual basis of accounting (that is, a special purpose framework) to comply with the provisions of that contract.
- Based on the provisions of the contract, management does not have a choice of financial reporting frameworks.

Independent Accountant's Review Report

[*Appropriate Addressee*]

I (We) have reviewed the accompanying financial statements of ABC Company, which comprise the assets and liabilities—contractual basis as of December 31, 20X2, and the revenue and expenses—contractual basis, changes in equity—contractual basis, and cash flows—contractual basis for the year then ended, and the related notes to the financial statements. A review includes primarily applying analytical procedures to management's (partners') financial data and making inquiries of company management (owners). A review is substantially less in scope than an audit, the objective of which is the expression of an opinion regarding the financial statement as a whole. Accordingly, I (we) do not express such an opinion.

Management's Responsibility for the Financial Statements

Management (Owners) is (are) responsible for the preparation and fair presentation of these financial statements in accordance with the financial reporting

 ©2017, AICPA

provisions of Section Z of the contract between ABC Company and DEF Company dated January 1, 20X2 (the contract). Management (Owners) is (are) also responsible for the design, implementation, and maintenance of internal control relevant to the preparation and fair presentation of financial statements that are free from material misstatement, whether due to fraud or error.

Accountant's Responsibility

My (Our) responsibility is to conduct the review engagement in accordance with Statements on Standards for Accounting and Review Services promulgated by the Accounting and Review Services Committee of the AICPA. Those standards require me (us) to perform procedures to obtain limited assurance as a basis for reporting whether I am (we are) aware of any material modifications that should be made to the financial statements for them to be in accordance with the financial reporting provisions of Section Z of the contract. I (We) believe that the results of my (our) procedures provide a reasonable basis for my (our) conclusion.

Accountant's Conclusion

Based on my (our) review, I am (we are) not aware of any material modifications that should be made to the accompanying financial statements in order for them to be in accordance with the financial reporting provisions of Section Z of the contract.

Basis of Accounting

I (We) draw attention to Note X of the financial statements, which describes the basis of accounting. The financial statements are prepared in accordance with the financial reporting provisions of Section Z of the contract, which is a basis of accounting other than accounting principles generally accepted in the United States of America, to comply with the financial reporting provisions of the contract referred to above. My (Our) conclusion is not modified with respect to this matter.

Restriction on Use

My (Our) report is intended solely for the information and use of ABC Company and DEF Company and is not intended to be and should not be used by anyone other than these specified parties.

[*Signature of accounting firm or accountant, as appropriate*]
[*Accountant's city and state*]
[*Date of the accountant's review report*]

Illustration 6—An Accountant's Review Report on Interim Financial Statements Prepared in Accordance With Accounting Principles Generally Accepted in the United States of America

Circumstances include the following:

- Review of a complete set of financial statements for the period ended September 30, 20X2, and for the three and nine months then ended.
- The financial statements are prepared in accordance with accounting principles generally accepted in the United States of America.

- The accountant appropriately performs the engagement in accordance with SSARSs (that is, AU-C section 930, *Interim Financial Information* [AICPA, *Professional Standards*], is not applicable).

Independent Accountant's Review Report

[*Appropriate Addressee*]

I (We) have reviewed the accompanying financial statements of XYZ Company, which comprise the balance sheet as of September 30, 20X2, and the related statements of income, changes in stockholders' equity, and cash flows for the three and nine months then ended, and the related notes to the financial statements. A review includes primarily applying analytical procedures to management's (owners') financial data and making inquiries of company management (owners). A review is substantially less in scope than an audit, the objective of which is the expression of an opinion regarding the financial statements as a whole. Accordingly, I (we) do not express such an opinion.

Management's Responsibility for the Financial Statements

Management (Owners) is (are) responsible for the preparation and fair presentation of these financial statements in accordance with accounting principles generally accepted in the United States of America; this includes the design, implementation, and maintenance of internal control relevant to the preparation and fair presentation of financial statements that are free from material misstatement whether due to fraud or error.

Accountant's Responsibility

My (Our) responsibility is to conduct the review engagement in accordance with Statements on Standards for Accounting and Review Services promulgated by the Accounting and Review Services Committee of the AICPA. Those standards require me (us) to perform procedures to obtain limited assurance as a basis for reporting whether I am (we are) aware of any material modifications that should be made to the financial statements for them to be in accordance with accounting standards generally accepted in the United States of America. I (We) believe that the results of my (our) procedures provide a reasonable basis for my (our) conclusion.

Accountant's Conclusion

Based on my (our) review, I am (we are) not aware of any material modifications that should be made to the accompanying financial statements in order for them to be in accordance with accounting principles generally accepted in the United States of America.

[*Signature of accounting firm or accountant, as appropriate*]
[*Accountant's city and state*]
[*Date of the accountant's review report*]

Illustration 7—An Accountant's Review Report on Comparative Financial Statements Disclosing a Departure From Accounting Principles Generally Accepted in the United States of America

Circumstances include the following:

- Review of a complete set of comparative financial statements.
- The financial statements contain a departure from accounting principles generally accepted in the United States of America.

 ©2017, AICPA

Independent Accountant's Review Report

[*Appropriate Addressee*]

I (We) have reviewed the accompanying financial statements of XYZ Company, which comprise the balance sheets as of December 31, 20X2 and 20X1, and the related statements of income, changes in stockholders' equity, and cash flows for the years then ended, and the related notes to the financial statements. A review includes primarily applying analytical procedures to management's (owners') financial data and making inquiries of company management (owners). A review is substantially less in scope than an audit, the objective of which is the expression of an opinion regarding the financial statements as a whole. Accordingly, I (we) do not express such an opinion.

Management's Responsibility for the Financial Statements

Management (Owners) is (are) responsible for the preparation and fair presentation of these financial statements in accordance with accounting principles generally accepted in the United States of America; this includes the design, implementation, and maintenance of internal control relevant to the preparation and fair presentation of financial statements that are free from material misstatement whether due to fraud or error.

Accountant's Responsibility

My (Our) responsibility is to conduct the review engagements in accordance with Statements on Standards for Accounting and Review Services promulgated by the Accounting and Review Services Committee of the AICPA. Those standards require me (us) to perform procedures to obtain limited assurance as a basis for reporting whether I am (we are) aware of any material modifications that should be made to the financial statements for them to be in accordance with accounting principles generally accepted in the United States of America. I (We) believe that the results of my (our) procedures provide a reasonable basis for my (our) conclusion.

Accountant's Conclusion

Based on my (our) reviews, except for the issue noted in the Known Departure From Accounting Principles Generally Accepted in the United States of America paragraph, I am (we are) not aware of any material modifications that should be made to the accompanying financial statements in order for them to be in accordance with accounting principles generally accepted in the United States of America.

Known Departure From Accounting Principles Generally Accepted in the United States of America

As disclosed in Note X to these financial statements, accounting principles generally accepted in the United States of America require that inventory cost consist of material, labor, and overhead. Management has informed me (us) that the inventory of finished goods and work in process is stated in the accompanying financial statements at material and labor cost only, and that the effects of this departure from accounting principles generally accepted in the United States of America on financial position, results of operations, and cash flows have not been determined.

or

As disclosed in Note X to these financial statements, the company has adopted [*description of newly adopted method*], whereas it previously used [*description of previous method*]. Although the [*description of newly adopted method*] is in accordance with accounting principles generally accepted in the United States of America, the company does not appear to have reasonable justification for making a change as required by FASB *Accounting Standards Codification* 250, *Accounting Changes and Error Corrections.*

[*Signature of accounting firm or accountant, as appropriate*]
[*Accountant's city and state*]
[*Date of the accountant's review report*]

Illustration 8—An Accountant's Review Report on Comparative Consolidated Financial Statements in Which the Accountant Makes Reference to the Work of Other Accountants Who Were Engaged to Review the Financial Statements of a Significant Component

Circumstances include the following:

- Review of a complete set of comparative consolidated financial statements.
- The financial statements of B Company, a wholly-owned subsidiary, whose financial statements reflect total assets constituting 20 percent and 22 percent, respectively, of consolidated total assets at December 31, 20X2 and 20X1, and total revenues constituting 18 percent and 20 percent, respectively, of consolidated total revenues for the years then ended, were reviewed by other accountants, and the accountant has decided to make reference to the work of other accountants in the accountant's review report.

Independent Accountant's Review Report

[*Appropriate Addressee*]

I (We) have reviewed the accompanying consolidated financial statements of XYZ Company and its subsidiaries, which comprise the consolidated balance sheets as of December 31, 20X2 and 20X1, and the related consolidated statements of income, changes in stockholders' equity, and cash flows for the years then ended, and the related notes to the financial statements. A review includes primarily applying analytical procedures to management's (owners') financial data and making inquiries of company management (owners). A review is substantially less in scope than an audit, the objective of which is the expression of an opinion regarding the financial statements as a whole. Accordingly, I (we) do not express such an opinion.

Management's Responsibility for the Financial Statements

Management (Owners) is (are) responsible for the preparation and fair presentation of these consolidated financial statements in accordance with accounting principles generally accepted in the United States of America; this includes the design, implementation, and maintenance of internal control relevant to the preparation and fair presentation of consolidated financial statements that are free from material misstatement whether due to fraud or error.

Accountant's Responsibility

My (Our) responsibility is to conduct the review engagements in accordance with Statements on Standards for Accounting and Review Services (SSARSs)

 ©2017, AICPA

promulgated by the Accounting and Review Services Committee of the AICPA. We have not reviewed the financial statements of B Company, a wholly-owned subsidiary, whose financial statements reflect total assets constituting 20 percent and 22 percent, respectively, of consolidated total assets at December 31, 20X2 and 20X1, and total revenues constituting 18 percent and 20 percent, respectively, of consolidated total revenues for the years then ended. Those statements were reviewed by other accountants, whose report has been furnished to me (us), and our conclusion, insofar as it relates to the amounts included for B Company, is based solely on the report of the other accountants.

SSARSs require me (us) to perform procedures to obtain limited assurance as a basis for reporting whether I am (we are) aware of any material modifications that should be made to the consolidated financial statements for them to be in accordance with accounting principles generally accepted in the United States of America. I (We) believe that the results of my (our) procedures provide a reasonable basis for our conclusion.

Accountant's Conclusion

Based on my (our) reviews, and the report of other accountants, I am (we are) not aware of any material modifications that should be made to the accompanying consolidated financial statements in order for them to be in accordance with accounting principles generally accepted in the United States of America.

[*Signature of accounting firm or accountant, as appropriate*]
[*Accountant's city and state*]
[*Date of the accountant's review report*]

Illustration 9—An Accountant's Review Report on Comparative Consolidated Financial Statements and all Required Supplementary Information Accompanies the Financial Statements and the Accountant Reviewed the Required Supplementary Information

Circumstances include the following:

- Review of a complete set of comparative financial statements of a homeowners' association.
- The financial statements are prepared in accordance with accounting principles generally accepted in the United States of America.
- The estimates of current or future costs of major repairs and replacements of common property that will be required in the future as required by FASB ASC 972-235-50-3 is included and the accountant has reviewed the information and no material departures from the prescribed guidelines have been identified.

Independent Accountant's Review Report

[*Appropriate Addressee*]

I (We) have reviewed the accompanying financial statements of XYZ Homeowners' Association, which comprise the balance sheets as of December 31, 20X2 and 20X1, and the related statements of revenues, expenses, and changes in fund balances and cash flows for the years then ended, and the related notes to the financial statements. A review includes primarily applying analytical procedures to management's (owners') financial data and making inquiries of association management (owners). A review is substantially less in scope than an audit, the objective of which is the expression of an opinion regarding the financial statements as a whole. Accordingly, I (we) do not express such an opinion.

Management's Responsibility for the Financial Statements

Management (Owners) is (are) responsible for the preparation and fair presentation of these financial statements in accordance with accounting principles generally accepted in the United States of America; this includes the design, implementation, and maintenance of internal control relevant to the preparation and fair presentation of financial statements that are free from material misstatement whether due to fraud or error.

Accountant's Responsibility

My (Our) responsibility is to conduct the review engagements in accordance with Statements on Standards for Accounting and Review Services promulgated by the Accounting and Review Services Committee of the AICPA. Those standards require me (us) to perform procedures to obtain limited assurance as a basis for reporting whether I am (we are) aware of any material modifications that should be made to the financial statements for them to be in accordance with accounting principles generally accepted in the United States of America. I (We) believe that the results of my (our) procedures provide a reasonable basis for my (our) conclusion.

Accountant's Conclusion

Based on my (our) reviews, I am (we are) not aware of any material modifications that should be made to the accompanying financial statements in order for them to be in accordance with accounting principles generally accepted in the United States of America.

Required Supplementary Information

Accounting principles generally accepted in the United States of America require that estimates of current or future costs of major repairs and replacements of common property that will be required in the future on page XX be presented to supplement the basic financial statements. Such information, although not a required part of the basic financial statements, is required by the Financial Accounting Standards Board who considers it to be an essential part of financial reporting and for placing the basic financial statements in an appropriate operational, economic, or historical context. The information is the representation of management. I (We) have reviewed the information and, based on my (our) review, I am (we are) not aware of any material modifications that should be made to the information in order for it to be in accordance with accounting principles generally accepted in the United States of America. I (We) have not audited the information and, accordingly, do not express an opinion on such information.

[*Signature of accounting firm or accountant, as appropriate*]
[*Accountant's city and state*]
[*Date of the accountant's review report*]

 ©2017, AICPA

Illustration 10—An Accountant's Review Report on Comparative Financial Statements Prepared in Accordance With Accounting Principles Generally Accepted in the United States of America and the Review Is Performed in Accordance With Statements on Standards for Accounting and Review Services and International Standard on Review Engagements 2400 (Revised) Issued by the International Auditing and Assurance Standards Board

Circumstances include the following:

- Review of a complete set of general purpose consolidated comparative financial statements.
- Financial statements are prepared in accordance with accounting principles generally accepted in the United States of America.
- The accountant performs the engagement in accordance with Statements on Standards for Accounting and Review Services and International Standard on Review Engagements 2400 (Revised) issued by the International Auditing and Assurance Standards Board.

Independent Accountant's Review Report

[*Appropriate Addressee*]

I (We) have reviewed the accompanying financial statements of XYZ Company, which comprise the balance sheets as of December 31, 20X2 and 20X1, and the related statements of income, changes in stockholders' equity, and cash flows for the years then ended, and the related notes to the financial statements. A review includes primarily applying analytical procedures to management (owners') financial data and making inquiries of company management (owners). A review is substantially less in scope than an audit, the objective of which is the expression of an opinion regarding the financial statements as a whole. Accordingly, I (we) do not express such an opinion.

Management's Responsibility for the Financial Statements

Management (Owners) is (are) responsible for the preparation and fair presentation of the financial statements in accordance with accounting principles generally accepted in the United States of America; this includes the design, implementation, and maintenance of internal control relevant to the preparation and fair presentation of the financial statements that are free from material misstatement whether due to fraud or error.

Accountant's Responsibility

My (our) responsibility is to conduct the review engagements in accordance with Statements on Standards for Accounting and Review Services promulgated by the Accounting and Review Services Committee of the AICPA and in accordance with International Standard on Review Engagements 2400 (Revised) issued by the International Auditing and Assurance Standards Board. Those standards require me (us) to perform procedures to obtain limited assurance as a basis for reporting whether I am (we are) aware of any material modifications that should be made to the financial statements for them to be in accordance with accounting principles generally accepted in the United States of America. I (We) believe that the results of my (our) procedures provide a reasonable basis for my (our) conclusion.

Accountant's Conclusion

Based on my (our) reviews, I am (we are) not aware of any material modifications that should be made to the accompanying financial statements in order for them to be in accordance with accounting principles generally accepted in the United States of America.

[*Signature of accounting firm or accountant, as appropriate*]
[*Accountant's city and state*]
[*Date of the accountant's review report*]

Illustration 11—An Accountant's Review Report on Comparative Financial Statements Prepared in Accordance With International Financial Reporting Standards as Issued by the International Accounting Standards Board and the Review is Performed in Accordance With Statements on Standards for Accounting and Review Services and International Standard on Review Engagements 2400 (Revised) Issued by the International Auditing and Assurance Standards Board

Circumstances include the following:

- Review of a complete set of comparative financial statements.
- The financial statements are prepared in accordance with International Financial Reporting Standards as issued by the International Accounting Standards Board.
- The accountant performs the engagement in accordance with Statements on Standards for Accounting and Review Services and International Standard on Review Engagements 2400 (Revised) issued by the International Auditing and Assurance Standards Board.

Independent Accountant's Review Report

[*Appropriate Addressee*]

I (We) have reviewed the accompanying financial statements of XYZ Company, which comprise the statements of financial position as of December 31, 20X2 and 20X1, and the related statements of comprehensive income, changes in equity, and cash flows for the years then ended, and the related notes to the financial statements. A review includes primarily applying analytical procedures to management's (owners') financial data and making inquiries of company management (owners). A review is substantially less in scope than an audit, the objective of which is the expression of an opinion regarding the financial statements as a whole. Accordingly, I (we) do not express such an opinion.

Management's Responsibility for the Financial Statements

Management (Owners) is (are) responsible for the preparation and fair presentation of these financial statements in accordance with International Financial Reporting Standards as Issued by the International Accounting Standards Board; this includes the design, implementation, and maintenance of internal control relevant to the preparation and fair presentation of financial statements that are free from material misstatement whether due to fraud or error.

 ©2017, AICPA

Accountant's Responsibility

My (Our) responsibility is to conduct the review engagements in accordance with Statements on Standards for Accounting and Review Services promulgated by the Accounting and Review Services Committee of the AICPA and in accordance with International Standard on Review Engagements 2400 (Revised) issued by the International Auditing and Assurance Standards Board. Those standards require me (us) to perform procedures to obtain limited assurance as a basis for reporting whether I am (we are) aware of any material modifications that should be made to the financial statements for them to be in accordance with International Financial Reporting Standards as Issued by the International Accounting Standards Board. I (We) believe that the results of my (our) procedures provide a reasonable basis for my (our) conclusion.

Accountant's Conclusion

Based on my (our) reviews, I am (we are) not aware of any material modifications that should be made to the accompanying financial statements in order for them to be in accordance with International Financial Reporting Standards as Issued by the International Accounting Standards Board.

[*Signature of accounting firm or accountant, as appropriate*]
[*Accountant's city and state*]
[*Date of the accountant's review report*]

Illustration 12—An Accountant's Review Report on Comparative Financial Statements Prepared in Accordance With a Financial Reporting Framework Generally Accepted in Another Country

Circumstances include the following:

- Review of a complete set of comparative financial statements.
- The financial statements are prepared in accordance with a financial reporting framework generally accepted in another country.

Independent Accountant's Review Report

[*Appropriate Addressee*]

I (We) have reviewed the accompanying financial statements of XYZ Company, which comprise the balance sheets as of December 31, 20X2 and 20X1, and the related statements of income, changes in stockholders' equity, and cash flows for the years then ended, and the related notes to the financial statements. A review includes primarily applying analytical procedures to management's (owners') financial data and making inquiries of company management (owners). A review is substantially less in scope than an audit, the objective of which is the expression of an opinion regarding the financial statements as a whole. Accordingly, I (we) do not express such an opinion.

Management's Responsibility for the Financial Statements

Management (Owners) is (are) responsible for the preparation and fair presentation of these financial statements in accordance with [*the financial reporting framework generally accepted in another country, including identification of the nationality of the framework*] and for determining that [*the financial reporting framework generally accepted in another country, including identification of the nationality of the framework*] is an acceptable financial reporting framework in the circumstances. Management (Owners) is (are) also responsible for the design, implementation, and maintenance of internal control relevant to the preparation and fair presentation of financial statements that are free from material misstatement whether due to fraud or error.

Accountant's Responsibility

My (Our) responsibility is to conduct the review engagements in accordance with Statements on Standards for Accounting and Review Services promulgated by the Accounting and Review Services Committee of the AICPA. Those standards require me (us) to perform procedures to obtain limited assurance as a basis for reporting whether I am (we are) aware of any material modifications that should be made to the financial statements for them to be in accordance with [*the financial reporting framework generally accepted in another country, including identification of the nationality of the framework*]. I (We) believe that the results of my (our) procedures provide a reasonable basis for my (our) conclusion.

Accountant's Conclusion

Based on my (our) reviews, I am (we are) not aware of any material modifications that should be made to the accompanying financial statements in order for them to be in accordance with [*the financial reporting framework generally accepted in another country, including identification of the nationality of the framework*].

Restriction on Use

Our report is intended solely for the information and use of [*specified parties*] and is not intended to be and should not be used by anyone other than these specified parties.

[*Signature of accounting firm or accountant, as appropriate*]
[*Accountant's city and state*]
[*Date of the accountant's review report*]

Illustration 13—An Accountant's Review Report on Comparative Financial Statements Prepared in Accordance With Accounting Principles Generally Accepted in the United States of America When the Financial Statements of the Prior Year Were Audited

Circumstances include the following:

- Review of a complete set financial statements for the current year.
- Audit of the complete set of financial statements of the prior year.
- Both sets of financial statements are prepared in accordance with accounting principles generally accepted in the United States of America.

<u>Independent Accountant's Review Report</u>

[*Appropriate Addressee*]

I (We) have reviewed the accompanying financial statements of XYZ Company, which comprise the balance sheet as of December 31, 20X2, and the related statements of income, changes in stockholders' equity, and cash flows for the year then ended, and the related notes to the financial statements. A review includes primarily applying analytical procedures to management's (owners') financial data and making inquiries of company management (owners). A review is substantially less in scope than an audit, the objective of which is the

©2017, AICPA

expression of an opinion regarding the financial statements as a whole. Accordingly, I (we) do not express such an opinion.

Management's Responsibility for the Financial Statements

Management (Owners) is (are) responsible for the preparation and fair presentation of these financial statements in accordance with accounting principles generally accepted in the United States of America; this includes the design, implementation, and maintenance of internal control relevant to the preparation and fair presentation of financial statements that are free from material misstatement whether due to fraud or error.

Accountant's Responsibility

My (Our) responsibility is to conduct the review engagement in accordance with Statements on Standards for Accounting and Review Services promulgated by the Accounting and Review Services Committee of the AICPA. Those standards require me (us) to perform procedures to obtain limited assurance as a basis for reporting whether I am (we are) aware of any material modifications that should be made to the financial statements for them to be in accordance with accounting principles generally accepted in the United States of America. I (We) believe that the results of my (our) procedures provide a reasonable basis for my (our) conclusion.

Accountant's Conclusion

Based on my (our) review, I am (we are) not aware of any material modifications that should be made to the accompanying financial statements in order for them to be in accordance with accounting principles generally accepted in the United States of America.

Report on 20X1 Financial Statements

The 20X1 financial statements were audited by me (us) and I (we) expressed an unmodified opinion on them in my (our) report dated March 1, 20X2. I (We) have not performed any auditing procedures since that date.

[*Signature of accounting firm or accountant, as appropriate*]
[*Accountant's city and state*]
[*Date of the accountant's review report*]

Illustration 14—An Accountant's Review Report on Comparative Financial Statements Prepared in Accordance With Accounting Principles Generally Accepted in the United States of America When the Accountant's Report on the Prior Period Includes a Changed Reference to a Departure From Accounting Principles Generally Accepted in the United States of America

Circumstances include the following:

- Review of a complete set of comparative financial statements.
- The financial statements are prepared in accordance with accounting principles generally accepted in the United States of America.
- The report on the prior period financial statements referenced a departure from accounting principles generally accepted in the United States of America. The entity restated the prior period financial statements to correct the misstatement.

Independent Accountant's Review Report

[*Appropriate Addressee*]

I (We) have reviewed the accompanying financial statements of XYZ Company, which comprise the balance sheets as of December 31, 20X2 and 20X1, and the related statements of income, changes in stockholders' equity, and cash flows for the years then ended, and the related notes to the financial statements. A review includes primarily applying analytical procedures to management's (owners') financial data and making inquiries of company management (owners). A review is substantially less in scope than an audit, the objective of which is the expression of an opinion regarding the financial statements as a whole. Accordingly, I (we) do not express such an opinion.

Management's Responsibility for the Financial Statements

Management (Owners) is (are) responsible for the preparation and fair presentation of these financial statements in accordance with accounting principles generally accepted in the United States of America; this includes the design, implementation, and maintenance of internal control relevant to the preparation and fair presentation of financial statements that are free from material misstatement whether due to fraud or error.

Accountant's Responsibility

My (Our) responsibility is to conduct the review engagements in accordance with Statements on Standards for Accounting and Review Services promulgated by the Accounting and Review Services Committee of the AICPA. Those standards require me (us) to perform procedures to obtain limited assurance as a basis for reporting whether I am (we are) aware of any material modifications that should be made to the financial statements for them to be in accordance with accounting principles generally accepted in the United States of America. I (We) believe that the results of my (our) procedures provide a reasonable basis for my (our) conclusion.

Accountant's Conclusion

Based on my (our) reviews, I am (we are) not aware of any material modifications that should be made to the accompanying financial statements in order for them to be in accordance with accounting principles generally accepted in the United States of America.

Report on 20X1 Financial Statements

In my (our) report dated March 1, 20X2, with respect to the 20X1 financial statements, we referred to a departure from accounting principles generally accepted in the United States of America because the company carried its land at appraised values. As described in Note X, the Company has changed its method of accounting for land and restated its 20X1 financial statements in accordance with accounting principles generally accepted in the United States of America. Accordingly, my (our) present statement on the 20X1 financial statements, as presented herein, that I am (we are) not aware of any material modifications that should be made to the accompanying financial statements is different from that expressed in our previous report.

[*Signature of accounting firm or accountant, as appropriate*]
[*Accountant's city and state*]
[*Date of the accountant's review report*]

 ©2017, AICPA

Illustration 15—An Accountant's Review Report on Comparative Financial Statements Prepared in Accordance With Accounting Principles Generally Accepted in the United States of America When the Prior Period Financial Statements Were Reviewed by a Predecessor Accountant and the Predecessor's Report Is Not Presented

Circumstances include the following:

- Review of a complete set of financial statements for the current year.
- Comparative prior year financial statements are presented and such financial statements were reviewed by a predecessor accountant and the predecessor's report is not presented.
- Both sets of financial statements are prepared in accordance with accounting principles generally accepted in the United States of America.

Independent Accountant's Review Report

[*Appropriate Addressee*]

I (We) have reviewed the accompanying financial statements of XYZ Company, which comprise the balance sheet as of December 31, 20X2, and the related statements of income, changes in stockholders' equity, and cash flows for the years then ended, and the related notes to the financial statements. A review includes primarily applying analytical procedures to management's (owners') financial data and making inquiries of company management (owners). A review is substantially less in scope than an audit, the objective of which is the expression of an opinion regarding the financial statements as a whole. Accordingly, I (we) do not express such an opinion.

Management's Responsibility for the Financial Statements

Management (Owners) is (are) responsible for the preparation and fair presentation of these financial statements in accordance with accounting principles generally accepted in the United States of America; this includes the design, implementation, and maintenance of internal control relevant to the preparation and fair presentation of financial statements that are free from material misstatement whether due to fraud or error.

Accountant's Responsibility

My (Our) responsibility is to conduct the review engagement in accordance with Statements on Standards for Accounting and Review Services promulgated by the Accounting and Review Services Committee of the AICPA. Those standards require me (us) to perform procedures to obtain limited assurance as a basis for reporting whether I am (we are) aware of any material modifications that should be made to the financial statements for them to be in accordance with accounting principles generally accepted in the United States of America. I (We) believe that the results of my (our) procedures provide a reasonable basis for my (our) conclusion.

Accountant's Conclusion

Based on my (our) review, I am (we are) not aware of any material modifications that should be made to the accompanying financial statements in order for them to be in accordance with accounting principles generally accepted in the United States of America.

Report on 20X1 Financial Statements

The financial statements of XYZ Company as of December 31, 20X1, were reviewed by other accountants whose report dated February 1, 20X2, stated that based on their procedures, they are not aware of any material modifications that should be made to the financial statements in order for them to be in accordance with accounting principles generally accepted in the United States of America.

[*Signature of accounting firm or accountant, as appropriate*]
[*Accountant's city and state*]
[*Date of the accountant's review report*]

Illustration 16—An Accountant's Review Report on Comparative Financial Statements Prepared in Accordance With Accounting Principles Generally Accepted in the United States of America When the Prior Period Financial Statements Were Reviewed by a Predecessor Accountant, the Predecessor's Report Is Not Presented, and the Successor Accountant Is Engaged to Review the Restatement Adjustments

Circumstances include the following:

- Review of a complete set of financial statements for the current year.
- Comparative prior year financial statements are presented and such financial statements were reviewed by a predecessor accountant and the predecessor's report is not presented.
- The successor accountant is engaged to review the restatement adjustments on the prior year financial statements
- Both sets of financial statements are prepared in accordance with accounting principles generally accepted in the United States of America.

Independent Accountant's Review Report

[*Appropriate Addressee*]

I (We) have reviewed the accompanying financial statements of XYZ Company, which comprise the balance sheet as of December 31, 20X2, and the related statements of income, changes in stockholders' equity, and cash flows for the years then ended, and the related notes to the financial statements. A review includes primarily applying analytical procedures to management's (owners') financial data and making inquiries of company management (owners). A review is substantially less in scope than an audit, the objective of which is the

 ©2017, AICPA

expression of an opinion regarding the financial statements as a whole. Accordingly, I (we) do not express such an opinion.

Management's Responsibility for the Financial Statements

Management (Owners) is (are) responsible for the preparation and fair presentation of these financial statements in accordance with accounting principles generally accepted in the United States of America; this includes the design, implementation, and maintenance of internal control relevant to the preparation and fair presentation of financial statements that are free from material misstatement whether due to fraud or error.

Accountant's Responsibility

My (Our) responsibility is to conduct the review engagement in accordance with Statements on Standards for Accounting and Review Services promulgated by the Accounting and Review Services Committee of the AICPA. Those standards require me (us) to perform procedures to obtain limited assurance as a basis for reporting whether I am (we are) aware of any material modifications that should be made to the financial statements for them to be in accordance with accounting principles generally accepted in the United States of America. I (We) believe that the results of my (our) procedures provide a reasonable basis for my (our) conclusion.

Accountant's Conclusion

Based on my (our) review, I am (we are) not aware of any material modifications that should be made to the accompanying financial statements in order for them to be in accordance with accounting principles generally accepted in the United States of America.

Report on 20X1 Financial Statements

The financial statements of XYZ Company as of December 31, 20X1, prior to restatement, were reviewed by other accountants whose report dated February 1, 20X2, stated that based on their procedures, they are not aware of any material modifications that should be made to the financial statements in order for them to be in accordance with accounting principles generally accepted in the United States of America.

Report on Restatement Adjustments to 20X1 Financial Statements

As part of our review of the 20X2 financial statements, we also reviewed the adjustments described in Note X that were applied to restate the 20X1 financial statements. Based on my (our) review, I am (we are) not aware of any material modifications that should be made to the adjustments that were applied to restate the 20X1 financial statements in order for the statements to be in accordance with accounting principles generally accepted in the United States of America.

[*Signature of accounting firm or accountant, as appropriate*]
[*Accountant's city and state*]
[*Date of the accountant's review report*]

Illustration 17—An Accountant's Review Report on Comparative Consolidated Financial Statements Prepared in Accordance With Accounting Principles Generally Accepted in the United States of America in Which the Accountant Makes Reference to the Review of the Financial Statements of a Significant Component Prepared Using the Same Financial Reporting Framework as That Used for the Financial Statements of the Reporting Entity and Performed by the Other Accountant in Accordance With Statements on Standards for Accounting and Review Services

Circumstances include the following:

- Accountant performing the review of the reporting entity is making reference to the review of the financial statements of a component by other accountants.
- Both the financial statements of the reporting entity and the component are prepared in accordance with accounting principles generally accepted in the United States of America.
- Both reviews were performed in accordance with Statements on Standards for Accounting and Review Services.

Independent Accountant's Review Report

[*Appropriate Addressee*]

I (We) have reviewed the accompanying consolidated financial statements of XYZ Company and its subsidiaries, which comprise the consolidated balance sheets as of December 31, 20X2 and 20X1, and the related consolidated statements of income, changes in stockholders' equity, and cash flows for the years then ended, and the related notes to the financial statements. A review includes primarily applying analytical procedures to management's (owners') financial data and making inquiries of company management (owners). A review is substantially less in scope than an audit, the objective of which is the expression of an opinion regarding the consolidated financial statements as a whole. Accordingly, I (we) do not express such an opinion.

Management's Responsibility for the Financial Statements

Management (Owners) is (are) responsible for the preparation and fair presentation of these consolidated financial statements in accordance with accounting principles generally accepted in the United States of America; this includes the design, implementation, and maintenance of internal control relevant to the preparation and fair presentation of consolidated financial statements that are free from material misstatement whether due to fraud or error.

Accountant's Responsibility

My (Our) responsibility is to conduct the review engagements in accordance with Statements on Standards for Accounting and Review Services promulgated by the Accounting and Review Services Committee of the AICPA. Those standards require me (us) to perform procedures to obtain limited assurance as a basis for reporting whether I am (we are) aware of any material modifications that should be made to the consolidated financial statements for them to

 ©2017, AICPA

be in accordance with accounting principles generally accepted in the United States of America. I (We) believe that the results of my (our) procedures provide a reasonable basis for my (our) conclusion.

We did not review the financial statements of ABC Company, a wholly-owned subsidiary, which statements reflect total assets constituting 20 percent and 22 percent, respectively, of consolidated total assets at December 31, 20X2 and 20X1, and total revenues constituting 18 percent and 20 percent, respectively, of consolidated total revenues for the years then ended. Those statements were reviewed by other accountants, whose report has been furnished to us, and our conclusion, insofar as it relates to the amounts included for ABC Company, is based solely on the report of the other accountants.

Accountant's Conclusion

Based on my (our) reviews and the report of the other accountants, I am (we are) not aware of any material modifications that should be made to the accompanying consolidated financial statements in order for them to be in accordance with accounting principles generally accepted in the United States of America.

[*Signature of accounting firm or accountant, as appropriate*]
[*Accountant's city and state*]
[*Date of the accountant's review report*]

Illustration 18—An Accountant's Review Report on Single Year Financial Statements Prepared in Accordance With Accounting Principles Generally Accepted in the United States of America and Supplementary Information Accompanies the Reviewed Financial Statements and the Accountant Subjected the Supplementary Information to the Review Procedures Applied in the Accountant's Review of the Basic Financial Statements

Circumstances include the following:

- Review of a complete set of single year financial statements.
- The financial statements are prepared in accordance with accounting principles generally accepted in the United States of America.
- Supplementary information accompanies the reviewed financial statements and has been subjected to the accountant's review procedures applied in the accountant's review of the basic financial statements.

Independent Accountant's Review Report

[*Appropriate Addressee*]

I (We) have reviewed the accompanying financial statements of XYZ Company, which comprise the balance sheet as of December 31, 20X1, and the related statements of income, changes in stockholders' equity, and cash flows for the year then ended, and the related notes to the financial statements. A review includes primarily applying analytical procedures to management's (owners') financial data and making inquiries of company management (owners). A review is substantially less in scope than an audit, the objective of which is the expression of an opinion regarding the financial statements as a whole. Accordingly, I (we) do not express such an opinion.

Management's Responsibility for the Financial Statements

Management (Owners) is (are) responsible for the preparation and fair presentation of these financial statements in accordance with accounting principles generally accepted in the United States of America; this includes the design, implementation, and maintenance of internal control relevant to the preparation and fair presentation of financial statements that are free from material misstatement whether due to fraud or error.

Accountant's Responsibility

My (Our) responsibility is to conduct the review engagement in accordance with Statements on Standards for Accounting and Review Services promulgated by the Accounting and Review Services Committee of the AICPA. Those standards require me (us) to perform procedures to obtain limited assurance as a basis for reporting whether I am (we are) aware of any material modifications that should be made to the financial statements for them to be in accordance with accounting principles generally accepted in the United States of America. I (We) believe that the results of my (our) procedures provide a reasonable basis for my (our) conclusion.

Accountant's Conclusion

Based on my (our) review, I am (we are) not aware of any material modifications that should be made to the accompanying financial statements in order for them to be in accordance with accounting principles generally accepted in the United States of America.

Supplementary Information

The accompanying [*describe the supplementary information, for example, "Schedule of Accounts Receivable as of December 31, 20X1*] is presented for purposes of additional analysis and is not a required part of the basic financial statements. The [*describe the supplementary information*] is the responsibility of management and was derived from, and relates directly to, the underlying accounting and other records used to prepare the financial statements. The [*describe the supplementary information*] has been subjected to the review procedures applied in my (our) review of the basic financial statements. I am (we are) not aware of any material modifications that should be made to the [*describe the supplementary information*]. I (We) have not audited the [*describe the supplementary information*] and do not express an opinion on it.

[*Signature of accounting firm or accountant, as appropriate*]
[*Accountant's city and state*]
[*Date of the accountant's review report*]

©2017, AICPA

Illustration 19—An Accountant's Review Report on Single Year Financial Statements Prepared in Accordance With Accounting Principles Generally Accepted in the United States of America and Supplementary Information Accompanies the Reviewed Financial Statements and the Accountant Did Not Subject the Supplementary Information to the Review Procedures Applied in the Accountant's Review of the Basic Financial Statements

Circumstances include the following:

- Review of a complete set of single year financial statements.
- The financial statements are prepared in accordance with accounting principles generally accepted in the United States of America.
- Supplementary information accompanies the reviewed financial statements and was not subjected to the accountant's review procedures applied in the accountant's review of the basic financial statements.

Independent Accountant's Review Report

[*Appropriate Addressee*]

I (We) have reviewed the accompanying financial statements of XYZ Company, which comprise the balance sheet as of December 31, 20X1, and the related statements of income, changes in stockholders' equity, and cash flows for the year then ended, and the related notes to the financial statements. A review includes primarily applying analytical procedures to management's (owners') financial data and making inquiries of company management (owners). A review is substantially less in scope than an audit, the objective of which is the expression of an opinion regarding the financial statements as a whole. Accordingly, I (we) do not express such an opinion.

Management's Responsibility for the Financial Statements

Management (Owners) is (are) responsible for the preparation and fair presentation of these financial statements in accordance with accounting principles generally accepted in the United States of America; this includes the design, implementation, and maintenance of internal control relevant to the preparation and fair presentation of financial statements that are free from material misstatement whether due to fraud or error.

Accountant's Responsibility

My (Our) responsibility is to conduct the review engagement in accordance with Statements on Standards for Accounting and Review Services promulgated by the Accounting and Review Services Committee of the AICPA. Those standards require me (us) to perform procedures to obtain limited assurance as a basis for reporting whether I am (we are) aware of any material modifications that should be made to the financial statements for them to be in accordance with accounting principles generally accepted in the United States of America. I (We) believe that the results of my (our) procedures provide a reasonable basis for my (our) conclusion.

©2017, AICPA

Accountant's Conclusion

Based on my (our) review, I am (we are) not aware of any material modifications that should be made to the accompanying financial statements in order for them to be in accordance with accounting principles generally accepted in the United States of America.

Supplementary Information

The accompanying [*describe the supplementary information, for example, "Schedule of Accounts Receivable as of December 31, 20X1*] is presented for purposes of additional analysis and is not a required part of the basic financial statements. The [*describe the supplementary information*] is the responsibility of management. I (We) have not audited or reviewed the [*describe the supplementary information*] and accordingly do not express an opinion, a conclusion, nor provide any assurance on it.

[*Signature of accounting firm or accountant, as appropriate*]
[*Accountant's city and state*]
[*Date of the accountant's review report*]

Illustration 20—An Accountant's Review Report on Single Year Financial Statements Prepared in Accordance With Accounting Principles Generally Accepted in the United States of America and Supplementary Information Is Presented on the Face of the Reviewed Financial Statements and the Accountant Did Not Subject the Supplementary Information to the Review Procedures Applied in the Accountant's Review of the Basic Financial Statements

Circumstances include the following:

- Review of a complete set of single year financial statements.
- The financial statements are prepared in accordance with accounting principles generally accepted in the United States of America.
- Supplementary information is presented as a separate column on the face of the reviewed financial statements and was not subjected to the accountant's review procedures applied in the accountant's review of the basic financial statements.

Independent Accountant's Review Report

[*Appropriate Addressee*]

I (We) have reviewed the accompanying financial statements of XYZ Company, which comprise the balance sheet as of December 31, 20X1, and the related statements of income, changes in stockholders' equity, and cash flows for the year then ended, and the related notes to the financial statements. A review includes primarily applying analytical procedures to management's (owners') financial data and making inquiries of company management (owners). A review is substantially less in scope than an audit, the objective of which is the expression of an opinion regarding the financial statements as a whole. Accordingly, I (we) do not express such an opinion.

 ©2017, AICPA

Management's Responsibility for the Financial Statements

Management (Owners) is (are) responsible for the preparation and fair presentation of these financial statements in accordance with accounting principles generally accepted in the United States of America; this includes the design, implementation, and maintenance of internal control relevant to the preparation and fair presentation of financial statements that are free from material misstatement whether due to fraud or error.

Accountant's Responsibility

My (Our) responsibility is to conduct the review engagement in accordance with Statements on Standards for Accounting and Review Services promulgated by the Accounting and Review Services Committee of the AICPA. Those standards require me (us) to perform procedures to obtain limited assurance as a basis for reporting whether I am (we are) aware of any material modifications that should be made to the financial statements for them to be in accordance with accounting principles generally accepted in the United States of America. I (We) believe that the results of my (our) procedures provide a reasonable basis for my (our) conclusion.

Accountant's Conclusion

Based on my (our) review, I am (we are) not aware of any material modifications that should be made to the accompanying financial statements in order for them to be in accordance with accounting principles generally accepted in the United States of America.

Supplementary Information

The [*describe the supplementary information*] presented on the face of the financial statements as a separate column is presented for purposes of additional analysis and is not a required part of the basic financial statements. The [*describe the supplementary information*] is the responsibility of management. I (We) have not audited or reviewed the [*describe the supplementary information*] and accordingly do not express an opinion, a conclusion, nor provide any assurance on it.

[*Signature of accounting firm or accountant, as appropriate*]
[*Accountant's city and state*]
[*Date of the accountant's review report*]

Chapter 2

Compilation of Financial Statements

Introduction

2.01 AR-C section 80, *Compilation Engagements* (AICPA, *Professional Standards*), applies when the accountant is engaged to perform a compilation of financial statements, prospective financial information, pro forma financial information,[1] or other historical financial information. The objective of the accountant in a compilation engagement is to apply accounting and financial reporting expertise to assist management in the presentation of financial statements and report in accordance with AR-C section 80, without undertaking to obtain or provide any assurance that there are no material modifications that should be made to the financial statements in order for them to be in accordance with the applicable financial reporting framework. Other historical financial information to which this section applies includes the following:

- Specified elements, accounts, or items of a financial statement, such as schedules of rentals, royalties, profit participation, or provision for income taxes
- Supplementary information
- Required supplementary information

2.02 Because a compilation engagement is not an assurance engagement, the accountant is not required to verify the accuracy or completeness of the information provided by management for the compilation engagement or otherwise gather evidence to express an opinion or a conclusion on the financial statements. Therefore, the accountant does not express an opinion or a conclusion nor provide any assurance in the compilation report on the financial statements.

Applicability

2.03 The preparation of financial statements, in whole or in part, is a nonattest service subject to the provisions of the "Nonattest Services" subtopic (AICPA, *Professional Standards*, ET sec. 1.295) under the "Independence Rule" (AICPA, *Professional Standards*, ET sec. 1.200.001). The preparation of financial statements is an accounting service and is always separate from the compilation service, which is a reporting service. The following table compares an engagement to prepare financial statements with a compilation engagement:

[1] In a compilation of pro forma financial information, the accountant is required to adhere to the requirements in AR-C section 120, *Compilation of Pro Forma Financial Information*, in addition to the requirements of AR-C section 80, *Compilation Engagements* (AICPA, *Professional Standards*). See chapter 4, *Compilation of Pro Forma Financial Information*, of this guide.

	Compilation Engagements	*Engagements to Prepare Financial Statements*
In addition to AR-C section 60, *General Principles for Engagements Performed in Accordance With Statements on Standards for Accounting and Review Services*, which AR-C section applies to the engagement?	AR-C section 80, *Compilation Engagements*	AR-C section 70, *Preparation of Financial Statements*
When is the accountant required to follow the applicable AR-C section?	When an accountant is engaged to perform a compilation	When an accountant is engaged to prepare financial statements
Is an engagement letter required?	Yes	Yes
Is the accountant required to determine if he or she is independent of the client?	Yes	No
If the accountant is not independent, is that fact required to be disclosed in the accountant's report?	Yes	Not applicable
Does the engagement require a report?	Yes	No (A statement on each page of the financial statements stating that no assurance is provided is required. If the accountant is unable to include the statement on each page of the financial statements, the accountant is required to issue a disclaimer.)
May the financial statements go to users outside of management?	Yes	Yes
May the financial statements omit note disclosures?	Yes	Yes

Requirements

General Principles for Performing and Reporting on Compilations of Financial Statements

2.04 In addition to complying with AR-C section 80, an accountant is required to comply with AR-C section 60, *General Principles for Engagements*

 ©2017, AICPA

Performed in Accordance With Statements of Standards for Accounting and Review Services (AICPA, *Professional Standards*). AR-C section 60 requires

- the accountant to comply with relevant ethical requirements;
- the accountant to exercise professional judgment in the performance of the engagement;
- the accountant to perform the engagement in accordance with Statements on Standards for Accounting and Review Services (SSARSs);
- the engagement partner to possess the competence and capabilities to perform the engagement and competence in financial reporting, appropriate to the engagement circumstances; and
- the engagement partner to take responsibility for certain quality control matters.

AR-C section 60 also includes certain preconditions for the performance of the engagement.

Engagement Level Quality Control in a Compilation Engagement

2.05 In a compilation engagement performed in accordance with SSARSs, the engagement partner is required to possess the competence and capabilities to perform the engagement and competence in financial reporting, appropriate to the engagement circumstances.

2.06 In a compilation engagement performed in accordance with SSARSs, the engagement partner is required to take responsibility for the following:

a. The overall quality of the engagement

b. The direction, supervision, planning, and performance of the engagement in compliance with professional standards and applicable legal and regulatory requirements

c. The accountant's report being appropriate in the circumstances

d. The engagement being performed in accordance with the firm's quality control policies and procedures, including the following:

  i. Being satisfied that appropriate procedures regarding the acceptance and continuance of client relationships and engagements have been followed, and that conclusions reached are appropriate, including considering whether there is information that would lead the engagement partner to conclude that management lacks integrity

  ii. Being satisfied that the engagement team collectively has the appropriate competence and capabilities to perform the engagement and expertise in financial reporting to

    (1) perform the engagement in accordance with professional standards and applicable legal and regulatory requirements and

    (2) enable a report that is appropriate in the circumstances to be issued, if applicable

  iii. Taking responsibility for appropriate engagement documentation being maintained

2.07 If the engagement partner obtains information that would have caused the firm to decline the engagement had that information been available earlier, the engagement partner is required to communicate that information promptly to the firm, so that the firm and the engagement partner can take the necessary action.

2.08 Throughout the engagement, the engagement partner is required to remain alert, through observation and making inquiries as necessary, for evidence of noncompliance with relevant ethical requirements by members of the engagement team. If matters come to the engagement partner's attention through the firm's system of quality control or otherwise that indicate that members of the engagement team have not complied with relevant ethical requirements, the engagement partner, in consultation with others in the firm, is required to determine the appropriate action.

2.09 An effective system of quality control for a firm includes a monitoring process designed to provide the firm with reasonable assurance that the firm's policies and procedures relating to the system of quality control are relevant, adequate, and operating effectively. The engagement partner is required to consider the results of the firm's monitoring process as evidenced in the latest information circulated by the firm and, if applicable, other network firms and whether deficiencies noted in that information may affect the engagement.

Independence

2.10 The accountant must determine whether the accountant is independent of the entity as part of a compilation engagement. The interpretations of the "Independence Rule" of the AICPA Code of Professional Conduct provide authoritative guidance with respect to independence. In the absence of an interpretation of the "Independence Rule" that addresses a particular relationship or circumstance, a member should apply the "Conceptual Framework for Independence" interpretation (AICPA, *Professional Standards*, ET sec. 1.210.010).

2.11 Although an accountant can prepare the financial statements that are the subject of the compilation engagement, the preparation of financial statements, in whole or in part, is a nonattest service separate from the compilation engagement. The preparation of financial statements is subject to the requirements of the "Nonattest Services" subtopic of the "Independence Rule." When an accountant prepares financial statements for an attest client, threats to compliance with the "Independence Rule" may exist. Pursuant to paragraph .01 of the "General Requirements for Performing Nonattest Services" interpretation (AICPA, *Professional Standards*, ET sec. 1.295.040) of the "Independence Rule," these threats would be at an acceptable level and independence would not be impaired when all of the following safeguards are met:

- Management agrees to
  - assume all management responsibilities as described in the "Management Responsibilities" interpretation (AICPA, *Professional Standards*, ET sec. 1.295.030) of the "Independence Rule."
  - oversee the service, by designating an individual, preferably within senior management, who possesses suitable skill, knowledge, or experience (or all of these qualities). The member should assess and be satisfied that such individual understands the services to be performed

©2017, AICPA

sufficiently to oversee them. However, the individual is not required to possess the expertise to perform or re-perform the services.

  - — evaluate the adequacy and results of the nonattest services performed.
  - — accept responsibility for the results of the services.

- The accountant does not assume management responsibilities when providing nonattest services and is satisfied that the client and its management will
  - — be able to meet all of the criteria listed in the aforementioned "management agrees to" section;
  - — make an informed judgment on the results of the accountant's nonattest services; and
  - — accept responsibility for making the significant judgments and decisions that are the proper responsibility of management.

If management is unable or unwilling to assume these responsibilities (for example, management cannot oversee the nonattest services provided or is unwilling to carry out such responsibilities due to lack of time or desire), the accountant's performance of nonattest services would impair independence.

- Before performing nonattest services the accountant establishes and documents in writing his or her understanding with management regarding
  - — objectives of the engagement,
  - — services to be performed,
  - — the client's acceptance of its responsibilities,
  - — accountant's responsibilities, and
  - — any limitations of the engagement.

Preconditions for Accepting a Compilation Engagement

2.12 In accordance with paragraph .25 of AR-C section 60, the accountant is precluded from accepting a compilation engagement if

a. the accountant has reason to believe that relevant ethical requirements will not be satisfied;

b. the accountant's preliminary understanding of the engagement circumstances indicates that information needed to perform the engagement is likely to be unavailable or unreliable; or

c. the accountant has cause to doubt management's integrity such that it is likely to affect the performance of the engagement.

2.13 An example of when the accountant may determine that information needed to perform the compilation engagement is likely to be unavailable or unreliable is when financial statements or accounting records necessary to perform the compilation are suspected to be substantially inaccurate and incomplete.

2.14 As a precondition for accepting a compilation engagement to be performed in accordance with SSARSs, certain items should be considered. In accordance with paragraph .26 of AR-C section 60 and paragraph .08 of AR-C section 80, the accountant is required to do the following:

a. Determine whether preliminary knowledge of the engagement circumstances indicate that ethical requirements regarding professional competence will be satisfied.

b. Determine whether the financial reporting framework selected by management to be applied in the preparation of the financial statements is acceptable.

2.15 Accounting principles generally accepted in the United States of America (GAAP) and International Financial Reporting Standards (IFRS) are general purpose frameworks and are presumed to be acceptable. In determining whether the financial reporting framework selected by management to be applied in the preparation of the financial statements is acceptable, the accountant may consider whether the financial reporting framework exhibits the characteristics of suitable criteria. Suitable criteria exhibit all of the following characteristics:

- *Relevance*. Criteria are relevant to the subject matter.
- *Objectivity*. Criteria are free from bias.
- *Measurability*. Criteria permit reasonably consistent measurements, qualitative or quantitative, of subject matter.
- *Completeness*. Criteria are complete when subject matter prepared in accordance with them does not omit relevant factors that could reasonably be expected to affect decisions of the intended users made on the basis of that subject matter.

The relative importance of each characteristic to a particular engagement is a matter of professional judgment. For example, even though a financial reporting framework designed for a special purpose may not result in the preparation of financial statements that is free from bias, that financial reporting framework may be acceptable in the circumstances.

2.16 Additionally, the accountant's determination of the acceptability for the financial reporting framework to be applied in the preparation of financial statements would include a consideration of the nature of the entity and the intended purpose and users of the financial statements. Financial statements prepared in accordance with a special purpose framework may not be suitable for general purposes as the users may not understand the financial reporting framework.

2.17 Additionally, as a precondition for accepting a compilation engagement, the accountant is required to obtain the agreement of management that it acknowledges and understands its responsibility

a. for the selection of the financial reporting framework to be applied in the preparation of financial statements.

b. for the preparation and fair presentation of financial statements in accordance with the applicable financial reporting framework and the inclusion of all informative disclosures that are appropriate for the applicable financial reporting framework used to prepare the entity's financial statements. If the financial statements

 ©2017, AICPA

are prepared in accordance with a special purpose framework, this includes

i. a description of the special purpose framework, including a summary of significant accounting policies, and how the framework differs from GAAP, the effect of which need not be quantified, and informative disclosures similar to those required by GAAP, in the case of special purpose financial statements that contain items that are the same as, or similar to, those in financial statements prepared in accordance with GAAP,

ii. a description of any significant interpretations of the contract on which the special purpose financial statements are prepared, in the case of financial statements prepared in accordance with a contractual-basis of accounting, and

iii. additional disclosures beyond those specifically required by the framework that may be necessary for the special purpose framework to achieve fair presentation.

c. for the design, implementation, and maintenance of internal control relevant to the preparation and fair presentation of the financial statements that are free from material misstatement, whether due to fraud or error, unless the accountant decides to accept responsibility for such internal control.

d. for preventing and detecting fraud.

e. for ensuring that the entity complies with laws and regulations applicable to its activities.

f. for the accuracy and completeness of the records, documents, explanations, and other information, including significant judgments provided by management for the preparation of financial statements.

g. to provide the accountant with

i. access to all information of which management is aware that is relevant to the preparation and fair presentation of the financial statements, such as records, documentation, and other matters.

ii. additional information that the accountant may request from management for the purpose of the engagement.

iii. unrestricted access to persons within the entity of whom the accountant determines it necessary to make inquiries.

h. to include the accountant's compilation report in any document containing financial statements that indicates that the entity's accountant has performed a compilation engagement on such financial statements unless a different understanding is reached.

Agreement on Engagement Terms

2.18 Paragraph .10 of AR-C section 80 states that the accountant should agree upon the terms of the engagement with management or those charged with governance, as appropriate. The agreed-upon terms of the engagement should be documented in an engagement letter or other suitable form of written agreement between the parties that is signed by both the accountant or the accountant's firm and management or those charged with governance, as appropriate. Ordinarily, this written communication will be what most practitioners refer to as an engagement letter.

2.19 Both management and the accountant have an interest in documenting the agreed-upon terms of the engagement before the commencement of the engagement. Such an understanding reduces the risk that the accountant or the client may misinterpret the needs or expectations of the other party. For example, it reduces the risk that management may inappropriately rely on the accountant to protect the entity against certain risks or to perform certain functions that are management's responsibility.

2.20 The accountant should ensure that the engagement letter includes the objectives of the engagement, management's responsibilities as set forth in paragraph 2.17, the accountant's responsibilities, the limitations of the engagement, identification of the applicable financial reporting framework for the preparation of the financial statements, and the expected form and content of the accountant's compilation report and a statement that there may be circumstances in which the report may differ from its expected form and content.

Observations and Suggestions

It is considered a best practice that an engagement letter be obtained at least annually. The engagement letter can cover multiple services and address both nonattest and attest services (for example, an engagement to prepare monthly financial statements and perform a compilation engagement on the annual financial statements for an entity).

2.21 Illustrations of engagement letters for compilation engagements are included in paragraph 2.100.

Knowledge and Understanding of the Entity's Financial Reporting Framework

2.22 Paragraph .12 of AR-C section 80 states that the accountant should obtain an understanding of the applicable financial reporting framework and significant accounting policies intended to be used in the preparation of the financial statements. This requirement does not prevent the accountant from accepting a compilation engagement for an entity in an industry in which the accountant has no previous experience. The accountant may obtain such an understanding during the course of the compilation engagement, but prior to the issuance of the accountant's compilation report.

2.23 Different financial reporting frameworks may be used to prepare and present financial statements. Some accountants refer to a financial reporting frameworks as a "basis of accounting." Management is responsible for the selection of the financial reporting framework to be applied in the preparation of financial statements. The financial reporting framework selected by management depends on the nature of the entity and the intended use of the information.

2.24 Management may select a general purpose financial reporting framework such as GAAP or IFRS established by the International Accounting

©2017, AICPA

Standards Board. Such frameworks are designed to meet the common financial information needs of a wide range of users.

2.25 Management may also select a special purpose financial reporting framework such as the cash- or tax-basis of accounting, a regulatory-basis of accounting, the contractual-basis of accounting, or the AICPA's Financial Reporting Framework for Small- and Medium-Sized Entities. Such bases of accounting are designed to meet the financial information needs of specific users.

2.26 Additionally, in cases in which the entity is not required to use an established financial reporting framework, management may select a basis of accounting that is appropriate for a narrow use and the entity's circumstances. For example, management may elect to use the cash-basis of accounting and incorporate certain accruals that are not based on cash transactions such as accounts receivable and accounts payable.

Reading the Financial Statements

2.27 Paragraph .13 of AR-C section 80 states that the accountant should read the financial statements in light of the accountant's understanding of the applicable financial reporting framework and the significant accounting policies adopted by management and consider whether such financial statements appear to be appropriate in form and free from obvious material misstatements. The following are examples of the types of issues that may be considered as part of the accountant's reading of the financial statements. The examples are not intended to be all inclusive, and professional judgment would still need to be applied.

- Are headings on the financial statements appropriate for the applicable financial reporting framework (such as the use of the heading "Statement of Cash Receipts and Disbursements" when the cash-basis of accounting is used)?
- Are major sections of the financial statements properly captioned (such as the use of "Current" and "Noncurrent" captions on a classified balance sheet)?
- Are accounts grouped in appropriate captions (such as land held for investment classified as "Other Assets")?
- Are there arithmetical errors in the financial statements (such as the individual financial statement line items for "Total Assets" not adding mathematically to the "Total Assets" presented on the balance sheet)?
- Are there clerical mistakes in the financial statements (such as typographical errors)?
- Are there obvious mistakes in the application of accounting principles (such as the reporting of property, plant, and equipment at cost with no accumulated depreciation in a balance sheet purporting to be in accordance with GAAP)?
- Are required financial statement disclosures omitted (such as the omission of the method used to account for inventories in a set of financial statements purporting to be prepared in accordance with GAAP)?

Consideration of Materiality in a Compilation Engagement

The accountant's consideration of materiality is made in the context of the applicable financial reporting framework. Some financial reporting frameworks discuss the concept of materiality in the context of the preparation and presentation of financial statements. Although financial reporting frameworks may discuss materiality in different terms, they generally explain that:

- Misstatements, including omissions, are considered to be material if they, individually or in the aggregate, could reasonably be expected to influence the economic decisions of users taken on the basis of the financial information;
- Judgments about materiality are made in light of surrounding circumstances, and are affected by the size or nature of a misstatement, or a combination of both; and
- Judgments about matters that are material to users of the financial information are based on a consideration of the common financial information needs of users as a group. The possible effect of misstatements on specific individual users, whose needs may vary widely, is not considered.

If present in the applicable financial reporting framework, a discussion of the concept of materiality provides a frame of reference for the accountant in determining, as required by paragraph .13 of AR-C section 80, whether the financial statements appear to be appropriate in form and free from obvious material misstatements. If the applicable financial reporting framework does not include a discussion of the concept of materiality, the characteristics referred to in the preceding paragraph provide the accountant with a frame of reference.

The accountant's perception of the needs of users of the financial information affects the accountant's view of materiality. In this context, it is reasonable for the accountant to assume that users:

- Have a reasonable knowledge of business and economic activities and accounting, and a willingness to study the financial information with reasonable diligence;
- Understand that financial information is prepared and presented to levels of materiality;
- Recognize the uncertainties inherent in the measurement of amounts based on the use of estimates, judgment and the consideration of future events; and
- Make reasonable economic decisions on the basis of the information in the financial information.

Other Compilation Procedures

2.28 In a compilation engagement, the accountant is not required to make inquiries or perform other procedures to verify, corroborate, or review information supplied by the entity. However, the accountant may have made inquiries or performed other procedures, often as part of other services performed for the client, such as bookkeeping, payroll, and tax services. The results of these inquiries or procedures, as well as knowledge gained from prior engagements, or the financial statements on their face may cause the accountant to recognize

 ©2017, AICPA

that the records, documents, explanations, or other information provided by management are incomplete, inaccurate, or otherwise unsatisfactory. In these instances, the accountant is required by paragraph .14 of AR-C section 80 to bring that to the attention of management and request additional or corrected information.

2.29 Paragraph .15 of AR-C section 80 states that if the accountant becomes aware during the course of the engagement that

a. the financial statements do not adequately refer to or describe the applicable financial reporting framework;

b. revisions to the financial statements are required for the financial statements to be in accordance with the applicable financial reporting framework; or

c. the financial statements are otherwise misleading

the accountant should propose the appropriate revisions to management.

2.30 When, during the performance of the compilation engagement, evidence or information that subsequent events that require adjustment of, or disclosure in, the financial statements comes to the accountant's attention, in accordance with paragraph .15 of AR-C section 80, the accountant should propose the appropriate revisions to management.

2.31 Paragraph .16 of AR-C section 80 states that the accountant should withdraw from the engagement and inform management of the reason for withdrawing if

a. the accountant is unable to complete the engagement because management has failed to provide records, documents, explanations, or other information, including significant judgments, as requested, or

b. management does not make appropriate revisions that are proposed by the accountant or does not disclose such departures in the financial statements, and the accountant determines to not disclose such departures in the accountant's compilation report.

2.32 The accountant has an ethical responsibility to not be associated with financial statements that he or she knows to be misleading. For example, an accountant who is engaged to perform a compilation engagement on the financial statements of XYZ Company is also separately engaged to prepare the personal income tax returns of the owner of XYZ Company and a family member. As part of the tax engagement, the accountant becomes aware that the family member owns another company that provides a material amount of management services to XYZ Company. In reading the financial statements, the accountant becomes aware that the related party relationship and transactions are not disclosed properly in the notes to the financial statements. In this case, the accountant should propose the appropriate revisions to management. If management does not make the appropriate revisions or does not disclose the departure in the financial statements and the accountant determines to not disclose the departures in the accountant's compilation report, the accountant should withdraw from the engagement.

2.33 As an additional example, the accountant may be performing a compilation engagement on the financial statements of a small manufacturing company. During the course of the compilation engagement, the accountant becomes aware that the company is being investigated for possible violations of the Fair Labor Standards Act. Because GAAP requires disclosure of uncertainties, such as litigation exposure, the accountant requests that management provide additional information with respect to the issue. If management refuses to provide the requested information and, therefore, the accountant is unable to complete the compilation, the accountant should withdraw from the engagement.

2.34 Although the accountant, in a compilation engagement, is not required to verify the accuracy or completeness of the information management provides to the accountant for the engagement or otherwise gather evidence for the purpose of expressing an opinion or a conclusion, the accountant may perform procedures customarily performed in a review or an audit but not in a compilation. In such instances, the engagement remains a compilation and the accountant is not required to change the engagement to a review or an audit. Nothing precludes the accountant from performing whatever additional procedures he or she deems necessary as part of the compilation engagement. However, if the accountant determines it is necessary to perform confirmation procedures as part of the compilation engagement, the wording of confirmation requests, or any other communications related to additional procedures performed in the course of the compilation engagement, is not to use phrases such as "as part of an audit of financial statements."

2.35 In instances when the accountant determines that procedures ordinarily performed in a review or an audit are appropriate, the accountant may want to reconsider the appropriateness of the compilation engagement. Management may not have understood the compilation, including the limitations of the engagement, and perhaps a more appropriate service would be a review, an audit, or an agreed-upon procedures engagement. The agreed-upon procedures engagement would be appropriate if management or a third party requests the performance of certain procedures.

Reporting—General

2.36 As part of the compilation engagement, the accountant is required to issue a compilation report. The accountant's compilation report minimizes the risk of misinterpretation of the degree of responsibility the accountant is assuming with respect to the financial statements. Paragraph .17 of AR-C section 80 states that the accountant's compilation report should be in writing and

a. include a statement that management (owners) is (are) responsible for the financial statements.

b. identify the financial statements that have been subjected to the compilation engagement.

c. identify the entity whose financial statements have been subjected to the compilation engagement.

d. specify the date or period covered by the financial statements.

e. include a statement that the accountant performed the compilation engagement in accordance with SSARSs promulgated by the Accounting and Review Services Committee of the AICPA.

f. include a statement that the accountant did not audit or review the financial statements nor was the accountant required to perform any procedures to verify the accuracy or completeness of the information provided by management and does not express an opinion, a conclusion, nor provide any assurance on the financial statements.

 ©2017, AICPA

g. include the signature of the accountant or the accountant's firm.

h. include the city and state where the accountant practices.

i. include the date of the report, which should be the date that the accountant has completed the procedures required by AR-C section 80.

Observations and Suggestions

FASB *Accounting Standards Codification* (ASC) 855-10-50-1 states that an entity should disclose the date through which subsequent events have been evaluated, as well as whether that date is the date the financial statements were issued or the date the financial statements were available to be issued. Because the accountant's compilation report should be dated as of the completion of the compilation, the date of the accountant's compilation report can never be earlier than management's subsequent event note date.

2.37 Illustrative compilation reports are included in paragraph 2.101.

Reporting—Financial Statements Prepared in Accordance With a Special Purpose Framework

2.38 Unless the entity elects to omit substantially all disclosures, when engaged to perform a compilation on financial statements prepared in accordance with a special purpose framework, in accordance with paragraph .18 of AR-C section 80, the accountant should modify the compilation report when that accountant becomes aware that the financial statements do not include

a. a description of the special purpose framework.

b. a summary of significant accounting policies.

c. an adequate description about how the special purpose framework differs from GAAP. The effects of these differences need not be quantified.

d. informative disclosures similar to those required by GAAP when the financial statements contain items that are the same as, or similar to, those in financial statements prepared in accordance with GAAP.

2.39 In the case of financial statements prepared in accordance with a contractual-basis of accounting, the accountant should modify the compilation report if the financial statements do not adequately describe any significant interpretations of the contract on which the financial statements are based.

2.40 In accordance with paragraph .20 of AR-C section 80, the accountant's compilation report on financial statements prepared in accordance with a special purpose framework should

a. make reference to management's responsibility for determining that the applicable financial reporting framework is acceptable in the circumstances when management has a choice of financial reporting frameworks in the preparation of such financial statements.

b. describe the purpose for which the financial statements are prepared or refer to a note in the financial statements that contains that information when the financial statements are prepared in accordance with a regulatory- or contractual-basis of accounting.

2.41 In accordance with paragraph .21 of AR-C section 80, the accountant's compilation report on financial statements prepared in accordance with a special purpose framework should include a separate paragraph that

a. indicates that the financial statements are prepared in accordance with the applicable special purpose framework,

b. refers to the note to the financial statements that describes the framework, if applicable, and

c. states that the special purpose framework is a basis of accounting other than GAAP.

Reporting—Financial Statements that Omit Substantially All the Disclosures Required by the Applicable Financial Reporting Framework

2.42 The entity may request that the accountant perform a compilation engagement on financial statements that omit substantially all disclosures required by the applicable financial reporting framework. Paragraph .26 of AR-C section 80 states that the accountant should not issue a compilation report on financial statements that omit substantially all disclosures required by the applicable financial reporting framework unless the omission of substantially all disclosures is not, to the accountant's knowledge, undertaken with the intention of misleading those who might reasonably be expected to use such financial statements.

> **Observations and Suggestions**
>
> *Financial statement disclosures* refer to the disclosures required by an applicable financial reporting framework, including disclosures that might appear in the body of the financial statements.

2.43 When reporting on financial statements that omit substantially all disclosures required by the applicable financial reporting framework, the accountant should include a separate paragraph in the accountant's compilation report that includes the following elements:

a. A statement that management has elected to omit substantially all the disclosures (and the statement of cash flows, if applicable) required by the applicable financial reporting framework (or ordinarily included in the financial statements if the financial statements are prepared in accordance with a special purpose framework)

b. A statement that if the omitted disclosures (and statement of cash flows, if applicable) were included in the financial statements, they might influence the user's conclusions about the entity's financial position, results of operations, and cash flows (or equivalent for presentations other than GAAP)

c. A statement that, accordingly, the financial statements are not designed for those who are not informed about such matters

2.44 The inclusion of the separate paragraph in the accountant's compilation report regarding the omission of substantially all disclosures does not alleviate the requirement for the accountant to disclose other known departures resulting from measurement or recognition issues from the applicable financial reporting framework in the accountant's compilation report. For example,

 ©2017, AICPA

the financial statements may omit substantially all disclosures required by accounting principles generally accepted in the United States of America (U.S. GAAP) and also may include land at appraised values (GAAP requires that land be recorded at cost). In such instances, the accountant would include separate paragraphs in the accountant's compilation report. An illustration of this example is included as illustration 9, "An Accountant's Compilation Report on Comparative Financial Statements That Omit Substantially All Disclosures and the Accountant Is Aware of an Additional Departure From Accounting Principles Generally Accepted in the United States of America."

2.45 In financial statements that omit substantially all disclosures required by the applicable financial reporting framework, an entity can include disclosures about only a few matters in the form of notes to the financial statements, such disclosures may be labeled "Selected Information—Substantially All Disclosures Required by [*identify the applicable financial reporting framework (for example 'accounting principles generally accepted in the United States of America')*] Are Not Included." However, when the financial statements include more than a few disclosures, this guidance is not appropriate. The omission of one or more notes, when substantially all other disclosures are presented, should be treated in a compilation report like any other departure from the applicable financial reporting framework, and the nature of the departure and its effects, if known, should be disclosed in accordance with paragraphs .29–.33 of AR-C section 80. The label "Selected Information—Substantially All Disclosures Required by [*identify the applicable financial reporting framework (for example 'accounting principles generally accepted in the United States of America')*] Are Not Included" is not intended to be used for the omission of (intentionally or unintentionally) one or more specific disclosures. In determining whether use of the label is appropriate, the accountant should apply professional judgment to all the facts and circumstances.

2.46 In financial statements that omit substantially all disclosures required by GAAP and an element of comprehensive income is present, the display of comprehensive income can be omitted. FASB ASC 220, *Comprehensive Income*, requires the display of comprehensive income when a full set of financial statements is presented in accordance with U.S. GAAP. However, the display of comprehensive income may be omitted by identifying the omission in the compilation report. An illustration of this example is included as illustration 4, "An Accountant's Compilation Report on Comparative Financial Statements Prepared in Accordance With Accounting Principles Generally Accepted in the United States of America and Management Has Elected to Omit Substantially All Disclosures Ordinarily Included in Financial Statements Prepared in Accordance With Accounting Principles Generally Accepted in the United States of America and the Display of Comprehensive Income."

2.47 If the accountant performs a compilation engagement on financial statements that include substantially all disclosures required by GAAP but omits the display of comprehensive income, the omission is a departure from GAAP. Additionally, if an element of comprehensive income has not been computed, for example, unrealized gains and losses arising from investments in marketable securities classified as "available for sale," then the accountant should consider it a departure from GAAP and follow the guidance in paragraphs .29–.33 of AR-C section 80.

2.48 The accountant may have reviewed or audited financial statements and subsequently be engaged to perform a compilation on financial statements for the same period which are included in a prescribed form which do not include the disclosures required by the applicable financial reporting framework. If differences between the reviewed or audited financial statements and the financial statements included in the prescribed form is limited to the omission of disclosures not required by the form and the measurement principles used do not cause the financial statements subject to the compilation engagement to be materially different from the financial statements that were reviewed or audited, the accountant's compilation report on the prescribed form may refer to the accountant's review or auditor's report.

2.49 Illustrative compilation reports on financial statements that omit substantially all disclosures required by the applicable financial reporting framework are included in paragraph 2.101.

Reporting—Comparative Financial Statements

2.50 When the accountant is engaged to perform a compilation engagement on comparative financial statements, in accordance with the requirement in paragraph .17 of AR-C section 80, the accountant's compilation report should specify the financial statement periods covered by the accountant's compilation report.

2.51 Whenever the accountant becomes aware that financial statements of other periods that have not been subjected to an audit, review, or compilation engagement have been presented in columnar form in a document with financial statements on which he or she has performed a compilation engagement and the accountant's compilation report thereon, the accountant may advise his or her client that a clear indication should be included so that a user does not inappropriately extend the accountant's compilation report to such financial statements.

2.52 When comparative financial statements are presented and a continuing accountant performed a compilation engagement in the preceding period but performed an engagement to prepare financial statements for the current period and, in accordance with AR-C section 70, *Preparation of Financial Statements* (AICPA, *Professional Standards*), the accountant did not issue a report on the current period financial statements, the accountant is not required to reissue the accountant's compilation report on the preceding period. However, the accountant may determine to reissue the compilation report on the prior year financial statements so that the accountant's responsibility with respect to the prior period financial statements is clear to users of the comparative financial statements.

2.53 Financial statements subjected to a compilation engagement that omit substantially all of the disclosures required by an applicable financial reporting framework are not comparable to financial statements that include such disclosures. Accordingly, it is not appropriate to issue a compilation report on comparative financial statements when statements for one or more, but not all, of the periods presented omit substantially all of the disclosures required by an applicable financial reporting framework.

2.54 A continuing accountant who performs the same or a higher level of service with respect to the financial statements of the current period would, in most circumstances, update his or her report on the financial statements of a prior period presented with those of the current period. A continuing accountant who performs a lower level of service with respect to the financial

 ©2017, AICPA

statements of the current period would either (*a*) include as a separate paragraph of his or her report a description of the responsibility assumed for the financial statements of the prior period (see paragraph 2.55) or (*b*) reissue his or her report on the financial statements of the prior period.

2.55 A continuing accountant who performs a compilation engagement of the current period financial statements and has previously reviewed or audited one or more prior period financial statements would report as indicated in either (*a*) or (*b*) that follow:

a. Issue a compilation report on the current period financial statements that includes a description of the responsibility assumed for the financial statements of the prior period. The description states the original date of the accountant's review or auditor's report and also states that he or she has not performed any procedures in connection with that review or audit engagement after that date.

b. Combine his or her compilation report on the financial statements of the current period with his or her reissued review or audit report on the financial statements of the prior period or present them separately. The combined report also states that the accountant has not performed any procedures in connection with that review or audit engagement after the date of his or her review or audit report.

2.56 During his or her current engagement, the accountant remains aware that circumstances or events may affect the prior period financial statements presented, including the adequacy of informative disclosures. The accountant considers the effects on his or her report on the prior period financial statements of circumstances or events coming to his or her attention.

2.57 When the accountant's compilation report on the financial statements of the prior period contains a changed reference to a departure from the applicable financial reporting framework, a separate explanatory paragraph in his or her report may indicate

a. the date of the accountant's previous report;

b. the circumstances or events that caused the reference to be changed;

c. when applicable, that the financial statements of the prior period have been changed.

2.58 Although a predecessor accountant or auditor may reissue his or her compilation, review, or audit report at the client's request, the predecessor is not required to do so. If the predecessor accountant does not reissue his or her compilation, review, or audit report on the financial statements of a prior period, a successor may make reference to the report of the predecessor.

2.59 When the financial statements of a prior period have been subjected to a compilation, review, or audit by a predecessor whose report is not presented and the successor has not performed a compilation of those financial statements, the successor may make reference in an additional paragraph(s) of his or her report on the current period financial statements to the predecessor's report on the prior period financial statements. Ordinarily, this reference would include the following matters:

a. A statement that the financial statements of the prior period were subjected to a compilation, review, or audit by another accountant (other accountants)[2]

b. The date of his or her (their) report

c. If the financial statements of the prior period were subjected to a compilation engagement, a statement that the other accountant(s) did not audit or review the financial statements and, accordingly, did not express an opinion or provide any assurance about whether the financial statements are in accordance with the applicable financial reporting framework

d. If the financial statements of the prior period were reviewed, a statement that, based on his or her review, the other accountant(s) are not aware of any material modifications that should be made to the financial statements in order for them to be in accordance with the applicable financial reporting framework, other than those modifications, if any, indicated in the report

e. If the financial statements of the prior period were audited, the type of opinion expressed on the prior period financial statements

f. A description or a quotation of any modifications of the standard report and of any paragraphs emphasizing a matter regarding the financial statements

2.60 If a predecessor becomes aware of information, including information about events or transactions occurring subsequent to the date of his or her previous report, that he or she believes may affect the prior period financial statements or his or her report on them, he or she would perform the compilation procedures he or she deems necessary in the circumstances. For example, the predecessor may wish to discuss this information with the successor or to review the engagement documentation of the successor as it relates to the matters affecting the prior period financial statements. If the predecessor decides, based on the information obtained, that his or her report on the prior period financial statements should be revised, he or she would follow the guidance in paragraphs 2.58–.59 and 2.61.

2.61 A predecessor's knowledge of the current affairs of his or her former client is obviously limited in the absence of a continuing relationship. Consequently, when reissuing his or her report on the prior period financial statements, a predecessor would use the date of his or her previous report to avoid any implication that he or she has performed procedures after that date. If the predecessor revises his or her report or if the financial statements are restated, he or she would dual-date his or her report (for example, "March 1, 20X1, except for note X, as to which the date is March 15, 20X2"). The predecessor's responsibility for events occurring subsequent to the completion of his or her engagement is limited to the specific event referred to in the note or otherwise disclosed. He or she would also obtain a written statement from the former client setting forth the information currently acquired and its effect on the prior period financial statements and, if applicable, expressing an understanding of its effect on the predecessor's reissued report.

---

[2] The successor accountant would not name the predecessor accountant in his or her report unless the predecessor accountant's practice was acquired by, or merged with, that of the successor accountant.

 ©2017, AICPA

2.62 When prior period financial statements have been restated, in practice the predecessor accountant rarely reissues his or her report. If the predecessor does not reissue his or her report, the successor accountant may be engaged to report on the financial statements for the prior year. If the predecessor accountant does not reissue his or her report and the successor accountant is not engaged to report on the prior year financial statements, to avoid confusion with respect to the accountant's association with the prior period financial statements, the successor accountant may, but is not required to, indicate in his or her compilation report that a predecessor accountant reported on the financial statements of the prior period before restatement. In addition, if the successor accountant is engaged to perform a compilation engagement on the restatement adjustment(s), he or she may also indicate in the accountant's report that he or she performed a compilation engagement on the adjustment(s) that was (were) applied to restate prior year financial statements. An example compilation report is included as illustration 14, "An Accountant's Compilation Report on Comparative Financial Statements When the Predecessor Accountant's Report Is Not Presented, and the Successor Accountant Is Engaged to Perform a Compilation Engagement on the Restatement Adjustment(s)" in paragraph 2.101.

Reporting—When the Accountant Is Not Independent

2.63 When the accountant performs a compilation engagement on financial statements for a client in situations in which the accountant is not independent, the accountant should indicate the accountant's lack of independence in a final paragraph of the accountant's compilation report. In making a judgment about whether he or she is independent, the accountant should be guided by the AICPA Code of Professional Conduct.

2.64 Although the accountant is not required to provide any details regarding the reasons for the independence impairment, he or she may choose to provide a description regarding the reason that his or her independence is impaired. If the accountant elects to disclose a description about the reasons his or her independence is impaired, the accountant should include all such reasons in the description.

Observations and Suggestions

Some accountants are more comfortable simply stating that they are not independent (without disclosing the reasons for the lack of independence). Those accountants are concerned that the disclosure of the reasons may be misinterpreted by the user of the financial statements. Other accountants, however, prefer to be able to describe the reason for the independence impairment. Those accountants feel that the users of the financial statements are better informed regarding the services provided by the accountant. In the end, it is a matter of professional judgment about which type of disclosure is best suited for the accountant's client and other users of the financial statements.

2.65 The exhibit, "Compilation Reporting Requirements When Independence Is Impaired," in this chapter provides additional discussion on compilation reporting requirements when an accountant's independence is impaired. Illustrations of compilation reports when the accountant's independence has been impaired are included in paragraph 2.101.

Reporting—Known Departures From the Applicable Financial Reporting Framework

2.66 In the course of performing a compilation engagement on the client's financial statements, the accountant may become aware of a departure from the applicable financial reporting framework (including inadequate disclosure) that is material to the financial statements. Such departure includes subsequent events that are not adequately accounted for or disclosed in the financial statements.

2.67 If the financial statements are not revised, or the departure is not disclosed in the notes to the financial statements, the accountant should modify the compilation report to disclose the departure. The departure would be disclosed in a separate paragraph of the report, including disclosure of the effects of the departure on the financial statements if such effects have been determined by management or are readily known to the accountant as the result of the accountant's procedures. The accountant is not required to determine the effects of a departure if management has not done so or such effects are not readily known to the accountant as a result of the accountant's procedures. However, in such circumstances, the accountant is required to state in the report that such determination has not been made by management.

2.68 If the accountant believes that modification of the standard report is not adequate to indicate the deficiencies in the financial statements as a whole, the accountant should withdraw from the compilation engagement and provide no further services with respect to those financial statements. The accountant also may wish to consult with his or her legal counsel in those circumstances.

2.69 The accountant should not modify the compilation report to include a statement that the financial statements are not in accordance with the applicable financial reporting framework as such a statement would be tantamount to expressing an adverse opinion on the financial statements as a whole. Such an opinion can be expressed only in the context of an audit engagement.

2.70 However, the accountant may emphasize the limitations of the financial statements in a separate paragraph of his or her compilation report, depending on his or her assessment of the possible dollar magnitude of the effects of the departures, the significance of the affected items to the entity, the pervasiveness and overall impact of the misstatements, and whether disclosure has been made of the effects of the departures. Such separate paragraph might read as follows:

> Because the significance and pervasiveness of the matters previously discussed makes it difficult to assess their impact on the financial statements as a whole, users of these financial statements should recognize that they might reach different conclusions about the company's financial position, results of operations, and cash flows if they had access to revised financial statements prepared in accordance with accounting principles generally accepted in the United States of America.

Inclusion of such a separate paragraph in the accountant's compilation report is not a substitute for disclosure of the specific departures or the effects of such departures when they have been determined by management or are known as a result of the accountant's procedures.

 ©2017, AICPA

2.71 Illustrations of compilation reports that disclose departures from the applicable financial reporting framework are included in paragraph 2.101.

Reporting—Supplementary Information That Accompanies Financial Statements and the Accountant's Compilation Report Thereon

2.72 When supplementary information accompanies financial statements and the accountant's compilation report thereon, pursuant to paragraph .34 of AR-C section 80, the accountant is required to clearly indicate the degree of responsibility, if any, the accountant is taking with respect to such information in either

a. a separate paragraph in the accountant's compilation report on the financial statements or

b. a separate report on the supplementary information.

2.73 When the accountant has performed a compilation engagement with respect to both the financial statements and the supplementary information, the accountant, pursuant to paragraph .35 of AR-C section 80, is required to include a separate paragraph in the accountant's compilation report on the financial statements or issue a separate report on the supplementary information that states

a. the supplementary information is presented for purposes of additional analysis and is not a required part of the basic financial statements;

b. the supplementary information is the responsibility of management;

c. the supplementary information was subject to the compilation engagement, and

d. the accountant has not audited or reviewed the supplementary information and does not express an opinion, a conclusion, nor provide any assurance on such information.

2.74 When the accountant has performed a compilation engagement with respect to the financial statements but the supplementary information was not subject to the compilation engagement, the accountant is required, in accordance with paragraph .36 of AR-C section 80, to include a separate paragraph in the accountant's compilation report on the financial statements or issue a separate report on the supplementary information that states

a. the supplementary information is presented for purposes of additional analysis and is not a required part of the basic financial statements;

b. the supplementary information is the responsibility of management; and

c. the supplementary information was not subject to the compilation engagement and the accountant does not express an opinion, a conclusion, nor provide any assurance on such information.

Reporting—Required Supplementary Information

2.75 With regard to the requirement in paragraph .34 of AR-C section 80, with respect to required supplementary information, the accountant is required to include a separate paragraph in the accountant's compilation report on the financial statements. Pursuant to paragraph .37 of AR-C section 80, the other-matter paragraph should include language to explain the following circumstances, as applicable:

a. The required supplementary information is included, and the accountant performed a compilation engagement on the required supplementary information.

b. The required supplementary information is included, and the accountant did not perform a compilation, review, or audit on the required supplementary information.

c. The required supplementary information is omitted.

d. Some required supplementary information is missing, and some is presented in accordance with the prescribed guidelines.

e. The accountant has identified departures from the prescribed guidelines.

f. The accountant has unresolved doubts about whether the required supplementary information is presented in accordance with prescribed guidelines.

2.76 If the entity has presented all or some of the required supplementary information and the accountant did not perform a compilation engagement on the required supplementary information, the other-matter paragraph in the accountant's compilation report referred to in paragraph .34 of AR-C section 80 should include the following elements:

a. A statement that [*identify the applicable financial reporting framework (for example, accounting principles generally accepted in the United States of America)*] requires that the [*identify the required supplementary information*] be presented to supplement the basic financial statements

b. A statement that such information, although not a part of the basic financial statements, is required by [*identify designated accounting standard-setter*], who considers it to be an essential part of financial reporting for placing the basic financial statements in an appropriate operational, economic, or historical context

c. A statement that the accountant did not perform a compilation, review, or audit on the required supplementary information and does not express an opinion, a conclusion, nor provide any assurance on the information

d. If some of the required supplementary information is omitted:

   i. A statement that management has omitted [*description of the missing required supplementary information*] that [*identify the applicable financial reporting framework (for example, accounting principles generally accepted in the United States of America)*] require to be presented to supplement the basic financial statements

   ii. A statement that such missing information, although not a part of the basic financial statements, is required by [*identify designated accounting standard- setter*], who considers it to be an essential part of financial reporting for placing the basic financial statements in an appropriate operational, economic, or historical context

 ©2017, AICPA

e. If the measurement or presentation of the required supplementary information departs materially from the prescribed guidelines, a statement that material departures from prescribed guidelines exist [*describe the material departures from the applicable financial reporting framework*]

f. If the accountant has unresolved doubts about whether the required supplementary information is measured or presented in accordance with prescribed guidelines, a statement that the accountant has doubts about whether material modifications should be made to the required supplementary information for it to be presented in accordance with guidelines established by [*identify designated accounting standard-setter*]

2.77 If all the required supplementary information is omitted, in accordance with paragraph .39 of AR-C section 80, the separate paragraph in the accountant's compilation report is required to include the following elements:

a. A statement that management has omitted [*description of the missing required supplementary information*] that [*identify the applicable financial reporting framework (for example, accounting principles generally accepted in the United States of America)*] require to be presented to supplement the basic financial statements

b. A statement that such missing information, although not a part of the basic financial statements, is required by [*identify designated accounting standard-setter*], who considers it to be an essential part of financial reporting for placing the basic financial statements in an appropriate operational, economic, or historical context

Reporting—Alert That Restricts the Use of the Accountant's Compilation Report

2.78 Although never required, the accountant is not precluded from including an alert, in a separate paragraph, that restricts the use of the accountant's compilation report.

2.79 An accountant's compilation report for general-use may be included in a document that also includes a separate restricted-use report. For example, the compilation report on financial statements may be included in a document that also includes an agreed-upon procedures report. The inclusion of the separate restricted-use report does not affect the intended use of the general-use report nor does the inclusion of the general-use report affect the intended use of the restricted-use report. The restricted-use report remains restricted as to use and the general-use report continues to be for general use.

Reporting—Emphasis-of-Matter or Other-Matter Paragraphs

2.80 AR-C section 80 does not preclude an accountant from including an emphasis-of-matter or an other-matter paragraph in the accountant's compilation report.

An illustration of a report that includes an emphasis-of-matter paragraph with respect to a going concern uncertainty is included as illustration 18, "An Accountant's Compilation Report on Comparative Financial Statements Prepared in Accordance With Accounting Principles Generally Accepted in the United States of America That Includes an Emphasis-of-Matter Paragraph With Respect to a Going Concern Uncertainty" in paragraph 2.101.

Reporting—Financial Statements Prepared in Accordance With a Prescribed Format

2.81 The accountant may be engaged to perform a compilation engagement on financial statements prepared in accordance with a prescribed format. A prescribed form is any standard preprinted form designed or adopted by the body to which it is to be submitted. Prescribed forms include, for example, forms used by industry trade associations, credit agencies, banks, and governmental and regulatory bodies other than those concerned with the sale or trading of securities. Importantly, a form designed or adopted by the entity whose financial statements are to be subjected to the compilation engagement is not considered to be a prescribed form.

2.82 There is a presumption that the information required by a prescribed form is sufficient to meet the needs of the body that designed or adopted the form and that there is no need for that body to be advised of departures from the applicable financial reporting framework required by the prescribed form or related instructions. However, if the accountant becomes aware of a departure from an applicable financial reporting framework other than departures that may be called for by the prescribed form or related instructions, he or she should follow the guidance in paragraphs .29–.33 of AR-C section 80 (discussed previously in this chapter) related to departures from the applicable financial reporting framework.

2.83 If the accountant becomes aware of a departure from the requirements of the prescribed form or related instructions, he or she should consider that departure as the equivalent of a departure from an applicable financial reporting framework in determining its effect on his or her report and follow the guidance in paragraphs .29–.33 of AR-C section 80.

2.84 Due to the nature of the financial statements prepared in accordance with a prescribed format and the accountant's compilation report thereon, as well as the potential for the report to be misunderstood when taken out of the context in which it was intended to be used, the accountant may determine to restrict the use of the accountant's compilation report on financial statements prepared in accordance with a prescribed format.

2.85 The accountant should not sign a preprinted report form that does not conform to the guidance in AR-C section 80. If the preprinted report form does not conform to the applicable requirements, the accountant should append an appropriate report to the prescribed form.

2.86 Illustrative compilation reports on prescribed forms are included in paragraph 2.101.

Compilation of Specified Elements, Accounts, or Items of a Financial Statement

2.87 Paragraph .01 of AR-C section 80 states that AR-C section 80 also applies to other historical financial information.

2.88 The performance, reporting, and documentation requirements of AR-C section 80 would apply to compilations of specified elements, accounts, or items of a financial statement.

 ©2017, AICPA

2.89 An illustration of an engagement letter for a compilation of specified elements, accounts, or items of a financial statement is presented in illustration 5, "Engagement Letter for a Compilation Engagement With Respect to One or More Compiled Specified Elements, Accounts, or Items of a Financial Statement" in paragraph 2.100.

2.90 An illustrative compilation report on specified elements, accounts, or items of a financial statement is presented in illustration 19, "An Accountant's Compilation Report on Specified Elements, Accounts, or Items of a Financial Statement Prepared in Accordance With Accounting Principles Generally Accepted in the United States of America" in paragraph 2.101.

Change in Engagement From Audit or Review to a Compilation Engagement

2.91 The accountant who has been engaged to audit financial statements in accordance with auditing standards generally accepted in the United States of America (GAAS) or the accountant who has been engaged to review financial statements in accordance with SSARSs may, before the completion of the audit or review, be requested to change the engagement to a compilation. A request to change the engagement may result from a change in circumstances affecting the entity's requirement for an audit or review; a misunderstanding regarding the nature of an audit, review, or compilation; or a restriction on the scope of the audit or review, whether imposed by the client or caused by circumstances.

2.92 Before the accountant who was engaged to perform an audit in accordance with GAAS or a review in accordance with SSARSs agrees to change the engagement to a compilation engagement, he or she would consider the following:

- *a.* The reason given for the client's request, particularly the implications of a restriction on the scope of the audit or review, whether imposed by the client or by circumstances
- *b.* The additional audit or review effort required to complete the audit or review
- *c.* The estimated additional cost to complete the audit or review

2.93 A change in circumstances that affects the entity's requirement for an audit or a review or a misunderstanding concerning the nature of an audit, a review, or compilation would ordinarily be considered a reasonable basis for requesting a change in the engagement.

2.94 In considering the implications of a restriction on the scope of the audit or review, the accountant evaluates the possibility that information affected by the scope restriction may be incorrect, incomplete, or otherwise unsatisfactory. Nevertheless, when the accountant has been engaged to audit an entity's financial statements and has been prohibited by the client from corresponding with the entity's legal counsel, the accountant ordinarily would be precluded from issuing a compilation report on the financial statements. If in an audit or a review engagement, a client does not provide the accountant with a signed representation letter, the accountant would ordinarily be precluded from issuing a compilation report on the financial statements.

©2017, AICPA

2.95 In all circumstances, if the audit or review procedures are substantially complete or the cost to complete such procedures is relatively insignificant, the accountant would consider the propriety of accepting a change in the engagement.

2.96 If the accountant concludes, based upon his or her professional judgment, that reasonable justification exists to change the engagement and if he or she complies with the standards applicable to a compilation engagement, the accountant should issue an appropriate compilation report. The report should not include reference to (*a*) the original engagement, (*b*) any audit or review procedures that may have been performed, or (*c*) scope limitations that resulted in the changed engagement.

Documentation Requirements

2.97 The accountant should prepare documentation in connection with each compilation engagement in sufficient detail to provide a clear understanding of the work performed. Documentation provides the principal support for the representation in the compilation report that the accountant performed the compilation engagement in accordance with SSARSs.

2.98 Although the form, content, and extent of documentation depend on the circumstances of the engagement, the methodology and tools used, and the accountant's professional judgment, the accountant's documentation should, at a minimum, include all of the following:

- *a.* The engagement letter or other suitable form of written documentation with management
- *b.* A copy of the financial statements
- *c.* A copy of the accountant's report

2.99 In addition to the minimum requirements set forth in paragraph 2.98, other documentation may include the following:

- *a.* Any findings or issues that, in the accountant's judgment, are significant. This includes, for example, the results of compilation procedures that indicate that the financial statements could be materially misstated, including actions taken to address such findings, and, to the extent that the accountant had any questions or concerns as a result of his or her compilation procedures, how those issues were resolved.
- *b.* Communications, whether oral or written, to the appropriate level of management regarding fraud or illegal acts that came to the accountant's attention.

Illustrative Engagement Letters

Notice to Readers

The illustrative engagement letters presented in this section are intended to show how the engagement letter can be presented assuming that the accountant has been engaged to perform a compilation engagement on the financial statements or financial information. The engagement letter will vary according to individual requirements and circumstances and may be

 ©2017, AICPA

modified to include other services that the accountant may be engaged to perform such as nonattest services. In those cases, the engagement letter may include management's acknowledgment of its responsibilities in accordance with the "Nonattest Services" subtopic of the "Independence Rule." The accountant may seek legal advice about whether the proposed letter is suitable.

2.100 The illustrative engagement letters in this paragraph are as follows:

Illustration 1—An Engagement Letter for a Compilation Engagement With Respect to Financial Statements Prepared in Accordance With Accounting Principles Generally Accepted in the United States of America

Illustration 2—An Engagement Letter for a Compilation Engagement With Respect to Financial Statements Prepared in Accordance With Accounting Principles Generally Accepted in the United States of America, Except the Financial Statements Omit the Statement of Cash Flows and Substantially All Disclosures Required by U.S. GAAP and in Which the Accountant's Independence Is Impaired Because the Accountant Accepts Responsibility for the Design, Implementation, and Maintenance of Internal Control Over Financial Reporting

Illustration 3—An Engagement Letter for a Compilation Engagement With Respect to Financial Statements Prepared in Accordance With the Tax-Basis of Accounting

Illustration 4—An Engagement Letter for a Compilation Engagement With Respect to Financial Statements Prepared in Accordance With a Prescribed Format

Illustration 5—Engagement Letter for a Compilation Engagement With Respect to One or More Compiled Specified Elements, Accounts, or Items of a Financial Statement

Illustration 1—An Engagement Letter for a Compilation Engagement With Respect to Financial Statements Prepared in Accordance With Accounting Principles Generally Accepted in the United States of America

Circumstances include the following:

- The accountant will prepare, as a nonattest service, the financial statements, including related notes, subject to the compilation engagement.
- The financial statements will be prepared in accordance with accounting principles generally accepted in the United States of America and will include all related notes required by accounting principles generally accepted in the United States of America.
- The accountant expects that his or her independence will not be impaired.

To the appropriate representative of management of ABC Company:[3]

[3] The addresses and references in the engagement letter would be those that are appropriate in the circumstances of the engagement, including the relevant jurisdiction. It is important to refer to the appropriate persons. See paragraph .A7 of AR-C section 80.

You[4] have requested that we prepare the financial statements of ABC Company (the Company), which comprise the balance sheet as of December 31, 20X2, and the related statements of income, changes in stockholders' equity, and cash flows for the year then ended, and the related notes to the financial statements, and perform a compilation engagement with respect to those financial statements.[5] We are pleased to confirm our acceptance and our understanding of this engagement by means of this letter.

Our Responsibilities

The objective of our engagement is to

a. prepare financial statements in accordance with accounting principles generally accepted in the United States of America based on information provided by you and

b. apply accounting and financial reporting expertise to assist you in the presentation of financial statements without undertaking to obtain or provide any assurance that there are no material modifications that should be made to the financial statements in order for them to be in accordance with accounting principles generally accepted in the United States of America.

We will conduct our compilation engagement in accordance with Statements on Standards for Accounting and Review Services (SSARSs) promulgated by the Accounting and Review Services Committee of the AICPA and comply with the AICPA's Code of Professional Conduct, including the ethical principles of integrity, objectivity, professional competence, and due care.

We are not required to, and will not, verify the accuracy or completeness of the information you will provide to us for the engagement or otherwise gather evidence for the purpose of expressing an opinion or a conclusion. Accordingly, we will not express an opinion or a conclusion nor provide any assurance on the financial statements.

Our engagement cannot be relied upon to identify or disclose any financial statement misstatements, including those caused by fraud or error, or to identify or disclose any wrongdoing within the Company or noncompliance with laws and regulations.

Your Responsibilities

The engagement to be performed is conducted on the basis that you acknowledge and understand that our role is to prepare financial statements in accordance with accounting principles generally accepted in the United States of America and assist you in the presentation of the financial statements in accordance with accounting principles generally accepted in the United States of America. You have the following overall responsibilities that are fundamental to our undertaking the engagement in accordance with SSARSs:

a. The selection of accounting principles generally accepted in the United States of America as the financial reporting framework to be applied in the preparation of financial statements

---

[4] Throughout this engagement letter, references to *you*, *we*, *us*, *management*, and *accountant* would be used or amended as appropriate in the circumstances.

[5] The accountant may include other nonattest services to be performed as part of the engagement, such as income tax preparation and bookkeeping services.

 ©2017, AICPA

b. The preparation and fair presentation of financial statements in accordance with accounting principles generally accepted in the United States of America and the inclusion of all informative disclosures that are appropriate for accounting principles generally accepted in the United States of America

c. The design, implementation, and maintenance of internal control relevant to the preparation and fair presentation of the financial statements

d. The prevention and detection of fraud

e. To ensure that the Company complies with the laws and regulations applicable to its activities

f. The accuracy and completeness of the records, documents, explanations, and other information, including significant judgments, you provide to us for the engagement

g. To provide us with

i. access to all information of which you are aware is relevant to the preparation and fair presentation of the financial statements, such as records, documentation, and other matters

ii. additional information that we may request from you for the purpose of the compilation engagement

iii. unrestricted access to persons within the Company of whom we determine it necessary to make inquiries

You are also responsible for all management decisions and responsibilities and for designating an individual with suitable skills, knowledge, and experience to oversee our preparation of your financial statements. You are responsible for evaluating the adequacy and results of the services performed and accepting responsibility for such services.

Our Report

As part of our engagement, we will issue a report that will state that we did not audit or review the financial statements and that, accordingly, we do not express an opinion, a conclusion, nor provide any assurance on them. There may be circumstances in which the report differs from the expected form and content.

You agree to include our accountant's compilation report in any document containing financial statements that indicates that we have performed a compilation engagement on such financial statements and, prior to inclusion of the report, to ask our permission to do so.

Other Relevant Information

Our fees for these services . . . .

[*The accountant may include language, such as the following, regarding limitation of or other arrangements regarding the liability of the accountant or the entity, such as indemnification to the accountant for liability arising from knowing misrepresentations to the accountant by management (regulators may restrict or prohibit such liability limitation arrangements):*

You agree to hold us harmless and to release, indemnify, and defend us from any liability or costs, including attorney's fees, resulting from management's knowing misrepresentations to us or resulting from any actions against us by

third parties relying on the financial statements described herein except for our own intentional wrongdoing]

If you request us to perform additional services not contemplated or described in this engagement letter, we will provide you with a separate agreement describing those additional services and fees.

Please sign and return the attached copy of this letter to indicate your acknowledgment of, and agreement with, the arrangements for our engagement to prepare the financial statements described herein and to perform a compilation engagement with respect to those same financial statements, and our respective responsibilities.

Sincerely yours,

____

[*Signature of accountant or accountant's firm*]

Acknowledged and agreed on behalf of ABC Company by:

____

[*Signed*]
[*Name and Title*]

____

[*Date*]

Illustration 2—An Engagement Letter for a Compilation Engagement With Respect to Financial Statements Prepared in Accordance With Accounting Principles Generally Accepted in the United States of America, Except the Financial Statements Omit the Statement of Cash Flows and Substantially All Disclosures Required by U.S. GAAP and in Which the Accountant's Independence Is Impaired Because the Accountant Accepts Responsibility for the Design, Implementation, and Maintenance of Internal Control Over Financial Reporting

Circumstances include the following:

- The accountant will prepare, as a nonattest service, the financial statements subject to the compilation engagement.
- The financial statements will be prepared in accordance with accounting principles generally accepted in the United States of America, except the statement of cash flows and substantially all disclosures required by accounting principles generally accepted in the United States of America will be omitted.
- The accountant's independence will be impaired because the accountant accepts responsibility for the design, implementation, and maintenance of internal control over financial reporting.

To the appropriate representative of management of ABC Company:[6]

---

[6] See footnote 2.

 ©2017, AICPA

You[7] have requested that we prepare the financial statements of ABC Company (the Company), which comprise the balance sheet as of December 31, 20X2, and the related statements of income and changes in stockholders' equity for the year then ended, and perform a compilation engagement with respect to those financial statements.[8] These financial statements will not include a statement of cash flows and related notes to the financial statements. We are pleased to confirm our acceptance and our understanding of this engagement by means of this letter.

Our Responsibilities

The objective of our engagement is to

a. prepare financial statements in accordance with accounting principles generally accepted in the United States of America based on information provided by you and

b. apply accounting and financial reporting expertise to assist you in the presentation of financial statements without undertaking to obtain or provide any assurance that there are no material modifications that should be made to the financial statements in order for them to be in accordance with accounting principles generally accepted in the United States of America.

We will conduct our compilation engagement in accordance with Statements on Standards for Accounting and Review Services (SSARSs) promulgated by the Accounting and Review Services Committee of the AICPA and comply with the AICPA's Code of Professional Conduct, including the ethical principles of integrity, objectivity, professional competence, and due care.

We are not required to, and will not, verify the accuracy or completeness of the information you will provide to us for the engagement or otherwise gather evidence for the purpose of expressing an opinion or a conclusion. Accordingly, we will not express an opinion, a conclusion, nor provide any assurance on the financial statements.

Our engagement cannot be relied upon to identify or disclose any financial statement misstatements, including those caused by fraud or error, or to identify or disclose any wrongdoing within the Company or noncompliance with laws and regulations.

Your Responsibilities

The compilation engagement to be performed is conducted on the basis that you acknowledge and understand that our role is to prepare financial statements in accordance with accounting principles generally accepted in the United States of America and assist you in the presentation of the financial statements in accordance with accounting principles generally accepted in the United States of America. You have the following overall responsibilities that are fundamental to our undertaking the engagement in accordance with SSARSs:

a. The selection of accounting principles generally accepted in the United States of America as the financial reporting framework to be applied in the preparation of financial statements.

---

[7] See footnote 3.

[8] See footnote 4.

b. The preparation and fair presentation of financial statements in accordance with accounting principles generally accepted in the United States of America

c. The prevention and detection of fraud

d. To ensure that the Company complies with the laws and regulations applicable to its activities

e. The accuracy and completeness of the records, documents, explanations, and other information, including significant judgments, you provide to us for the engagement

f. To provide us with

i. access to all information of which you are aware is relevant to the preparation and fair presentation of the financial statements, such as records, documentation, and other matters.

ii. additional information that we may request from you for the purpose of the compilation engagement.

iii. unrestricted access to persons within the entity of whom we determine it necessary to make inquiries.

Our Report

As part of our engagement, we will issue a report that will state that we did not audit or review the financial statements and that, accordingly, we do not express an opinion, a conclusion, nor provide any assurance on them. There may be circumstances in which the report differs from the expected form and content.

Our report will disclose that the Company's management has elected to omit the statement of cash flows and substantially all of the disclosures required by accounting principles generally accepted in the United States of America. If the statement of cash flows and omitted disclosures were to be included in the financial statements, they might influence the user's conclusions about the Company's financial position, results of operations, and cash flows. Accordingly, the financial statements will not be designed for those who are not informed about such matters.

We will also disclose that we are not independent in our report.

You agree to include our accountant's compilation report in any document containing financial statements that indicates that we have performed a compilation engagement on such financial statements and, prior to inclusion of the report, to ask our permission to do so.

Other Relevant Information

Our fees for these services . . . .

[*The accountant may include language, such as the following, regarding limitation of, or other arrangements regarding, the liability of the accountant or the entity, such as indemnification to the accountant for liability arising from knowing misrepresentations to the accountant by management (regulators may restrict or prohibit such liability limitation arrangements):*

You agree to hold us harmless and to release, indemnify, and defend us from any liability or costs, including attorneys' fees, resulting from management's knowing misrepresentations to us or resulting from any actions against us by

©2017, AICPA

third parties relying on the financial statements described herein except for our own intentional wrongdoing.]

If you request us to perform additional services not contemplated or described in this engagement letter, we will provide you with a separate agreement describing those additional services and fees.

Please sign and return the attached copy of this letter to indicate your acknowledgment of, and agreement with, the arrangements for our engagement to prepare the financial statements described herein and to perform a compilation engagement with respect to those same financial statements, and our respective responsibilities.

Sincerely yours,

____

[*Signature of accountant or accountant's firm*]

Acknowledged and agreed on behalf of ABC Company by:

____

[*Signed*]
[*Name and Title*]

____

[*Date*]

Illustration 3—An Engagement Letter for a Compilation Engagement With Respect to Financial Statements Prepared in Accordance With the Tax-Basis of Accounting

Circumstances include the following:

- The accountant will prepare, as a nonattest service, the financial statements subject to the compilation engagement.
- The financial statements will be prepared in accordance with the tax-basis of accounting.
- The accountant expects that his or her independence will not be impaired.

To the appropriate representative of management of ABC Company:[9]

You[10] have requested that we prepare the financial statements of ABC Company (the Company), which comprise the statement of assets, liabilities, and equity—tax-basis as of December 31, 20X2, and the related statements of operations and related earnings—tax-basis, and cash flows—tax-basis for the year then ended, and the related notes to the financial statements and perform a compilation engagement with respect to those financial statements.[11,12] We are

---

[9] See footnote 2.

[10] See footnote 3.

[11] If the accountant is to be engaged to prepare financial statements that omit the statement of cash flows—tax-basis and the related notes and perform a compilation engagement with respect to those financial statements, the sentence may be revised to read, "You have requested that we prepare the financial statements of ABC Company, which comprise the statement of assets, liabilities, and equity—tax-basis as of December 31, 20X2, and the related statement of operations and retained earnings—tax-basis, and perform a compilation engagement with respect to those financial statements." The following additional sentence may then be added: "These financial statements will not include a statement of cash flows—tax-basis and related notes to the financial statements."

[12] See footnote 4.

pleased to confirm our acceptance and our understanding of this compilation engagement by means of this letter.

Our Responsibilities

The objective of our engagement is to

a. prepare financial statements in accordance with the tax-basis of accounting based on information provided by you and

b. apply accounting and financial reporting expertise to assist you in the presentation of financial statements without undertaking to obtain or provide any assurance that there are no material modifications that should be made to the financial statements in order for them to be in accordance with the tax-basis of accounting.

We will conduct our compilation engagement in accordance with Statements on Standards for Accounting and Review Services (SSARSs) promulgated by the Accounting and Review Services Committee of the AICPA and comply with the AICPA's Code of Professional Conduct, including the ethical principles of integrity, objectivity, professional competence, and due care.

We are not required to, and will not, verify the accuracy or completeness of the information you will provide to us for the engagement or otherwise gather evidence for the purpose of expressing an opinion or a conclusion. Accordingly, we will not express an opinion, a conclusion, nor provide any assurance on the financial statements.

Our engagement cannot be relied upon to identify or disclose any financial statement misstatements, including those caused by fraud or error, or to identify or disclose any wrongdoing within the entity or noncompliance with laws and regulations.

Your Responsibilities

The engagement to be performed is conducted on the basis that you acknowledge and understand that our role is to prepare financial statements in accordance with the tax-basis of accounting and assist you in the presentation of the financial statements in accordance with the tax-basis of accounting. You have the following overall responsibilities that are fundamental to our undertaking the engagement in accordance with SSARSs:

a. The selection of the tax-basis of accounting as the financial reporting framework to be applied in the preparation of financial statements.

b. The preparation and fair presentation of financial statements in accordance with the tax-basis of accounting

c. The inclusion of all informative disclosures that is appropriate for the tax-basis of accounting. This includes

   i. a description of the tax-basis of accounting, including a summary of significant accounting policies, and how the tax-basis of accounting differs from accounting principles generally accepted in the United States of America, the effects of which need not be quantified and

 ©2017, AICPA

ii. informative disclosures similar to those required by accounting principles generally accepted in the United States of America.[13]

d. The design, implementation, and maintenance of internal control relevant to the preparation and fair presentation of the financial statements

e. The prevention and detection of fraud

f. To ensure that the Company complies with the laws and regulations applicable to its activities

g. The accuracy and completeness of the records, documents, explanations, and other information, including significant judgments, you provide to us for the compilation engagement

h. To provide us with

i. access to all information of which you are aware is relevant to the preparation and fair presentation of the financial statements, such as records, documentation, and other matters.

ii. additional information that we may request from you for the purpose of the compilation engagement.

iii. unrestricted access to persons within the entity of whom we determine it necessary to make inquiries.

You are also responsible for all management decisions and responsibilities and for designating an individual with suitable skills, knowledge, and experience to oversee our preparation of your financial statements. You are responsible for evaluating the adequacy and results of the services performed and accepting responsibility for such services.

Our Report

As part of our engagement, we will issue a report that will state that we did not audit or review the financial statements and that, accordingly, we do not express an opinion, a conclusion, nor provide any assurance on them. There may be circumstances in which the report differs from the expected form and content.

Our report will disclose that the financial statements are prepared in accordance with the income tax basis of accounting, which is a basis of accounting other than accounting principles generally accepted in the United States of America.

You agree to include our accountant's compilation report in any document containing financial statements that indicates that we have performed a compilation engagement on such financial statements and, prior to inclusion of the report, to ask our permission to do so.

Other Relevant Information

Our fees for these services . . . .

[*The accountant may include language, such as the following, regarding limitation of, or other arrangements regarding, the liability of the accountant or the entity, such as indemnification to the accountant for liability arising from*

---

[13] The responsibility described in *b*(ii) need not be included if the financial statements omit substantially all disclosures required by the financial reporting framework.

knowing misrepresentations to the accountant by management (regulators may restrict or prohibit such liability limitation arrangements):

You agree to hold us harmless and to release, indemnify, and defend us from any liability or costs, including attorneys' fees, resulting from management's knowing misrepresentations to us or resulting from any actions against us by third parties relying on the financial statements described herein except for our own intentional wrongdoing.]

If you request us to perform additional services not contemplated or described in this engagement letter, we will provide you with a separate agreement describing those additional services and fees.

Please sign and return the attached copy of this letter to indicate your acknowledgment of, and agreement with, the arrangements for our engagement to prepare the financial statements described herein and perform a compilation engagement with respect to those same financial statements and our respective responsibilities.

Sincerely yours,

____

[*Signature of accountant or accountant's firm*]

Acknowledged and agreed on behalf of ABC Company by:

____

[*Signed*]
[*Name and Title*]

____

[*Date*]

Illustration 4—An Engagement Letter for a Compilation Engagement With Respect to Financial Statements Prepared in Accordance With a Prescribed Format

Circumstances include the following:

- The accountant will prepare, as a nonattest service, the financial statements, including related notes, subject to the compilation engagement.
- The financial statements will be prepared in accordance with a prescribed format and in accordance with accounting principles generally accepted in the United States of America.
- The accountant expects that his or her independence will not be impaired.

To the appropriate representative of management of ABC Company:[14]

You[15] have requested that we prepare the financial statements of ABC Company (the Company) as of and for the year ended December 31, 20X2 in the form prescribed by (*developer of the format of the financial statements*) in accordance with accounting principles generally accepted in the United States of America, and perform a compilation engagement with respect to those financial

[14] See footnote 2.

[15] See footnote 3.

 ©2017, AICPA

statements.[16] We are pleased to confirm our acceptance and our understanding of this engagement by means of this letter.

Our Responsibilities

The objective of our engagement is to

a. prepare financial statements in accordance with the format prescribed by (*developer of the format of the financial statements*) and in accordance with accounting principles generally accepted in the United States of America

b. apply accounting and financial reporting expertise to assist you in the presentation of financial statements without undertaking to obtain or provide any assurance that there are no material modifications that should be made to the financial statements in order for them to be in accordance with the format prescribed by (*developer of the format of the financial statements*) and accounting principles generally accepted in the United States of America

We will conduct our compilation engagement in accordance with Statements on Standards for Accounting and Review Services (SSARSs) promulgated by the Accounting and Review Services Committee of the AICPA and comply with the AICPA's Code of Professional Conduct, including the ethical principles of integrity, objectivity, professional competence, and due care.

We are not required to, and will not, verify the accuracy or completeness of the information you will provide to us for the engagement or otherwise gather evidence for the purpose of expressing an opinion or a conclusion. Accordingly, we will not express an opinion or a conclusion nor provide any assurance on the financial statements.

Our engagement cannot be relied upon to identify or disclose any financial statement misstatements, including those caused by fraud or error, or to identify or disclose any wrongdoing within the entity or noncompliance with laws and regulations.

Your Responsibilities

The engagement to be performed is conducted on the basis that you acknowledge and understand that our role is to prepare financial statements in accordance with the format prescribed by (*developer of the format of the financial statements*) and accounting principles generally accepted in the United States of America and assist you in the presentation of the financial statements in accordance with the format prescribed by (*developer of the format of the financial statements*) and accounting principles generally accepted in the United States of America. You have the following overall responsibilities that are fundamental to our undertaking the engagement in accordance with SSARSs:

a. The selection of the format prescribed by (developer of the format of the financial statements) and accounting principles generally accepted in the United States of America as the financial reporting framework to be applied in the preparation of financial statements

b. The preparation and fair presentation of financial statements in accordance with the format prescribed by (developer of the format of the financial statements) and accounting principles generally accepted in the United States of America

[16] See footnote 4.

c. The design, implementation, and maintenance of internal control relevant to the preparation and fair presentation of the financial statements

d. The prevention and detection of fraud

e. To ensure that the Company complies with the laws and regulations applicable to its activities

f. The accuracy and completeness of the records, documents, explanations, and other information, including significant judgments, you provide to us for the engagement

g. To provide us with

i. access to all information of which you are aware is relevant to the preparation and fair presentation of the financial statements, such as records, documentation, and other matters.

ii. additional information that we may request from you for the purpose of the compilation engagement.

iii. unrestricted access to persons within the Company of whom we determine it necessary to make inquiries.

You are also responsible for all management decisions and responsibilities and for designating an individual with suitable skills, knowledge, and experience to oversee our preparation of your financial statements. You are responsible for evaluating the adequacy and results of the services performed and accepting responsibility for such services.

Our Report

As part of our engagement, we will issue a report that will state that we did not audit or review the financial statements and that, accordingly, we do not express an opinion, a conclusion, nor provide any assurance on them. There may be circumstances in which the report differs from the expected form and content.

Our report will disclose that the financial statements are presented in a prescribed form in accordance with the requirements of [*developer of the format of the financial statements*] and are not intended to be a presentation in accordance with accounting principles generally accepted in the United States of America.

You agree to include our accountant's compilation report in any document containing financial statements that indicates that we have performed a compilation engagement on such financial statements and, prior to inclusion of the report, to ask our permission to do so.

Other Relevant Information

Our fees for these services . . . .

[*The accountant may include language, such as the following, regarding limitation of or other arrangements regarding the liability of the accountant or the entity, such as indemnification to the accountant for liability arising from knowing misrepresentations to the accountant by management (regulators may restrict or prohibit such liability limitation arrangements):*

You agree to hold us harmless and to release, indemnify, and defend us from any liability or costs, including attorney's fees, resulting from management's knowing misrepresentations to us or resulting from any actions against us by

©2017, AICPA

third parties relying on the financial statements described herein except for our own intentional wrongdoing.]

If you request us to perform additional services not contemplated or described in this engagement letter, we will provide you with a separate agreement describing those additional services and fees.

Please sign and return the attached copy of this letter to indicate your acknowledgment of, and agreement with, the arrangements for our engagement to prepare the financial statements described herein and to perform a compilation engagement with respect to those same financial statements, and our respective responsibilities.

Sincerely yours,

____

[*Signature of accountant or accountant's firm*]

Acknowledged and agreed on behalf of ABC Company by:

____

[*Signed*]
[*Name and Title*]

____

[*Date*]

Illustration 5—Engagement Letter for a Compilation Engagement With Respect to One or More Specified Elements, Accounts, or Items of a Financial Statement

Circumstances include the following:

- The accountant will prepare, as a nonattest service, the specified element(s), account(s) or item(s) of a financial statement subject to the compilation engagement.
- The element(s), account(s) or item(s) of a financial statement will be prepared in accordance with accounting principles generally accepted in the United States of America.
- The accountant expects that his or her independence will not be impaired.

To the appropriate representative of management of ABC Company:[17]

You[18] have requested that we prepare the [*identify specified element, account, or item of the financial statement, for example, schedule of accounts receivable, or schedule of depreciation*] of ABC Company (the Company) as of December 31, 20X2, and perform a compilation engagement with respect to the [*identify specified element, account, or item of the financial statement, for example, schedule of accounts receivable, or schedule of depreciation*] We are pleased to confirm our acceptance and our understanding of this engagement by means of this letter.

---

[17] See footnote 2.

[18] See footnote 3.

Our Responsibilities

The objective of our engagement is to

a. prepare the [*identify specified element, account, or item of the financial statement, for example, schedule of accounts receivable, or schedule of depreciation*] in accordance with accounting principles generally accepted in the United States of America based on information provided by you and

b. apply accounting and financial reporting expertise to assist you in the presentation of [*identify specified element, account, or item of the financial statement, for example, schedule of accounts receivable, or schedule of depreciation*] without undertaking to obtain or provide any assurance that there are no material modifications that should be made to the [*identify specified element, account, or item of the financial statement, for example, schedule of accounts receivable, or schedule of depreciation*] in order for it to be in accordance with accounting principles generally accepted in the United States of America.

We will conduct our compilation engagement in accordance with Statements on Standards for Accounting and Review Services (SSARSs) promulgated by the Accounting and Review Services Committee of the AICPA and comply with the AICPA's Code of Professional Conduct, including the ethical principles of integrity, objectivity, professional competence, and due care.

We are not required to, and will not, verify the accuracy or completeness of the information you will provide to us for the engagement or otherwise gather evidence for the purpose of expressing an opinion or a conclusion. Accordingly, we will not express an opinion or a conclusion nor provide any assurance on the [*identify specified element, account, or item of the financial statement, for example, schedule of accounts receivable, or schedule of depreciation*].

Our engagement cannot be relied upon to identify or disclose any misstatements, including those caused by fraud or error, or to identify or disclose any wrongdoing within the entity or noncompliance with laws and regulations.

Your Responsibilities

The engagement to be performed is conducted on the basis that you acknowledge and understand that our role is to prepare the [*identify specified element, account, or item of the financial statement, for example, schedule of accounts receivable, or schedule of depreciation*] in accordance with accounting principles generally accepted in the United States of America and assist you in the presentation of the [*identify specified element, account, or item of the financial statement, for example, schedule of accounts receivable, or schedule of depreciation*] in accordance with accounting principles generally accepted in the United States of America. You have the following overall responsibilities that are fundamental to our undertaking the engagement in accordance with SSARSs:

a. The selection of accounting principles generally accepted in the United States of America as the financial reporting framework to be applied in the preparation of the [*identify specified element, account, or item of the financial statement, for example, schedule of accounts receivable, or schedule of depreciation*]

b. The preparation and fair presentation of the [*identify specified element, account, or item of the financial statement, for example, schedule of accounts receivable, or schedule of depreciation*] in accordance

 ©2017, AICPA

with accounting principles generally accepted in the United States of America

c. The design, implementation, and maintenance of internal control relevant to the preparation and fair presentation of the [*identify specified element, account, or item of the financial statement, for example, schedule of accounts receivable, or schedule of depreciation*]

d. The prevention and detection of fraud

e. To ensure that the Company complies with the laws and regulations applicable to its activities

f. The accuracy and completeness of the records, documents, explanations, and other information, including significant judgments, you provide to us for the engagement

g. To provide us with

   i. access to all information of which you are aware is relevant to the preparation and fair presentation of the [*identify specified element, account, or item of the financial statement, for example, schedule of accounts receivable, or schedule of depreciation*], such as records, documentation, and other matters.

   ii. additional information that we may request from you for the purpose of the compilation engagement.

   iii. unrestricted access to persons within the Company of whom we determine it necessary to make inquiries.

You are also responsible for all management decisions and responsibilities and for designating an individual with suitable skills, knowledge, and experience to oversee our preparation of your [*identify specified element, account, or item of the financial statement, for example, schedule of accounts receivable, or schedule of depreciation*]. You are responsible for evaluating the adequacy and results of the services performed and accepting responsibility for such services.

Our Report

As part of our engagement, we will issue a report that will state that we did not audit or review the [*identify specified element, account, or item of the financial statement, for example, schedule of accounts receivable, or schedule of depreciation*] and that, accordingly, we do not express an opinion, a conclusion, nor provide any assurance on it. There may be circumstances in which the report differs from the expected form and content.

You agree to include our accountant's compilation report in any document containing the [*identify specified element, account, or item of the financial statement, for example, schedule of accounts receivable, or schedule of depreciation*] that indicates that we have performed a compilation engagement on such [*identify specified element, account, or item of the financial statement, for example, schedule of accounts receivable, or schedule of depreciation*] and, prior to inclusion of the report, to ask our permission to do so.

Other Relevant Information

Our fees for these services . . . .

[*The accountant may include language, such as the following, regarding limitation of or other arrangements regarding the liability of the accountant or the entity, such as indemnification to the accountant for liability arising from knowing misrepresentations to the accountant by management (regulators may restrict or prohibit such liability limitation arrangements):*

You agree to hold us harmless and to release, indemnify, and defend us from any liability or costs, including attorney's fees, resulting from management's knowing misrepresentations to us or resulting from any actions against us by third parties relying on the financial statements described herein except for our own intentional wrongdoing.

If you request us to perform additional services not contemplated or described in this engagement letter, we will provide you with a separate agreement describing those additional services and fees.

Please sign and return the attached copy of this letter to indicate your acknowledgment of, and agreement with, the arrangements for our engagement to prepare the [*identify specified element, account, or item of the financial statement, for example, schedule of accounts receivable, or schedule of depreciation*] described herein and to perform a compilation engagement with respect to the [*identify specified element, account, or item of the financial statement, for example, schedule of accounts receivable, or schedule of depreciation*], and our respective responsibilities.

Sincerely yours,

____

[*Signature of accountant or accountant's firm*]

Acknowledged and agreed on behalf of ABC Company by:

____

[*Signed*]
[*Name and Title*]

____

[*Date*]

Illustrative Examples of the Accountant's Compilation Report on Financial Statements

2.101 The illustrative compilation reports in this paragraph are as follows:

Illustration 1—An Accountant's Compilation Report on Comparative Financial Statements Prepared in Accordance With Accounting Principles Generally Accepted in the United States of America

Illustration 2—An Accountant's Compilation Report on Comparative Financial Statements Prepared in Accordance With the AICPA's Financial Reporting Framework for Small- and Medium-Sized Entities

Illustration 3—An Accountant's Compilation Report on Comparative Financial Statements Prepared in Accordance With International Financial Reporting Standards as Issued by the International Accounting Standards Board

Illustration 4—An Accountant's Compilation Report on Comparative Financial Statements Prepared in Accordance With Accounting Principles Generally Accepted in the United States of America and Management Has Elected to Omit Substantially All Disclosures Required by Accounting Principles Generally Accepted in the United States of America and the Display of Comprehensive Income

 ©2017, AICPA

Illustration 5—An Accountant's Compilation Report on Comparative Financial Statements Prepared in Accordance With the Tax-Basis of Accounting, and Management Has Elected to Omit Substantially All Disclosures Ordinarily Included in Financial Statements Prepared in Accordance With the Tax-Basis of Accounting

Illustration 6—An Accountant's Compilation Report on Comparative Financial Statements Prepared in Accordance With Accounting Principles Generally Accepted in the United States of America When the Accountant's Independence Is Impaired, and the Accountant Determines to Not Disclose the Reasons for the Independence Impairment

Illustration 7—An Accountant's Compilation Report on Comparative Financial Statements Prepared in Accordance With the AICPA's Financial Reporting Framework for Small- and Medium-Sized Entities When the Accountant's Independence Has Been Impaired Due to the Accountant Having a Financial Interest in the Entity, and the Accountant Decides to Disclose the Reason for the Independence Impairment

Illustration 8—An Accountant's Compilation Report on Comparative Financial Statements, and the Accountant Is Aware of Departures From Accounting Principles Generally Accepted in the United States of America

Illustration 9—An Accountant's Compilation Report on Comparative Financial Statements That Omit Substantially All Disclosures and the Accountant Is Aware of an Additional Departure From Accounting Principles Generally Accepted in the United States of America

Illustration 10—An Accountant's Compilation Report on Comparative Financial Statements Prepared in Accordance With a Financial Reporting Framework Generally Accepted in Another Country

Illustration 11—An Accountant's Compilation Report When the Financial Statements of the Current Year Have Been Subjected to a Compilation Engagement and Those of the Prior Year Have Been Reviewed

Illustration 12—An Accountant's Compilation Report on Comparative Financial Statements When the Accountant's Report Includes a Changed Reference to a Departure From Accounting Principles Generally Accepted in the United States of America

Illustration 13—An Accountant's Compilation Report on Comparative Financial Statements When the Prior Period Financial Statements Were Subjected to a Compilation Engagement by a Predecessor Accountant and the Predecessor's Report Is Not Presented

Illustration 14—An Accountant's Compilation Report on Comparative Financial Statements When the Predecessor Accountant's Report Is Not Presented, and the Successor Accountant Is Engaged to Perform a Compilation Engagement on the Restatement Adjustment(s)

Illustration 15—An Accountant's Compilation Report When the Financial Statements Are Included in a Prescribed Form That Calls for a Presentation Departure From Accounting Principles Generally Accepted in the United States of America

Illustration 16—An Accountant's Compilation Report on Comparative Consolidated Financial Statements and all Required Supplementary Information Accompanies the Financial Statements and the

Illustration 1—An Accountant's Compilation Report on Comparative Financial Statements Prepared in Accordance With Accounting Principles Generally Accepted in the United States of America

Management is responsible for the accompanying financial statements of XYZ Company, which comprise the balance sheets as of December 31, 20X2 and 20X1 and the related statements of income, changes in stockholders' equity, and cash flows for the years then ended, and the related notes to the financial statements in accordance with accounting principles generally accepted in the United States of America. I (We) have performed compilation engagements in accordance with Statements on Standards for Accounting and Review Services promulgated by the Accounting and Review Services Committee of the AICPA. I (We) did not audit or review the financial statements nor was (were) I (we) required to perform any procedures to verify the accuracy or completeness of the information provided by management. I (we) do not express an opinion, a conclusion, nor provide any assurance on these financial statements.

[*Signature of accounting firm or accountant, as appropriate*]
[*Accountant's city and state*]
[*Date of the accountant's report*]

Illustration 2—An Accountant's Compilation Report on Comparative Financial Statements Prepared in Accordance With the AICPA's Financial Reporting Framework for Small- and Medium-Sized Entities

Management is responsible for the accompanying financial statements of XYZ Company, which comprise the statements of financial position as of December 31, 20X2 and 20X1 and the related statements of operations and cash flows for the years then ended, and the related notes to the financial statements in accordance with the AICPA's Financial Reporting Framework for Small- and Medium-Sized Entities, and for determining that the AICPA's Financial Reporting Framework for Small- and Medium-Sized Entities is an acceptable financial reporting

 ©2017, AICPA

framework. I (We) have performed compilation engagements in accordance with Statements on Standards for Accounting and Review Services promulgated by the Accounting and Review Services Committee of the AICPA. I (We) did not audit or review the financial statements nor was (were) I (we) required to perform any procedures to verify the accuracy or completeness of the information provided by management. I (we) do not express an opinion, a conclusion, nor provide any assurance on these financial statements.

I (We) draw attention to Note X of the financial statements, which describes the basis of accounting. The financial statements are prepared in accordance with the AICPA's Financial Reporting Framework for Small- and Medium-Sized Entities, which is a basis of accounting other than accounting principles generally accepted in the United States of America.

[*Signature of accounting firm or accountant, as appropriate*]
[*Accountant's city and state*]
[*Date of the accountant's report*]

Illustration 3—An Accountant's Compilation Report on Comparative Financial Statements Prepared in Accordance With International Financial Reporting Standards as Issued by the International Accounting Standards Board

Management is responsible for the accompanying financial statements of XYZ Company, which comprise the statements of financial position as of December 31, 20X2 and 20X1 and the related statements of comprehensive income, changes in equity, and cash flows for the years then ended, and the related notes to the financial statements in accordance with International Financial Reporting Standards as issued by the International Accounting Standards Board. I (We) have performed compilation engagements in accordance with Statements on Standards for Accounting and Review Services promulgated by the Accounting and Review Services Committee of the AICPA. I (We) did not audit or review the financial statements nor was (were) I (we) required to perform any procedures to verify the accuracy or completeness of the information provided by management. I (we) do not express an opinion, a conclusion, nor provide any assurance on these financial statements.

[*Signature of accounting firm or accountant, as appropriate*]
[*Accountant's city and state*]
[*Date of the accountant's report*]

Illustration 4—An Accountant's Compilation Report on Comparative Financial Statements Prepared in Accordance With Accounting Principles Generally Accepted in the United States of America and Management Has Elected to Omit Substantially All Disclosures Required by Accounting Principles Generally Accepted in the United States of America and the Display of Comprehensive Income

Management is responsible for the accompanying financial statements of XYZ Company, which comprise the balance sheets as of December

31, 20X2 and 20X1 and the related statements of income, changes in stockholders' equity, and cash flows for the years then ended in accordance with accounting principles generally accepted in the United States of America. I (We) have performed compilation engagements in accordance with Statements on Standards for Accounting and Review Services promulgated by the Accounting and Review Services Committee of the AICPA. I (We) did not audit or review the financial statements nor was (were) I (we) required to perform any procedures to verify the accuracy or completeness of the information provided by management. I (we) do not express an opinion, a conclusion, nor provide any assurance on these financial statements.

Management has elected to omit substantially all the disclosures and the display of comprehensive income required by accounting principles generally accepted in the United States of America. If the omitted disclosures and the display of comprehensive income were included in the financial statements, they might influence the user's conclusions about the company's financial position, results of operations, and cash flows. Accordingly, the financial statements are not designed for those who are not informed about such matters.

[*Signature of accounting firm or accountant, as appropriate*]
[*Accountant's city and state*]
[*Date of the accountant's report*]

Illustration 5—An Accountant's Compilation Report on Comparative Financial Statements Prepared in Accordance With the Tax-Basis of Accounting, and Management Has Elected to Omit Substantially All Disclosures Ordinarily Included in Financial Statements Prepared in Accordance With the Tax-Basis of Accounting

Management is responsible for the accompanying financial statements of XYZ Partnership, which comprise the statements of assets, liabilities, and partners' capital—tax-basis as of December 31, 20X2 and 20X1 and the related statements of revenue and expenses—tax-basis, and changes in partners' capital—tax-basis for the years then ended in accordance with the tax-basis of accounting, and for determining that the tax-basis of accounting is an acceptable financial reporting framework. I (We) have performed compilation engagements in accordance with Statements on Standards for Accounting and Review Services promulgated by the Accounting and Review Services Committee of the AICPA. I (We) did not audit or review the financial statements nor was (were) I (we) required to perform any procedures to verify the accuracy or completeness of the information provided by management. I (we) do not express an opinion, a conclusion, nor provide any assurance on these financial statements.

The financial statements are prepared in accordance with the tax-basis of accounting, which is a basis of accounting other than accounting principles generally accepted in the United States of America.

Management has elected to omit substantially all the disclosures ordinarily included in financial statements prepared in accordance with the tax-basis of accounting. If the omitted disclosures were included in

 ©2017, AICPA

the financial statements, they might influence the user's conclusions about the company's assets, liabilities, equity, revenue, and expenses. Accordingly, the financial statements are not designed for those who are not informed about such matters.

[*Signature of accounting firm or accountant, as appropriate*]
[*Accountant's city and state*]
[*Date of the accountant's report*]

Illustration 6—An Accountant's Compilation Report on Comparative Financial Statements Prepared in Accordance With Accounting Principles Generally Accepted in the United States of America When the Accountant's Independence Is Impaired, and the Accountant Determines to Not Disclose the Reasons for the Independence Impairment

Management is responsible for the accompanying financial statements of XYZ Company, which comprise the balance sheets as of December 31, 20X2 and 20X1 and the related statements of income, changes in stockholders' equity, and cash flows for the years then ended, and the related notes to the financial statements in accordance with accounting principles generally accepted in the United States of America. I (We) have performed compilation engagements in accordance with Statements on Standards for Accounting and Review Services promulgated by the Accounting and Review Services Committee of the AICPA. I (We) did not audit or review the financial statements nor was (were) I (we) required to perform any procedures to verify the accuracy or completeness of the information provided by management. I (we) do not express an opinion, a conclusion, nor provide any assurance on these financial statements.

I am (We are) not independent with respect to XYZ Company.

[*Signature of accounting firm or accountant, as appropriate*]
[*Accountant's city and state*]
[*Date of the accountant's report*]

Illustration 7—An Accountant's Compilation Report on Comparative Financial Statements Prepared in Accordance With the AICPA's Financial Reporting Framework for Small- and Medium-Sized Entities When the Accountant's Independence Has Been Impaired Due to the Accountant Having a Financial Interest in the Entity, and the Accountant Decides to Disclose the Reason for the Independence Impairment

Management is responsible for the accompanying financial statements of XYZ Company, which comprise the statements of financial position as of December 31, 20X2 and 20X1, and the related statements of operations and cash flows for the years then ended, and the related notes to the financial statements in accordance with the AICPA's Financial Reporting Framework for Small- and Medium-Sized Entities, and for determining that the AICPA's Financial Reporting Framework for

Small- and Medium-Sized Entities is an acceptable financial reporting framework. I (We) have performed compilation engagements in accordance with Statements on Standards for Accounting and Review Services promulgated by the Accounting and Review Services Committee of the AICPA. I (We) did not audit or review the financial statements nor was (were) I (we) required to perform any procedures to verify the accuracy or completeness of the information provided by management. I (we) do not express an opinion, a conclusion, nor provide any assurance on these financial statements.

I (We) draw attention to Note X of the financial statements, which describes the basis of accounting. The financial statements are prepared in accordance with the AICPA's Financial Reporting Framework for Small- and Medium-Sized Entities, which is a basis of accounting other than accounting principles generally accepted in the United States of America.

I am (We are) not independent with respect to XYZ Company as of and during the year ended December 31, 20X2 because I (a member of the engagement team) had a direct financial interest in XYZ Company.

[*Signature of accounting firm or accountant, as appropriate*]
[*Accountant's city and state*]
[*Date of the accountant's report*]

Illustration 8—An Accountant's Compilation Report on Comparative Financial Statements, and the Accountant Is Aware of Departures From Accounting Principles Generally Accepted in the United States of America

Management is responsible for the accompanying financial statements of XYZ Company, which comprise the balance sheets as of December 31, 20X2 and 20X1 and the related statements of income, changes in stockholders' equity, and cash flows for the years then ended, and the related notes to the financial statements in accordance with accounting principles generally accepted in the United States of America. I (We) have performed compilation engagements in accordance with Statements on Standards for Accounting and Review Services promulgated by the Accounting and Review Services Committee of the AICPA. I (We) did not audit or review the financial statements nor was (were) I (we) required to perform any procedures to verify the accuracy or completeness of the information provided by management. I (we) do not express an opinion, a conclusion, nor provide any assurance on these financial statements.

Accounting principles generally accepted in the United States of America require that land be stated at cost. Management has informed me (us) that XYZ Company has stated its land at appraised value and that if accounting principles generally accepted in the United States of America had been followed, the land account and stockholders' equity would have been decreased by $500,000.

[*Signature of accounting firm or accountant, as appropriate*]
[*Accountant's city and state*]
[*Date of the accountant's report*]

 ©2017, AICPA

Illustration 9—An Accountant's Compilation Report on Comparative Financial Statements That Omit Substantially All Disclosures and the Accountant Is Aware of an Additional Departure From Accounting Principles Generally Accepted in the United States of America

Management is responsible for the accompanying financial statements of XYZ Company, which comprise the balance sheets as of December 31, 20X2 and 20X1 and the related statements of income, changes in stockholders' equity, and cash flows for the years then ended in accordance with accounting principles generally accepted in the United States of America. I (We) have performed compilation engagements in accordance with Statements on Standards for Accounting and Review Services promulgated by the Accounting and Review Services Committee of the AICPA. I (We) did not audit or review the financial statements nor was (were) I (we) required to perform any procedures to verify the accuracy or completeness of the information provided by management. I (we) do not express an opinion, a conclusion, nor provide any assurance on these financial statements.

Management has elected to omit substantially all the disclosures required by accounting principles generally accepted in the United States of America. If the omitted disclosures were included in the financial statements, they might influence the user's conclusions about the company's financial position, results of operations, and cash flows. Accordingly, the financial statements are not designed for those who are not informed about such matters.

Additionally, accounting principles generally accepted in the United States of America require that land be stated at cost. Management has informed me (us) that XYZ Company has stated its land at appraised value and that if accounting principles generally accepted in the United States of America had been followed, the land account and stockholders' equity would have been decreased by $500,000.

[*Signature of accounting firm or accountant, as appropriate*]
[*Accountant's city and state*]
[*Date of the accountant's report*]

Illustration 10—An Accountant's Compilation Report on Comparative Financial Statements Prepared in Accordance With a Financial Reporting Framework Generally Accepted in Another Country

Management is responsible for the accompanying financial statements of XYZ Company, which comprise the balance sheets as of December 31, 20X2 and 20X1 and the related statements of income, changes in stockholders' equity, and cash flows for the years then ended, and the related notes to the financial statements in accordance with [*the financial reporting framework generally accepted in another country, including identification of the nationality of the framework*]. I (We) have performed compilation engagements in accordance with Statements on Standards for Accounting and Review Services promulgated by the

Accounting and Review Services Committee of the AICPA. I (We) did not audit or review the financial statements nor was (were) I (we) required to perform any procedures to verify the accuracy or completeness of the information provided by management. I (we) do not express an opinion, a conclusion, nor provide any assurance on these financial statements.

I (We) draw attention to Note X of the financial statements, which describes the basis of accounting. The financial statements are prepared in accordance with [*the financial reporting framework generally accepted in another country, including identification of the nationality of the framework*], which is a basis of accounting other than accounting principles generally accepted in the United States of America.

This report is intended solely for the information and use of [*specified parties*] and is not intended to be and should not be used by anyone other than the specified parties.

[*Signature of accounting firm or accountant, as appropriate*]
[*Accountant's city and state*]
[*Date of the accountant's report*]

Illustration 11—An Accountant's Compilation Report When the Financial Statements of the Current Year Have Been Subjected to a Compilation Engagement and Those of the Prior Year Have Been Reviewed

Management is responsible for the accompanying financial statements of XYZ Company, which comprise the balance sheet as of December 31, 20X2 and the related statements of income, changes in stockholders' equity, and cash flows for the year then ended, and the related notes to the financial statements in accordance with accounting principles generally accepted in the United States of America. I (We) have performed a compilation engagement in accordance with Statements on Standards for Accounting and Review Services promulgated by the Accounting and Review Services Committee of the AICPA. I (We) did not audit or review the financial statements nor was (were) I (we) required to perform any procedures to verify the accuracy or completeness of the information provided by management. I (we) do not express an opinion, a conclusion, nor provide any assurance on these financial statements.

The accompanying 20X1 financial statements were previously reviewed by me (us) and I (we) stated that I was (we were) not aware of any material modifications that should be made to those financial statements in order for them to be in accordance with accounting principles generally accepted in the United States of America in my (our) report dated March 31, 20X2, but I (we) have not performed any procedures in connection with that review engagement since that date.

[*Signature of accounting firm or accountant, as appropriate*]
[*Accountant's city and state*]
[*Date of the accountant's report*]

 ©2017, AICPA

Illustration 12—An Accountant's Compilation Report on Comparative Financial Statements When the Accountant's Report Includes a Changed Reference to a Departure From Accounting Principles Generally Accepted in the United States of America

Management is responsible for the accompanying financial statements of XYZ Company, which comprise the balance sheets as of December 31, 20X2 and 20X1 and the related statements of income, changes in stockholders' equity, and cash flows for the years then ended, and the related notes to the financial statements in accordance with accounting principles generally accepted in the United States of America. I (We) have performed compilation engagements in accordance with Statements on Standards for Accounting and Review Services promulgated by the Accounting and Review Services Committee of the AICPA. I (We) did not audit or review the financial statements nor was (were) I (we) required to perform any procedures to verify the accuracy or completeness of the information provided by management. I (we) do not express an opinion, a conclusion, nor provide any assurance on these financial statements.

In my (our) report dated March 1, 20X2 with respect to the 20X1 financial statements, we referred to a departure from accounting principles generally accepted in the United States of America because the company carried its land at appraised values. As described in Note X, the Company has changed its method of accounting for land and restated its 20X1 financial statements to be in accordance with accounting principles generally accepted in the United States of America.

[*Signature of accounting firm or accountant, as appropriate*]
[*Accountant's city and state*]
[*Date of the accountant's report*]

Illustration 13—An Accountant's Compilation Report on Comparative Financial Statements When the Prior Period Financial Statements Were Subjected to a Compilation Engagement by a Predecessor Accountant and the Predecessor's Report Is Not Presented

Management is responsible for the accompanying financial statements of XYZ Company, which comprise the balance sheet as of December 31, 20X2 and the related statements of income, changes in stockholders' equity, and cash flows for the year then ended, and the related notes to the financial statements in accordance with accounting principles generally accepted in the United States of America. I (We) have performed a compilation engagement in accordance with Statements on Standards for Accounting and Review Services promulgated by the Accounting and Review Services Committee of the AICPA. I (We) did not audit or review the 20X2 financial statements nor was (were) I (we) required to perform any procedures to verify the accuracy or completeness of the information provided by management. I (we) do not express an opinion, a conclusion, nor provide any assurance on these financial statements.

The financial statements of XYZ Company as of December 31, 20X1, were subjected to a compilation engagement by other accountants whose report dated February 1, 20X2 stated that they have not audited or reviewed the 20X1 financial statements and do not express an opinion, a conclusion, nor provide any assurance on those financial statements.

[*Signature of accounting firm or accountant, as appropriate*]
[*Accountant's city and state*]
[*Date of the accountant's report*]

Illustration 14—An Accountant's Compilation Report on Comparative Financial Statements When the Predecessor Accountant's Report Is Not Presented, and the Successor Accountant Is Engaged to Perform a Compilation Engagement on the Restatement Adjustment(s)

Management is responsible for the accompanying financial statements of XYZ Company, which comprise the balance sheet as of December 31, 20X2 and the related statements of income, changes in stockholders' equity, and cash flows for the year then ended, and the related notes to the financial statements in accordance with accounting principles generally accepted in the United States of America. I (We) have performed a compilation engagement in accordance with Statements on Standards for Accounting and Review Services promulgated by the Accounting and Review Services Committee of the AICPA. I (We) did not audit or review the 20X2 financial statements nor was (were) I (we) required to perform any procedures to verify the accuracy or completeness of the information provided by management. I (we) do not express an opinion, a conclusion, nor provide any assurance on these financial statements.

I (We) also performed a compilation engagement on the adjustments described in Note X that were applied to restate the 20X1 financial statements. I (We) have not audited or reviewed the adjustments described in Note X that were applied to restate the 20X1 financial statements and do not express an opinion, a conclusion, nor provide any assurance on the adjustments.

The financial statements prior to adjustment of XYZ Company as of December 31, 20X1, were subjected to a compilation engagement by other accountants whose report dated February 1, 20X2, stated that they have not audited or reviewed the 20X1 financial statements and do not express an opinion, a conclusion, nor provide any assurance on those financial statements.

[*Signature of accounting firm or accountant, as appropriate*]
[*Accountant's city and state*]
[*Date of the accountant's report*]

 ©2017, AICPA

Illustration 15—An Accountant's Compilation Report When the Financial Statements Are Included in a Prescribed Form That Calls for a Presentation Departure From Accounting Principles Generally Accepted in the United States of America

Management is responsible for the [*identification of the financial statements, including period covered and the name of entity*] included in the accompanying prescribed form in accordance with accounting principles generally accepted in the United States of America. I (We) have performed a compilation engagement in accordance with Statements on Standards for Accounting and Review Services promulgated by the Accounting and Review Services Committee of the AICPA. I (We) did not audit or review the financial statements included in the accompanying prescribed form, nor was (were) I (we) required to perform any procedures to verify the accuracy or completeness of the information provided by management. I (we) do not express an opinion, a conclusion, nor provide any assurance on the financial statements included in the accompanying prescribed form.

The financial statements included in the accompanying prescribed form are presented in accordance with the requirements of [*developer of the format of the financial statements*], and are not intended to be a presentation in accordance with accounting principles generally accepted in the United States of America.

This report is intended solely for the information and use of [*the specified parties*] and is not intended to be and should not be used by anyone other than these specified parties.

[*Signature of accounting firm or accountant, as appropriate*]
[*Accountant's city and state*]
[*Date of the accountant's report*]

Illustration 16—An Accountant's Compilation Report on Comparative Consolidated Financial Statements and all Required Supplementary Information Accompanies the Financial Statements and the Accountant Performed a Compilation of the Required Supplementary Information

Management is responsible for the accompanying financial statements of XYZ Homeowners' Association, which comprise the balance sheets as of December 31, 20X2 and 20X1 and the related statements of revenues, expenses, and changes in fund balances and cash flows for the years then ended, and the related notes to the financial statements in accordance with accounting principles generally accepted in the United States of America. I (We) have performed compilation engagements in accordance with Statements on Standards for Accounting and Review Services promulgated by the Accounting and Review Services Committee of the AICPA. I (We) did not audit or review the financial statements nor was (were) I (we) required to perform any procedures to verify the accuracy or completeness of the information provided by management. I (we) do not express an opinion, a conclusion, nor provide any assurance on these financial statements.

Accounting principles generally accepted in the United States of America require that estimates of current or future costs of major repairs and replacements of common property that will be required in the future on page XX be presented to supplement the basic financial statements. Such information is presented for purposes of additional analysis and, although not a required part of the basic financial statements, is required by the Financial Accounting Standards Board who considers it to be an essential part of financial reporting and for placing the basic financial statements in an appropriate operational, economic, or historical context. The information is the responsibility of management. The information was subjected to my (our) compilation engagement; however, I (we) have not audited or reviewed the information and do not express an opinion, a conclusion, nor provide any assurance on such information.

[*Signature of accounting firm or accountant, as appropriate*]
[*Accountant's city and state*]
[*Date of the accountant's report*]

Illustration 17—An Accountant's Compilation Report on Financial Statements Prepared in Accordance With a Special Purpose Framework Prescribed by Contract or Regulation and That Framework Prescribes a Format for the Financial Information

Management is responsible for the [*identification of the financial statements, including period covered and the name of entity*] included in the accompanying prescribed form. I (We) have performed a compilation engagement in accordance with Statements on Standards for Accounting and Review Services promulgated by the Accounting and Review Services Committee of the AICPA. I (We) did not audit or review the financial statements included in the accompanying prescribed form, nor was (were) I (we) required to perform any procedures to verify the accuracy or completeness of the information provided by management. I (we) do not express an opinion, a conclusion, nor provide any assurance on the financial statements included in the accompanying prescribed form.

The financial statements included in the accompanying prescribed form are presented in accordance with the requirements of [*describe contract or regulation*], and are not intended to be a complete presentation of [*name of entity's*] assets and liabilities.

This report is intended solely for the information and use of [*the specified parties*] and is not intended to be and should not be used by anyone other than these specified parties.

[*Signature of accounting firm or accountant, as appropriate*]
[*Accountant's city and state*]
[*Date of the accountant's report*]

 ©2017, AICPA

Illustration 18—An Accountant's Compilation Report on Comparative Financial Statements Prepared in Accordance With Accounting Principles Generally Accepted in the United States of America That Includes an Emphasis-of-Matter Paragraph With Respect to a Going Concern Uncertainty

Management is responsible for the accompanying financial statements of XYZ Company, which comprise the balance sheets as of December 31, 20X2 and 20X1 and the related statements of income, changes in stockholders' equity, and cash flows for the years then ended, and the related notes to the financial statements in accordance with accounting principles generally accepted in the United States of America. I (We) have performed compilation engagements in accordance with Statements on Standards for Accounting and Review Services promulgated by the Accounting and Review Services Committee of the AICPA. I (We) did not audit or review the financial statements nor was (were) I (we) required to perform any procedures to verify the accuracy or completeness of the information provided by management. I (we) do not express an opinion, a conclusion, nor provide any assurance on these financial statements.

As discussed in Note X, certain conditions indicate that the Company may be unable to continue as a going concern. The accompanying financial statements do not include any adjustments that might be necessary should the Company be unable to continue as a going concern.

[*Signature of accounting firm or accountant, as appropriate*]
[*Accountant's city and state*]
[*Date of the accountant's report*]

Illustration 19—An Accountant's Compilation Report on Specified Elements, Accounts, or Items of a Financial Statement Prepared in Accordance With Accounting Principles Generally Accepted in the United States of America

Management is responsible for the preparation and fair presentation of the accompanying [*identify specified element, account, or item of the financial statement, for example, schedule of accounts receivable, or schedule of depreciation*] of XYZ Company as of December 31, 20X2 in accordance with accounting principles generally accepted in the United States of America. I (We) have performed a compilation engagement in accordance with Statements on Standards for Accounting and Review Services promulgated by the Accounting and Review Services Committee of the AICPA. I (We) did not audit or review the [*identify specified element, account, or item of the financial statement, for example, schedule of accounts receivable, or schedule of depreciation*] nor was (were) I (we) required to perform any procedures to verify the accuracy or completeness of the information provided by management. I (we) do not express an opinion, a conclusion, nor provide any assurance on the [*identify specified element, account, or item of the financial statement, for example, schedule of accounts receivable, or schedule of depreciation*].

[*Signature of accounting firm or accountant, as appropriate*]
[*Accountant's city and state*]
[*Date of the accountant's report*]

Exhibit—Compilation Reporting Requirements When Independence Is Impaired

2.102 Many accountants are finding that their independence with respect to a compilation client is impaired for a number of reasons. Examples of impairments include the performance of certain nonattest services, ownership in the client's business, or having certain relationships with the client. An accountant, if he or she chooses, is permitted to state the reasons for an independence impairment in the accountant's compilation report.

Question—Does Statements on Standards for Accounting and Review Services (SSARSs) require me to state the reasons why I'm not independent with respect to a compilation client?

Answer—No. SSARSs permits, but does not require, the accountant to disclose the reasons. You may simply state that you are not independent with respect to the client without disclosing the reasons.

Question—May I disclose the reasons for the lack of independence in one period and then not disclose the reasons in a subsequent period for the same client?

Answer—Yes. Each period for which a compilation report is issued for a client is treated as a separate compilation. For example, you may decide to disclose the reasons in a compilation report on financial statements for the period ended March 31, 20X1, and then decide to not disclose the reasons in a compilation report on financial statements for the period ended June 30, 20X1, or vice versa.

Question—Are there factors that I should consider before deciding to disclose the reason(s) for the impairment?

Answer—An accountant should exercise his or her professional judgment in making that decision. That judgment might include consideration of such factors as the number of reasons for independence impairment or the ability of the user of the financial statements that were subjected to the compilation engagement to understand the nature of the impairments.

Paragraph .23 of AR-C section 80, *Compilation Engagements* (AICPA, *Professional Standards*), states, "If the accountant elects to disclose a description about the reasons the accountant's independence is impaired, the accountant should include all such reasons in the description." Therefore, if the accountant's independence is impaired for three reasons (for example, ownership, nonattest services, and family relationships), the accountant may decide that describing all three would make the report too lengthy or too confusing. Consequently, the accountant might decide to merely say that he or she is not independent. On the other hand, an accountant who is providing a nonattest service that impairs independence may feel that this information would be beneficial for users to know. Therefore, that accountant may decide to disclose the reason.

Question—Are there any limitations on what the report may say?

Answer—No. SSARSs do not prescribe any requirements except that if an election is made to describe, then all the reasons for the impairment should be

 ©2017, AICPA

described. That means that an accountant could, if he or she chooses, write a paragraph three pages long to describe the reasons for the impairment. Although that length certainly isn't expected, some accountants may determine to go into far greater detail than others.

Question—Assuming an accountant is not independent for two reasons (for example, a family relationship and ownership) does each reason need to be in a separate paragraph?

Answer—No. An accountant may combine the reasons into a single paragraph. For example, assuming the accountant held an ownership interest in the client and the accountant's spouse was the CFO of the company, a description paragraph may be drafted, such as the following:

> I am not independent with respect to XYZ Company as of and for the year ended December 31, 20X2, because I am a minority shareholder in XYZ Company and my spouse is an officer of XYZ Company.

Question—Assuming an accountant's independence is impaired because the accountant maintains a number of controls for the client, does each area of internal control need to be listed by the accountant, or may the accountant merely say that his or her independence is impaired because he or she maintained internal controls?

Answer—The provision is flexible and allows an accountant to provide as much detail as he or she feels appropriate in the circumstances. Therefore, the accountant may either state the areas of internal control maintained by the accountant or provide a general description of the reason or give no reason at all and merely say that he or she is not independent. In making this decision, the accountant should make sure that his or her description is not misleading. For example, if the accountant is maintaining only small aspects of internal control over financial reporting, the accountant would not want to describe the reason by saying that he or she is maintaining all controls for the client. Such a statement would be misleading and inaccurate.

Chapter 3

Preparation of Financial Statements

Introduction

3.01 AR-C section 70, *Preparation of Financial Statements* (AICPA, *Professional Standards*), applies when an accountant in public practice is engaged to prepare financial statements or prospective financial information. The objective of the accountant in an engagement to prepare financial statements is to prepare the financial statements pursuant to a specified financial reporting framework. An engagement to prepare financial statements is a nonattest service and does not require a determination about whether the accountant is independent of the entity. Additionally, an engagement to prepare financial statements does not require the accountant to verify the accuracy or completeness of the information provided by management or otherwise gather evidence to express an opinion or a conclusion on the financial statements or otherwise report on the financial statements. AR-C section 70 may also be applied, adapted as appropriate in the circumstances, to the preparation of other historical financial information, including

- a single financial statement.
- specified elements, accounts, or items of a financial statement such as schedules of rentals, royalties, profit participation, or provision for income taxes.
- supplementary information.
- required supplementary information.
- pro forma financial information.

Applicability of This Chapter

Although AR-C section 70 applies to the preparation of prospective financial information, this guide does not address such engagements. For additional guidance on engagements to prepare prospective financial information, readers should refer to the AICPA Guide *Prospective Financial Information*.

Applicability

Observations and Suggestions

To be "engaged" does not mean to obtain an engagement letter. Instead, it is what the accountant is hired to do. Obtaining an engagement letter is a required procedure after the accountant has been engaged. The understanding with the entity about what the accountant is engaged (that is, hired) to do is paramount in determining whether AR-C section 70 applies.

Observations and Suggestions

As part of the accountant's bookkeeping services, the accountant may provide certain financial presentations to the client (for example, a trial balance) that do not constitute a financial statement. As such, although the accountant may apply, adapted as necessary, the provisions of AR-C section 70 to the preparation of a trial balance, the accountant is not required to do so.

In making a judgment about whether the presentation is a financial statement (to which AR-C section 70 would apply if the accountant is engaged to prepare) or is a trial balance (which would not require the accountant to apply AR-C section 70), the accountant may consider, among other matters, the following attributes:

- Generally, a financial statement features the combination of similar general ledger accounts to create classifications or account groupings with corresponding subtotals and totals of dollar amounts. Some examples of these classifications or account groupings are current assets, long-term debt, and revenues. In addition, contra accounts are generally netted against the related primary accounts in financial statement presentations (for example, accounts receivable net of allowance for doubtful accounts). In contrast, a trial balance consists of a listing of all of the general ledger accounts and their corresponding debit or credit balances.
- Financial statements generally contain titles that identify the presentation as one intended to present financial position, results of operations, or cash flows. Typical titles for financial statements include the following:
  - — Balance Sheet
  - — Income Statement or Statement of Operations
  - — Statement of Comprehensive Income
  - — Statement of Retained Earnings
  - — Statement of Cash Flows
  - — Statement of Changes in Owners' Equity or Statement of Changes in Stockholders' Equity
  - — Statement of Assets and Liabilities (with or without owners' equity accounts)
  - — Statement of Revenue and Expenses
  - — Statement of Financial Position
  - — Statement of Activities
  - — Summary of Operations
  - — Statement of Operations by Product Lines
  - — Statement of Cash Receipts and Disbursements

  Examples of typical titles for trial balance presentations are as follows:

  - — Trial Balance
  - — Working Trial Balance
  - — Adjusted Trial Balance
  - — Listing of General Ledger Accounts

 ©2017, AICPA

- The balance sheet in a set of financial statements segregates asset, liability, and owners' equity accounts and presents these three elements based on the following basic example equation:

  Assets = Liabilities + Owners' Equity

  The elements of the income statement and their relationship to net income are presented based on the following basic example equation:

  Revenues – Expenses + Gains – Losses = Net Income

  In a trial balance, no attempt is made to establish a mathematical relationship among the elements except that total debits equal total credits.

- The income statement in a set of financial statements generally contains a caption such as "Net Income" or "Net Revenues Over Expenses" that identifies the net results of operations. Trial balance presentations generally do not contain similar captions.
- The balance sheet in a set of financial statements usually presents assets in the order of their liquidity and liabilities in the order of their maturity. In a trial balance, the accounts are generally listed in account number order as they appear in the general ledger.
- In a set of financial statements, the income statement articulates with the balance sheet because the net results of operations are added to or subtracted from opening retained earnings. In a trial balance, the net results of operations are generally not closed out to retained earnings.

The accountant's use of judgment is important when considering these attributes to determine whether the financial presentation constitutes a financial statement or a trial balance. When making this determination, the accountant may consider the preponderance of the attributes of the financial presentation. For example, a trial balance that contains one or two attributes of a financial statement may, in the accountant's judgment, still constitute a trial balance.

3.02 AR-C section 70 applies when engaged to prepare financial statements regardless of who the end user(s) is (are). There may be a number of different users of financial statements such as management of the company; other accountants engaged to audit, review, or perform a compilation engagement on the financial statements; bankers; bonding agents; and other third parties.

3.03 In addition, AR-C section 70 applies when an accountant in public practice provides an entity with controllership or other management services and is engaged to prepare financial statements as part of the controllership or other management services agreement.

3.04 AR-C section 70 does not apply to accountants who are not in public practice. Additionally, AR-C section 70 does not apply when an accountant in public practice prepares financial statements

- and is engaged to perform an audit, review, or compilation of those financial statements,
- solely for submission to taxing authorities,
- for inclusion in written personal financial plans prepared by the accountant,

- in conjunction with litigation services that involve pending or potential legal or regulatory proceedings, or
- in conjunction with business valuation services.

3.05 It is very important to understand exactly what services the client is engaging the accountant to perform. Professional judgment should be applied by the accountant to determine if the client is requesting the accountant to prepare the financial statements or merely assist in preparing portions of the financial statements. Assisting in preparing or drafting a portion of the financial statements is not subject to AR-C section 70.

3.06 The following table provides examples of services that the accountant may be engaged to perform and whether AR-C section 70 would apply. The table is not intended to be all inclusive, and professional judgment would still need to be applied.

Examples of Services for Which AR-C Section 70 Applies	Examples of Accountant Services for Which AR-C Section 70 Does Not Apply
Preparation of financial statements prior to audit or review by another accountant	Preparation of financial statements when the accountant is engaged to perform an audit, review, or compilation of such financial statements
Preparation of financial statements for an entity to be presented alongside the entity's tax return	Preparation of financial statements with a tax return solely for submission to taxing authorities
Preparation of personal financial statements for presentation alongside a financial plan	Personal financial statements that are prepared for inclusion in written personal financial plans prepared by the accountant
	Financial statements prepared in conjunction with litigation services that involve pending or potential legal or regulatory proceedings
	Financial statements prepared in conjunction with business valuation services
	Maintaining depreciation schedules
	Preparing or proposing certain adjustments, such as those applicable to deferred income taxes, depreciation, or leases
Preparation of a single financial statement, such as a balance sheet or income statement, or preparing financial statements with substantially all disclosures omitted	Drafting financial statement notes
Using the information in a general ledger to prepare financial statements outside of an accounting software system	Entering general ledger transactions or processing payments (general bookkeeping) in an accounting software system

 ©2017, AICPA

3.07 When performing an engagement to prepare financial statements, the accountant may be asked to submit draft financial statements to the client to provide management with an opportunity to read and analyze the financial statements prior to final issuance. To prevent any confusion, the accountant would label each page of the draft financial statements with words such as "Draft," "Preliminary Draft," "Draft—Subject to Changes," or "Working Draft."

Independence

3.08 An engagement to prepare financial statements is a nonattest service and does not require a determination about whether the accountant is independent of the entity. However, it is important to note that the performance of nonattest services for attest clients could impair independence. Therefore, if the accountant anticipates being engaged to perform a review or audit engagement for the entity, the accountant will want to take steps necessary to ensure that independence is not impaired as a result of preparing the financial statements. If the accountant anticipates being engaged to perform a compilation engagement for the entity, the accountant may want to take such steps as the accountant can perform the compilation engagement if his or her independence is impaired but would be required to disclose the lack of independence in the accountant's compilation report.

3.09 The "Nonattest Services" subtopic (AICPA, *Professional Standards*, ET sec. 1.295) under the "Independence Rule" of the AICPA Code of Professional Conduct addresses the accountant's considerations with respect to independence when performing nonattest services for attest clients. For example, the accountant may prepare monthly or other interim financial statements and be engaged to perform an audit, review, or compilation engagement with respect to the annual financial statements. The accountant should be aware that the performance of the preparation services may impair independence unless the safeguards described in this subtopic are met.

Requirements

General Principles for Performing Engagements to Prepare Financial Statements

3.10 In addition to complying with AR-C section 70, an accountant is required to comply with AR-C section 60, *General Principles for Engagements Performed in Accordance With Statements of Standards for Accounting and Review Services* (AICPA, *Professional Standards*). AR-C section 60 requires

- the accountant to comply with relevant ethical requirements;
- the accountant to exercise professional judgment in the performance of the engagement;
- the accountant to perform the engagement in accordance with SSARSs;
- the engagement partner to possess the competence and capabilities to perform the engagement and competence in financial reporting, appropriate to the engagement circumstances; and
- the engagement partner to take responsibility for certain quality control matters.

©2017, AICPA

AR-C section 60 also includes certain preconditions for the performance of the engagement.

Engagement Level Quality Control in an Engagement to Prepare Financial Statements

3.11 In an engagement to prepare financial statements, the engagement partner is required to possess the competence and capabilities to perform the engagement and competence in financial reporting, appropriate to the engagement circumstances.

3.12 In an engagement to prepare financial statements, the engagement partner is required to take responsibility for the following:

a. The overall quality of the engagement

b. The direction, supervision, planning, and performance of the engagement in compliance with professional standards and applicable legal and regulatory requirements

c. The engagement being performed in accordance with the firm's quality control policies and procedures, including the following:

   i. Being satisfied that appropriate procedures regarding the acceptance and continuance of client relationships and engagements have been followed, and that conclusions reached are appropriate, including considering whether there is information that would lead the engagement partner to conclude that management lacks integrity

   ii. Being satisfied that the engagement team collectively has the appropriate competence and capabilities to perform the engagement and expertise in financial reporting to perform the engagement in accordance with professional standards and applicable legal and regulatory requirements

   iii. Taking responsibility for appropriate engagement documentation being maintained

3.13 If the engagement partner obtains information that would have caused the firm to decline the engagement had that information been available earlier, the engagement partner is required to communicate that information promptly to the firm, so that the firm and the engagement partner can take the necessary action.

3.14 Throughout the engagement, the engagement partner is required to remain alert, through observation and making inquiries as necessary, for evidence of noncompliance with relevant ethical requirements by members of the engagement team. If matters come to the engagement partner's attention through the firm's system of quality control or otherwise that indicate that members of the engagement team have not complied with relevant ethical requirements, the engagement partner, in consultation with others in the firm, is required to determine the appropriate action.

3.15 An effective system of quality control for a firm includes a monitoring process designed to provide the firm with reasonable assurance that the firm's policies and procedures relating to the system of quality control are relevant, adequate, and operating effectively. The engagement partner is required

 ©2017, AICPA

to consider the results of the firm's monitoring process as evidenced in the latest information circulated by the firm and, if applicable, other network firms and whether deficiencies noted in that information may affect the engagement.

Preconditions for Accepting an Engagement to Prepare Financial Statements

3.16 In accordance with paragraph .25 of AR-C section 60, the accountant is precluded from accepting an engagement to prepare financial statements if

a. the accountant has reason to believe that relevant ethical requirements will not be satisfied;

b. the accountant's preliminary understanding of the engagement circumstances indicates that information needed to perform the engagement is likely to be unavailable or unreliable; or

c. the accountant has cause to doubt management's integrity such that it is likely to affect the performance of the engagement.

3.17 As a precondition for accepting an engagement to prepare financial statements, certain items should be considered. In accordance with paragraph .26 of AR-C section 60, the accountant is required to

a. determine whether preliminary knowledge of the engagement circumstances indicate that ethical requirements regarding professional competence will be satisfied.

b. determine whether the financial reporting framework selected by management to be applied in the preparation of the financial statements is acceptable.

3.18 Additionally, as a condition for accepting an engagement to prepare financial statements, the accountant is required to obtain the agreement of management that it acknowledges and understands its responsibility

a. for the selection of the financial reporting framework to be applied in the preparation of financial statements.

b. for the design, implementation, and maintenance of internal control relevant to the preparation and fair presentation of the financial statements that are free from material misstatement, whether due to fraud or error, unless the accountant decides to accept responsibility for such internal control.

c. for preventing and detecting fraud.

d. for ensuring that the entity complies with laws and regulations applicable to its activities.

e. for the accuracy and completeness of the records, documents, explanations, and other information, including significant judgments provided by management for the preparation of financial statements.

f. to provide the accountant with

i. access to all information of which management is aware that is relevant to the preparation and fair presentation of the financial statements, such as records, documentation, and other matters;

ii. additional information that the accountant may request from management for the purpose of the engagement; and

iii. unrestricted access to persons within the entity of whom the accountant determines it necessary to make inquiries.

g. that each page of the financial statements will include a statement indicating that no assurance is provided on the financial statements or the accountant will be required to issue a disclaimer that makes clear that no assurance is provided on the financial statements.

Observations and Suggestions

Although management is responsible for the selection of the financial reporting framework to be applied in the preparation of financial statements, in many smaller entities management will seek the advice of the accountant in the selection of the framework. The accountant is permitted to provide such advice, and this provides the accountant with an opportunity to help management understand the various frameworks that may be applicable, including, for example, accounting principles generally accepted in the United States of America, the cash- or tax-basis of accounting, or the AICPA's Financial Reporting Framework for Small- and Medium-Sized Entities (FRF for SMEs™). The accountant may also help management assess the needs of third-party users of the financial statements, such as bankers or owners.

Agreement on Engagement Terms

3.19 Paragraph .10 of AR-C section 70 states that the accountant should agree upon the terms of the engagement with management or those charged with governance, as appropriate. The agreed-upon terms of the engagement should be documented in an engagement letter or other suitable form of written agreement that is signed by both the accountant and management or those charged with governance, as appropriate. Ordinarily, this written communication will be what most practitioners refer to as an engagement letter.

3.20 Both management and the accountant have an interest in documenting the agreed-upon terms of the engagement before the commencement of the engagement. Such an understanding reduces the risk that the accountant or the client may misinterpret the needs or expectations of the other party. For example, it reduces the risk that management may inappropriately rely on the accountant to protect the entity against certain risks or to perform certain functions that are management's responsibility.

3.21 The accountant should ensure that the engagement letter includes the following:

- The objective of the engagement
- The responsibilities of management as set forth in paragraph 3.18
- The responsibilities of the accountant
- The limitations of the engagement to prepare financial statements
- Identification of the applicable financial reporting framework for the preparation of the financial statements

 ©2017, AICPA

- Whether the financial statements are to contain a known departure or departures from the applicable financial reporting framework (including inadequate disclosure) or omit substantially all disclosures required by the applicable financial reporting framework

> **Observations and Suggestions**
>
> It is considered a best practice that an engagement letter be obtained at least annually. The engagement letter can cover multiple services and address both nonattest and attest services (for example, an engagement to prepare monthly financial statements and perform a compilation engagement on the annual financial statements for an entity).

3.22 Illustrations of engagement letters for an engagement to prepare financial statements are included in paragraph 3.50.

Knowledge and Understanding of the Entity's Financial Reporting Framework

3.23 Paragraph .12 of AR-C section 70 states that the accountant should obtain an understanding of the financial reporting framework and the significant accounting policies intended to be used in the preparation of the financial statements. This requirement does not prevent the accountant from accepting an engagement to prepare financial statements for an entity in an industry in which the accountant has no previous experience. The accountant may obtain such an understanding during the course of the engagement to prepare financial statements, but prior to the issuance of the financial statements.

3.24 Different financial reporting frameworks may be used to prepare and present financial statements. Some accountants refer to a financial reporting framework as a "basis of accounting." Management is responsible for the selection of the financial reporting framework to be applied in the preparation of financial statements. The financial reporting framework selected by management depends on the nature of the entity and the intended use of the information.

3.25 Management may select a general purpose financial reporting framework such as accounting principles generally accepted in the United States of America (GAAP) or International Financial Reporting Standards (IFRS) established by the International Accounting Standards Board (IASB). Such frameworks are designed to meet the common financial information needs of a wide range of users.

3.26 Management may also select a special purpose financial reporting framework such as the cash- or tax-basis of accounting, a regulatory basis of accounting, the contractual basis of accounting, or the AICPA's FRF for SMEs accounting framework. Such bases of accounting are designed to meet the financial information needs of specific users.

3.27 Additionally, in cases in which the entity is not required to use an established financial reporting framework, management may select a basis of accounting that is appropriate for a narrow use and the entity's circumstances. For example, management may elect to use the cash basis of accounting and incorporate certain accruals that are not based on cash transactions such as accounts receivable and accounts payable.

Preparing the Financial Statements

3.28 The accountant is required to prepare the financial statements using the records, documents, explanations, and other information provided by management.

3.29 Paragraph .14 of AR-C section 70 states that the accountant should ensure that a statement is included on each page of the financial statements indicating, at a minimum, that "no assurance is provided" on the financial statements. This statement is commonly referred to as a legend and would normally be placed on the bottom of each page of the financial statements and related notes.

3.30 The accountant is not precluded from including the accountant's or accountant's firm name in the legend. The decision to disclose the accountant's or accountant's firm name is a risk management decision that requires professional judgment.

3.31 The legend can include many different wording alternatives as long as the minimum requirement of stating that no assurance is provided is included. The accountant is not precluded from including positive statements in the legend.

3.32 Examples of language that can be used in the legend are as follows:

- No assurance is provided on these financial statements.
- These financial statements have not been subjected to an audit or review or compilation engagement, and no assurance is provided on them.
- No assurance is provided by ABC CPAs on these financial statements.
- ABC CPAs did not perform an audit, review, or compilation engagement on these financial statements, and no assurance is provided on them.
- ABC CPAs adhered to AICPA professional standards in the preparation of these financial statements. No assurance is provided on these financial statements.

3.33 The legend is intended to avoid misunderstanding on the part of users with respect to the accountant's involvement with the financial statements. This legend is included at management's discretion; however, if management refuses to allow the legend to be placed on each page of the financial statements and related notes, or the accountant is otherwise unable to include the legend, the accountant should issue a disclaimer that makes clear that no assurance is provided on the financial statements; perform an attest engagement in which a report is issued, such as a compilation engagement in accordance with AR-C section 80, *Compilation Engagements* (AICPA, *Professional Standards*); or withdraw from the engagement.

3.34 An example of a disclaimer that the accountant may issue is as follows:

©2017, AICPA

The accompanying financial statements of XYZ Company as of and for the year ended December 31, 20X2, were not subjected to an audit, review, or compilation engagement by me (us) and I (we) do not express an opinion, a conclusion, nor provide any assurance on them.

[*Signature of accounting firm or accountant, as appropriate*]

[*Accountant's city and state*]

[*Date*]

Observations and Suggestions

The issuance of a disclaimer is intended to be used when the accountant is engaged to prepare financial statements but either cannot include the required legend on each page of the financial statements or there is another reason that the inclusion of the legend is not practical. For example, if the accountant is engaged to prepare financial statements but management's software is not compatible with the inclusion of a legend, the accountant can perform the preparation engagement and issue the disclaimer. However, if at the time of engagement the intent is that the accountant will issue a report to be used by management or third parties, the accountant would likely perform a compilation engagement on the financial statements that the accountant prepared.

Preparation of Financial Statements in Accordance With a Special Purpose Framework

3.35 Paragraph .15 of AR-C section 70 states that when preparing financial statements in accordance with a special purpose framework, the accountant should include a description of the financial reporting framework on the face of the financial statements or in a note to the financial statements. Ordinarily the description of the special purpose framework is placed immediately next to the title of the financial statements. Examples of this are as follows:

- Balance sheet—income tax-basis
- Statement of assets, liabilities, and stockholder's equity—income tax-basis
- Statement of revenue and expenses—income tax-basis
- Statement of assets and owner's equity—cash-basis
- Statements of revenue collected and expenses—modified cash-basis

3.36 When engaged to prepare financial statements in accordance with a special purpose framework, it is important for the accountant to determine that the presentation is not intended to mislead users of the financial statements. Professional judgment should be used in making this determination.

Preparation of Financial Statements That Contain a Known Departure or Departures From the Applicable Financial Reporting Framework

3.37 The accountant, after discussions with management, may prepare financial statements that contain a known departure or departures from the applicable financial reporting framework (including inadequate disclosure). In such cases, the accountant is required to disclose the material misstatement or misstatements in the financial statements. The disclosure may be on the face of the financial statements or in a note to the financial statements.

3.38 The accountant may be engaged to prepare financial statements in accordance with an applicable financial reporting framework, and management directs that the financial statements contain numerous departures from the framework (for example, management directs that the financial statements be prepared in accordance with accounting principles generally accepted in the United States of America but do not include accruals). If such cases, it would be unrealistic to disclose all such departures from the applicable financial reporting framework on the face of or in a note to the financial statements, and the financial reporting framework selected by management would not be acceptable, therefore, precluding the accountant from accepting the engagement to prepare financial statements. The accountant may suggest an alternative framework (for example, the cash-basis of accounting if management does not want to reflect accruals).

Preparation of Financial Statements That Omit Substantially All Disclosures Required by the Applicable Financial Reporting Framework

3.39 When, after discussions with management, the accountant prepares financial statements that omit substantially all disclosures required by the applicable financial reporting framework, the accountant should disclose such omission in the financial statements. The disclosure of the omission may be made on the face of the financial statements or in a selected note to the financial statements. For example, the accountant may disclose the omission in the financial statement titles as follows:

XYZ Company

Balance Sheet

Substantially All Disclosures Required by GAAP Omitted

December 31, 20X2

3.40 The accountant may prepare financial statements that include disclosures about only a few matters in the notes to the financial statements. Such disclosures may be labeled "Selected Information—Substantially All Disclosures Required by [*the applicable financial reporting framework*] Are Not Included." However, when the financial statements include more than a few disclosures, this guidance is not appropriate. The omission of one or more notes, when substantially all other disclosures are presented, should be treated like any other departure from the applicable financial reporting framework, and the nature of the departure should be disclosed on the face of the statement or in a note to the financial statements. In determining whether use of the label is appropriate, the accountant should apply professional judgment to all the facts and circumstances.

3.41 The accountant is precluded from preparing financial statements that omit substantially all disclosures required by the applicable financial reporting framework if the accountant becomes aware that the omission of substantially all disclosures was undertaken with the intention of misleading users of such financial statements. For example, management may direct that financial statements be prepared that omit substantially all disclosures because management does not want a user of the financial statements to be aware of negative information, such as a going concern or other uncertainties, or other

©2017, AICPA

information, such as related parties or related party transactions. If the accountant is aware of management's intention to mislead users of the financial statements, the accountant is precluded from preparing the financial statements.

Preparation of Financial Statements Included in a Prescribed Form

3.42 When the accountant is engaged to prepare financial statements included in a prescribed form, certain matters are to be considered. A prescribed form is any standard preprinted form designed or adopted by the body to which it is to be submitted. For example, prescribed forms include forms used by industry trade associations, credit agencies, banks, and governmental and regulatory bodies other than those concerned with the sale or trading of securities.

3.43 There is a presumption that the information required by a prescribed form is sufficient to meet the needs of the body that designed or adopted the form and that there is no need for that body to be advised of departures from the applicable financial reporting framework required by the prescribed form or related instructions. However, if the accountant becomes aware of a departure from an applicable financial reporting framework other than departures that may be called for by the prescribed form or related instructions, he or she should follow the guidance in paragraph .18 of AR-C section 70 related to departures from the applicable financial reporting framework.

3.44 If the accountant becomes aware of a departure from the requirements of the prescribed form or related instructions, he or she would consider that departure as the equivalent of a departure from an applicable financial reporting framework in determining its effect on his or her report and follow the guidance in paragraph .18 of AR-C section 70.

Communication With Management

3.45 If, during the preparation of financial statements, the accountant assists management with significant judgments regarding amounts or disclosures to be reflected in the financial statements, the accountant should discuss those judgments with management so management understands the significant judgments reflected in financial statements and accepts responsibility for those judgments.

3.46 If the accountant becomes aware that the records, documents, explanations, or other information, including significant judgments, used in the preparation of the financial statement are incomplete, inaccurate, or otherwise unsatisfactory, the accountant should bring that to the attention of management and request additional or corrected information.

Documentation Requirements

3.47 The accountant should prepare documentation in connection with each preparation engagement in sufficient detail to provide a clear understanding of the work performed.

3.48 Although the form, content, and extent of documentation depend on the circumstances of the engagement, the methodology and tools used, and the accountant's professional judgment, the accountant's documentation should, at a minimum, include all of the following:

a. The engagement letter or other suitable form of written documentation with management

b. A copy of the financial statements that the accountant prepared

3.49 In addition to the minimum requirements set forth previously, other documentation may include the following:

a. Communications, whether oral or written, to the appropriate level of management regarding fraud or illegal acts that came to the accountant's attention

b. Documentation of significant consultations or significant professional judgments made throughout the engagement

Illustrative Engagement Letters

Notice to Readers

The illustrative engagement letters presented in the following paragraph are intended to show how the engagement letter can be presented assuming that the accountant has been engaged to prepare financial statements or financial information. The engagement letter will vary according to individual requirements and circumstances and may be modified to include other nonattest services that the accountant may be engaged to perform. The accountant may seek legal advice about whether a proposed letter is suitable.

3.50 The illustrative engagement letters in this paragraph are as follows:

Illustration 1—An Engagement Letter for an Engagement to Prepare Financial Statements in Accordance With Accounting Principles Generally Accepted in the United States of America

Illustration 2—An Engagement Letter for an Engagement to Prepare Financial Statements of a Not-for-Profit Entity in Accordance With the Modified Cash Basis of Accounting Except the Financial Statements Are to Include Accounts Receivable and Accounts Payable (Departures From the Modified Cash Basis of Accounting)

Illustration 3—An Engagement Letter for an Engagement to Prepare Financial Statements in Accordance With Accounting Principles Generally Accepted in the United States of America, Except the Financial Statements Omit the Statement of Cash Flows and Substantially All Disclosures Required by U.S. GAAP

Illustration 4—An Engagement Letter for an Engagement to Prepare Financial Statements in Accordance With the Tax-Basis of Accounting

Illustration 5—An Engagement Letter for an Engagement to Prepare Financial Statements in Accordance With a Prescribed Format

Illustration 6—An Engagement Letter for an Engagement to Prepare One or More Specified Elements, Accounts, or Items of a Financial Statement

 ©2017, AICPA

Illustration 1—An Engagement Letter for an Engagement to Prepare Financial Statements in Accordance With Accounting Principles Generally Accepted in the United States of America

To the appropriate representative of ABC Company:[1]

You[2] have requested that we prepare the financial statements of ABC Company (the Company), which comprise the balance sheet as of December 31, 20X2, and the related statements of income, changes in stockholders' equity, and cash flows for the year then ended and the related notes to the financial statements.[3] We are pleased to confirm our acceptance and our understanding of this engagement by means of this letter.

Our Responsibilities

The objective of our engagement is to prepare financial statements in accordance with accounting principles generally accepted in the United States of America based on information provided by you. We will conduct our engagement in accordance with Statements on Standards for Accounting and Review Services (SSARSs) promulgated by the Accounting and Review Services Committee of the AICPA and comply with the AICPA's Code of Professional Conduct, including the ethical principles of integrity, objectivity, professional competence, and due care.

We are not required to, and will not, verify the accuracy or completeness of the information you will provide to us for the engagement or otherwise gather evidence for the purpose of expressing an opinion or a conclusion. Accordingly, we will not express an opinion or a conclusion or provide any assurance on the financial statements.

Our engagement cannot be relied upon to identify or disclose any financial statement misstatements, including those caused by fraud or error, or to identify or disclose any wrongdoing within the Company or noncompliance with laws and regulations.

Management Responsibilities

The engagement to be performed is conducted on the basis that management acknowledges and understands that our role is to prepare financial statements in accordance with accounting principles generally accepted in the United States of America. Management has the following overall responsibilities that are fundamental to our undertaking the engagement to prepare your financial statements in accordance with SSARSs:

a. The selection of accounting principles generally accepted in the United States of America as the financial reporting framework to be applied in the preparation of financial statements.

b. The design, implementation, and maintenance of internal control relevant to the preparation and fair presentation of financial

---

[1] The addresses and references in the engagement letter would be those that are appropriate in the circumstances of the engagement to prepare financial statements, including the relevant jurisdiction. It is important to refer to the appropriate persons. See paragraph .A8 of AR-C section 70, *Preparation of Financial Statements* (AICPA, *Professional Standards*).

[2] Throughout this engagement letter, references to *you*, *we*, *us*, *management*, and *accountant* would be used or amended as appropriate in the circumstances.

[3] The accountant may include other nonattest services to be performed as part of the engagement, such as income tax preparation and bookkeeping services.

statements that are free from material misstatement, whether due to fraud or error

c. The prevention and detection of fraud

d. To ensure that the Company complies with the laws and regulations applicable to its activities

e. The accuracy and completeness of the records, documents, explanations, and other information, including significant judgments, you provide to us for the engagement to prepare financial statements

f. To provide us with:

i. Access to all information of which you are aware that is relevant to the preparation and presentation of the financial statements, such as records, documentation, and other matters,

ii. Additional information that may be requested for the purpose of the preparation of the financial statements, and

iii. Unrestricted access to persons within the Company of whom we determine necessary to communicate

The financial statements will not be accompanied by a report. However, you agree that the financial statements will clearly indicate that no assurance is provided on them.

[*If the accountant expects to issue a disclaimer, instead of the preceding paragraph, the following may be added:*

As part of our engagement, we will issue a disclaimer that will state that the financial statements were not subjected to an audit, review, or compilation engagement by us and we do not express an opinion, a conclusion, nor provide any assurance on them.]

Other Relevant Information

Our fees for these services . . . .

[*The accountant may include language, such as the following, regarding limitation of, or other arrangements regarding, the liability of the accountant or the entity, such as indemnification to the accountant for liability arising from knowing misrepresentations to the accountant by management (regulators may restrict or prohibit such liability limitation arrangements):*

You agree to hold us harmless and to release, indemnify, and defend us from any liability or costs, including attorney's fees, resulting from management's knowing misrepresentations to us or resulting from any actions against us by third parties relying on the financial statements described herein except for our own intentional wrongdoing.]

If you request us to perform additional services not contemplated or described in this engagement letter, we will provide you with a separate agreement describing those additional services and fees.

Please sign and return the attached copy of this letter to indicate your acknowledgment of, and agreement with, the arrangements for our engagement to

 ©2017, AICPA

prepare the financial statements described herein, and our respective responsibilities.

Sincerely yours,

____

[*Signature of accountant or accountant's firm*]

Acknowledged and agreed on behalf of ABC Company by:

____

[*Signed*]
[*Name and Title*]

____

[*Date*]

Illustration 2—An Engagement Letter for an Engagement to Prepare Financial Statements of a Not-for-Profit Entity in Accordance With the Modified Cash-Basis of Accounting Except the Financial Statements Are to Include Accounts Receivable and Accounts Payable (Departures From the Modified Cash-Basis of Accounting)

To the appropriate representative of ABC Organization:[4]

You[5] have requested that we prepare the financial statements of ABC Organization (the Organization), which comprise the statement of assets and net assets—modified cash-basis as of December 31, 20X2, and the related statements of revenue, expenses, and changes in net assets and statement of functional expenses—modified cash-basis for the year then ended and the related notes to the financial statements.[6] We are pleased to confirm our acceptance and our understanding of this engagement by means of this letter.

Our Responsibilities

The objective of our engagement is to prepare financial statements in accordance with the modified cash-basis of accounting based on information provided by you. You have directed that we incorporate accounts receivable and accounts payable, which are not appropriate modifications to the cash-basis of accounting. We will conduct our engagement in accordance with Statements on Standards for Accounting and Review Services (SSARSs) promulgated by the Accounting and Review Services Committee of the AICPA and comply with the AICPA's Code of Professional Conduct, including the ethical principles of integrity, objectivity, professional competence, and due care.

We are not required to, and will not, verify the accuracy or completeness of the information you will provide to us for the engagement or otherwise gather evidence for the purpose of expressing an opinion or a conclusion. Accordingly, we will not express an opinion or a conclusion or provide any assurance on the financial statements.

---

[4] See footnote 1.

[5] See footnote 2.

[6] See footnote 3.

Our engagement cannot be relied upon to identify or disclose any financial statement misstatements, including those caused by fraud or error, or to identify or disclose any wrongdoing within the Organization or noncompliance with laws and regulations.

Management Responsibilities

The engagement to be performed is conducted on the basis that management acknowledges and understands that our role is to prepare financial statements in accordance with the modified cash-basis of accounting incorporating accounts receivable and accounts payable. Management has the following overall responsibilities that are fundamental to our undertaking the engagement to prepare your financial statements in accordance with SSARSs:

a. The selection of the modified cash-basis of accounting incorporating accounts receivable and accounts payable as the financial reporting framework to be applied in the preparation of financial statements. Management acknowledges that the financial statements are intended to be used only by those who understand that the incorporation of accounts receivable and accounts payable is not an appropriate modification of the cash-basis of accounting.

b. The design, implementation, and maintenance of internal control relevant to the preparation and fair presentation of financial statements that are free from material misstatement, whether due to fraud or error

c. The prevention and detection of fraud

d. To ensure that the Organization complies with the laws and regulations applicable to its activities

e. The accuracy and completeness of the records, documents, explanations, and other information, including significant judgments, you provide to us for the engagement to prepare financial statements

f. To provide us with:

i. Access to all information of which you are aware that is relevant to the preparation and presentation of the financial statements, such as records, documentation, and other matters,

ii. Additional information that may be requested for the purpose of the preparation of the financial statements, and

iii. Unrestricted access to persons within the Organization of whom we determine necessary to communicate

The financial statements will not be accompanied by a report. However, you agree that the financial statements will clearly indicate that no assurance is provided on them.

[*If the accountant expects to issue a disclaimer, instead of the preceding paragraph, the following may be added:*

As part of our engagement, we will issue a disclaimer that will state that the financial statements were not subjected to an audit, review, or compilation engagement by us and we do not express an opinion, a conclusion, nor provide any assurance on them.]

 ©2017, AICPA

Other Relevant Information

Our fees for these services . . . .

[*The accountant may include language, such as the following, regarding limitation of, or other arrangements regarding, the liability of the accountant or the entity, such as indemnification to the accountant for liability arising from knowing misrepresentations to the accountant by management (regulators may restrict or prohibit such liability limitation arrangements):*

You agree to hold us harmless and to release, indemnify, and defend us from any liability or costs, including attorney's fees, resulting from management's knowing misrepresentations to us or resulting from any actions against us by third parties relying on the financial statements described herein except for our own intentional wrongdoing.]

If you request us to perform additional services not contemplated or described in this engagement letter, we will provide you with a separate agreement describing those additional services and fees.

Please sign and return the attached copy of this letter to indicate your acknowledgment of, and agreement with, the arrangements for our engagement to prepare the financial statements described herein, and our respective responsibilities.

Sincerely yours,

____

[*Signature of accountant or accountant's firm*]

Acknowledged and agreed on behalf of ABC Organization by:

____

[*Signed*]
[*Name and Title*]

____

[*Date*]

Illustration 3—An Engagement Letter for an Engagement to Prepare Financial Statements in Accordance With Accounting Principles Generally Accepted in the United States of America, Except the Financial Statements Omit the Statement of Cash Flows and Substantially All Disclosures Required by U.S. GAAP

To the appropriate representative of ABC Company:[7]

You[8] have requested that we prepare the financial statements of ABC Company (the Company), which comprise the balance sheet as of December 31, 20X2, and the related statements of income and changes in stockholders' equity. These financial statements will not include a statement of cash flows and related notes to the financial statements as required by accounting principles generally accepted in the United States of America.[9] We are pleased to confirm our acceptance and our understanding of this engagement by means of this letter.

---

[7] See footnote 1.

[8] See footnote 2.

[9] See footnote 3.

Our Responsibilities

The objective of our engagement is to prepare financial statements in accordance with accounting principles generally accepted in the United States of America based on information provided by you. We will conduct our engagement in accordance with Statements on Standards for Accounting and Review Services (SSARSs) promulgated by the Accounting and Review Services Committee of the AICPA and comply with the AICPA's Code of Professional Conduct, including the ethical principles of integrity, objectivity, professional competence, and due care.

We are not required to, and will not, verify the accuracy or completeness of the information you will provide to us for the engagement or otherwise gather evidence for the purpose of expressing an opinion or a conclusion. Accordingly, we will not express an opinion or a conclusion or provide any assurance on the financial statements.

Our engagement cannot be relied upon to identify or disclose any financial statement misstatements, including those caused by fraud or error, or to identify or disclose any wrongdoing within the Company or noncompliance with laws and regulations.

Management Responsibilities

The engagement to be performed is conducted on the basis that management acknowledges and understands that our role is to prepare financial statements in accordance with accounting principles generally accepted in the United States of America. Management has the following overall responsibilities that are fundamental to our undertaking the engagement to prepare your financial statements in accordance with SSARSs:

a. The selection of accounting principles generally accepted in the United States of America as the financial reporting framework to be applied in the preparation of financial statements.

b. The design, implementation, and maintenance of internal control relevant to the preparation and fair presentation of financial statements that are free from material misstatement, whether due to fraud or error

c. The prevention and detection of fraud

d. To ensure that the Company complies with the laws and regulations applicable to its activities

e. The accuracy and completeness of the records, documents, explanations, and other information, including significant judgments, you provide to us for the engagement to prepare financial statements

f. To provide us with:

  i. Access to all information of which you are aware that is relevant to the preparation and presentation of the financial statements, such as records, documentation, and other matters,

  ii. Additional information that may be requested for the purpose of the preparation of the financial statements, and

  iii. Unrestricted access to persons within the Company of whom we determine necessary to communicate.

 ©2017, AICPA

The financial statements will not be accompanied by a report. However, you agree that the financial statements will clearly indicate that no assurance is provided on them.

[*If the accountant expects to issue a disclaimer, instead of the preceding paragraph, the following may be added:*

As part of our engagement, we will issue a disclaimer that will state that the financial statements were not subjected to an audit, review, or compilation engagement by us and we do not express an opinion, a conclusion, nor provide any assurance on them.]

Other Relevant Information

Our fees for these services . . . .

[*The accountant may include language, such as the following, regarding limitation of, or other arrangements regarding, the liability of the accountant or the entity, such as indemnification to the accountant for liability arising from knowing misrepresentations to the accountant by management (regulators may restrict or prohibit such liability limitation arrangements):*

You agree to hold us harmless and to release, indemnify, and defend us from any liability or costs, including attorney's fees, resulting from management's knowing misrepresentations to us or resulting from any actions against us by third parties relying on the financial statements described herein except for our own intentional wrongdoing.]

If you request us to perform additional services not contemplated or described in this engagement letter, we will provide you with a separate agreement describing those additional services and fees.

Please sign and return the attached copy of this letter to indicate your acknowledgment of, and agreement with, the arrangements for our engagement to prepare the financial statements described herein, and our respective responsibilities.

Sincerely yours,

____

[*Signature of accountant or accountant's firm*]

Acknowledged and agreed on behalf of ABC Company by:

____

[*Signed*]
[*Name and Title*]

____

[*Date*]

Illustration 4—An Engagement Letter for an Engagement to Prepare Financial Statements in Accordance With the Tax-Basis of Accounting

To the appropriate representative of ABC Company:[10]

[10] See footnote 1.

You[11] have requested that we prepare the financial statements of ABC Company (the Company), which comprise the statement of assets, liabilities, and equity—tax-basis as of December 31, 20X2, and the related statements of operations and retained earnings—tax-basis, and cash flows—tax-basis for the year then ended and the related notes to the financial statements.[12,13] We are pleased to confirm our acceptance and our understanding of this engagement by means of this letter.

Our Responsibilities

The objective of our engagement is to prepare financial statements in accordance with the tax-basis of accounting based on information provided by you. We will conduct our engagement in accordance with Statements on Standards for Accounting and Review Services (SSARSs) promulgated by the Accounting and Review Services Committee of the AICPA and comply with the AICPA's Code of Professional Conduct, including the ethical principles of integrity, objectivity, professional competence, and due care.

We are not required to, and will not, verify the accuracy or completeness of the information you will provide to us for the engagement or otherwise gather evidence for the purpose of expressing an opinion or a conclusion. Accordingly, we will not express an opinion or a conclusion or provide any assurance on the financial statements.

Our engagement cannot be relied upon to identify or disclose any financial statement misstatements, including those caused by fraud or error, or to identify or disclose any wrongdoing within the Company or noncompliance with laws and regulations.

Management Responsibilities

The engagement to be performed is conducted on the basis that management acknowledges and understands that our role is to prepare financial statements in accordance with the tax-basis of accounting. Management has the following overall responsibilities that are fundamental to our undertaking the engagement to prepare your financial statements in accordance with SSARSs:

a. The selection of the tax-basis of accounting as the financial reporting framework to be applied in the preparation of financial statements.

b. The design, implementation, and maintenance of internal control relevant to the preparation and fair presentation of financial statements that are free from material misstatement, whether due to fraud or error

---

[11] See footnote 2.

[12] If the accountant is to be engaged to prepare financial statements that omit the statement of cash flows—tax-basis and the related notes, the sentence may be revised to read, "You have requested that we prepare the financial statements of ABC Company (the Company), which comprise the statement of assets, liabilities, and equity—tax-basis as of December 31, 20X2, and the related statements of operations and retained earnings-tax-basis." The following additional sentence may then be added: "These financial statements will not include a statement of cash flows—tax-basis and related notes to the financial statements."

[13] See footnote 3.

 ©2017, AICPA

c. The prevention and detection of fraud

d. To ensure that the Company complies with the laws and regulations applicable to its activities

e. The accuracy and completeness of the records, documents, explanations, and other information, including significant judgments, you provide to us for the engagement to prepare financial statements

f. To provide us with:

i. Access to all information of which you are aware that is relevant to the preparation and presentation of the financial statements, such as records, documentation, and other matters,

ii. Additional information that may be requested for the purpose of the preparation of the financial statements, and

iii. Unrestricted access to persons within the Company of whom we determine necessary to communicate

The financial statements will not be accompanied by a report. However, you agree that the financial statements will clearly indicate that no assurance is provided on them.

[*If the accountant expects to issue a disclaimer, instead of the preceding paragraph, the following may be added:*

As part of our engagement, we will issue a disclaimer that will state that the financial statements were not subjected to an audit, review, or compilation engagement by us and we do not express an opinion, a conclusion, nor provide any assurance on them.]

Other Relevant Information

Our fees for these services . . . .

[*The accountant may include language, such as the following, regarding limitation of, or other arrangements regarding, the liability of the accountant or the entity, such as indemnification to the accountant for liability arising from knowing misrepresentations to the accountant by management (regulators may restrict or prohibit such liability limitation arrangements):*

You agree to hold us harmless and to release, indemnify, and defend us from any liability or costs, including attorney's fees, resulting from management's knowing misrepresentations to us or resulting from any actions against us by third parties relying on the financial statements described herein except for our own intentional wrongdoing.]

If you request us to perform additional services not contemplated or described in this engagement letter, we will provide you with a separate agreement describing those additional services and fees.

Please sign and return the attached copy of this letter to indicate your acknowledgment of, and agreement with, the arrangements for our engagement to prepare the financial statements described herein, and our respective responsibilities.

Sincerely yours,

____

[*Signature of accountant or accountant's firm*]

Acknowledged and agreed on behalf of ABC Company by:

____

[*Signed*]
[*Name and Title*]

____

[*Date*]

Illustration 5—An Engagement Letter for an Engagement to Prepare Financial Statements in Accordance With a Prescribed Format

To the appropriate representative of ABC Company:[14]

You[15] have requested that we prepare the financial statements of ABC Company (the Company) as of and for the year ended December 31, 20X2 in the form prescribed by (*developer of the format of the financial statements*) in accordance with accounting principles generally accepted in the United States of America.[16] We are pleased to confirm our acceptance and our understanding of this engagement by means of this letter.

Our Responsibilities

The objective of our engagement is to prepare financial statements in accordance with the format prescribed by (*developer of the format of the financial statements*) and in accordance with accounting principles generally accepted in the United States of America based on information provided by you. We will conduct our engagement in accordance with Statements on Standards for Accounting and Review Services (SSARSs) promulgated by the Accounting and Review Services Committee of the AICPA and comply with the AICPA's Code of Professional Conduct, including the ethical principles of integrity, objectivity, professional competence, and due care.

We are not required to, and will not, verify the accuracy or completeness of the information you will provide to us for the engagement or otherwise gather evidence for the purpose of expressing an opinion or a conclusion. Accordingly, we will not express an opinion or a conclusion or provide any assurance on the financial statements.

Our engagement cannot be relied upon to identify or disclose any financial statement misstatements, including those caused by fraud or error, or to identify or disclose any wrongdoing within the Company or noncompliance with laws and regulations.

---

[14] See footnote 1.

[15] See footnote 2.

[16] See footnote 3.

 ©2017, AICPA

Management Responsibilities

The engagement to be performed is conducted on the basis that management acknowledges and understands that our role is to prepare financial statements in accordance with the format prescribed by (*developer of the format of the financial statements*) and accounting principles generally accepted in the United States of America. Management has the following overall responsibilities that are fundamental to our undertaking the engagement to prepare your financial statements in accordance with SSARSs:

a. The selection of the format prescribed by (*developer of the format of the financial statements*) and accounting principles generally accepted in the United States of America as the financial reporting framework to be applied in the preparation of financial statements.

b. The design, implementation, and maintenance of internal control relevant to the preparation and fair presentation of financial statements that are free from material misstatement, whether due to fraud or error

c. The prevention and detection of fraud

d. To ensure that the Company complies with the laws and regulations applicable to its activities

e. The accuracy and completeness of the records, documents, explanations, and other information, including significant judgments, you provide to us for the engagement to prepare financial statements

f. To provide us with:

i. Access to all information of which you are aware that is relevant to the preparation and presentation of the financial statements, such as records, documentation, and other matters,

ii. Additional information that may be requested for the purpose of the preparation of the financial statements, and

iii. Unrestricted access to persons within the Company of whom we determine necessary to communicate

The financial statements will not be accompanied by a report. However, you agree that the financial statements will clearly indicate that no assurance is provided on them.

[*If the accountant expects to issue a disclaimer, instead of the preceding paragraph, the following may be added:*

As part of our engagement, we will issue a disclaimer that will state that the financial statements were not subjected to an audit, review, or compilation engagement by us and we do not express an opinion, a conclusion, nor provide any assurance on them.]

Other Relevant Information

Our fees for these services . . . .

[*The accountant may include language, such as the following, regarding limitation of, or other arrangements regarding, the liability of the accountant or the entity, such as indemnification to the accountant for liability arising from knowing misrepresentations to the accountant by management (regulators may restrict or prohibit such liability limitation arrangements):*

You agree to hold us harmless and to release, indemnify, and defend us from any liability or costs, including attorney's fees, resulting from management's knowing misrepresentations to us or resulting from any actions against us by third parties relying on the financial statements described herein except for our own intentional wrongdoing.]

If you request us to perform additional services not contemplated or described in this engagement letter, we will provide you with a separate agreement describing those additional services and fees.

Please sign and return the attached copy of this letter to indicate your acknowledgment of, and agreement with, the arrangements for our engagement to prepare the financial statements described herein, and our respective responsibilities.

Sincerely yours,

____

[*Signature of accountant or accountant's firm*]

Acknowledged and agreed on behalf of ABC Company by:

____

[*Signed*]
[*Name and Title*]

____

[*Date*]

Illustration 6—An Engagement Letter for an Engagement to Prepare One or More Specified Elements, Accounts, or Items of a Financial Statement

To the appropriate representative of ABC Company:[17]

You[18] have requested that we prepare the [*identify the specified element, account, or item of the financial statement, for example, schedule of accounts receivable or schedule of depreciation*] of ABC Company (the Company) as of December 31, 20X2.[19] We are pleased to confirm our acceptance and our understanding of this engagement by means of this letter.

Our Responsibilities

The objective of our engagement is to prepare the [*identify the specified element, account, or item of the financial statement, for example, schedule of accounts receivable or schedule of depreciation*] in accordance with accounting principles generally accepted in the United States of America based on information provided by you. We will conduct our engagement in accordance with Statements on Standards for Accounting and Review Services (SSARSs) promulgated by the Accounting and Review Services Committee of the AICPA and comply with

---

[17] See footnote 1.

[18] See footnote 2.

[19] See footnote 3.

 ©2017, AICPA

the AICPA's Code of Professional Conduct, including the ethical principles of integrity, objectivity, professional competence, and due care.

We are not required to, and will not, verify the accuracy or completeness of the information you will provide to us for the engagement or otherwise gather evidence for the purpose of expressing an opinion or a conclusion. Accordingly, we will not express an opinion or a conclusion or provide any assurance on the [*identify the specified element, account, or item of the financial statement, for example, schedule of accounts receivable or schedule of depreciation*].

Our engagement cannot be relied upon to identify or disclose any [*identify the specified element, account, or item of the financial statement, for example, schedule of accounts receivable or schedule of depreciation*] misstatements, including those caused by fraud or error, or to identify or disclose any wrongdoing within the Company or noncompliance with laws and regulations.

Management Responsibilities

The engagement to be performed is conducted on the basis that management acknowledges and understands that our role is to prepare the [*identify the specified element, account, or item of the financial statement, for example, schedule of accounts receivable or schedule of depreciation*] in accordance with accounting principles generally accepted in the United States of America. Management has the following overall responsibilities that are fundamental to our undertaking the engagement to prepare your [*identify the specified element, account, or item of the financial statement, for example, schedule of accounts receivable or schedule of depreciation*] in accordance with SSARSs:

a. The selection of accounting principles generally accepted in the United States of America as the financial reporting framework to be applied in the preparation of the [*identify the specified element, account, or item of the financial statement, for example, schedule of accounts receivable or schedule of depreciation*]

b. The design, implementation, and maintenance of internal control relevant to the preparation and fair presentation of [*identify the specified element, account, or item of the financial statement, for example, schedule of accounts receivable or schedule of depreciation*] that is free from material misstatement, whether due to fraud or error

c. The prevention and detection of fraud

d. To ensure that the Company complies with the laws and regulations applicable to its activities

e. The accuracy and completeness of the records, documents, explanations, and other information, including significant judgments, you provide to us for the engagement to prepare the [*identify the specified element, account, or item of the financial statement, for example, schedule of accounts receivable or schedule of depreciation*]

f. To provide us with:

   i. Access to all information of which you are aware that is relevant to the preparation and presentation of the [*identify the specified element, account, or item of the financial statement, for example, schedule of accounts receivable or schedule of depreciation*], such as records, documentation, and other matters,

ii. Additional information that may be requested for the purpose of the preparation of the [*identify the specified element, account, or item of the financial statement, for example, schedule of accounts receivable or schedule of depreciation*], and

iii. Unrestricted access to persons within the Company of whom we determine necessary to communicate

The [*identify the specified element, account, or item of the financial statement, for example, schedule of accounts receivable or schedule of depreciation*] will not be accompanied by a report. However, you agree that the [*identify the specified element, account, or item of the financial statement, for example, schedule of accounts receivable or schedule of depreciation*] will clearly indicate that no assurance is provided on them.

[*If the accountant expects to issue a disclaimer, instead of the preceding paragraph, the following may be added:*

As part of our engagement, we will issue a disclaimer that will state that the [identify the specified element, account, or item of the financial statement, for example, schedule of accounts receivable or schedule of depreciation] *was not subjected to an audit, review, or compilation engagement by us and we do not express an opinion, a conclusion, nor provide any assurance on it.*]

Other Relevant Information

Our fees for these services . . .

[*The accountant may include language, such as the following, regarding limitation of, or other arrangements regarding, the liability of the accountant or the entity, such as indemnification to the accountant for liability arising from knowing misrepresentations to the accountant by management (regulators may restrict or prohibit such liability limitation arrangements):*

You agree to hold us harmless and to release, indemnify, and defend us from any liability or costs, including attorney's fees, resulting from management's knowing misrepresentations to us or resulting from any actions against us by third parties relying on the financial statements described herein except for our own intentional wrongdoing.]

If you request us to perform additional services not contemplated or described in this engagement letter, we will provide you with a separate agreement describing those additional services and fees.

Please sign and return the attached copy of this letter to indicate your acknowledgment of, and agreement with, the arrangements for our engagement to prepare the [*identify the specified element, account, or item of the financial*

 ©2017, AICPA

statement, for example, schedule of accounts receivable or schedule of depreciation] described herein, and our respective responsibilities.

Sincerely yours,

____

[*Signature of accountant or accountant's firm*]

Acknowledged and agreed on behalf of ABC Company by:

____

[*Signed*]
[*Name and Title*]

____

[*Date*]

Chapter 4

Compilation of Pro Forma Financial Information

Introduction

4.01 AR-C section 120, *Compilation of Pro Forma Financial Information* (AICPA, *Professional Standards*), contains performance and reporting requirements and application guidance for accountants engaged to perform a compilation engagement on pro forma financial information. The accountant's objective in a compilation of pro forma financial information is to apply accounting and financial reporting expertise to assist management in the presentation of pro forma financial information and report in accordance with AR-C section 120 without undertaking to obtain or provide any assurance on the pro forma financial information.

Applicability

4.02 Pro forma financial information shows what the significant effects on historical financial information might have been had a consummated or proposed transaction (or event) occurred at an earlier date. Pro forma financial information is developed by applying pro forma adjustments to historical financial information. Appropriate pro forma adjustments are based on management's assumptions, give effect to all significant effects directly attributable to the transaction (or event), and are stated on a basis consistent with the financial reporting framework of the reporting entity and its accounting policies under that framework. Pro forma financial information is commonly used to show the effects of a transaction such as the following:

- Business combination
- Change in capitalization
- Disposition of a significant portion of the business
- Change in the form of business organization or status as an autonomous entity
- Proposed sale of securities and the application of the proceeds

4.03 Adequately disclosed pro forma financial information is labeled as such to distinguish it from other historical financial information. In addition, adequately disclosed pro forma financial information

- describes the transaction (or event) that is reflected in the pro forma financial information, the date on which the transaction (or event) is assumed to occur, the financial reporting framework of the financial statements, the source of the historical financial information on which it is based, the significant assumptions used in developing the pro forma adjustments, and any significant uncertainties about those assumptions.
- indicates that the pro forma financial information should be read in conjunction with the related historical financial information

and that the pro forma financial information is not necessarily indicative of the results (such as financial position, results of operations, and cash flows, as applicable) that would have been attained had the transaction (or event) actually taken place earlier.

Requirements

General Principles for Compilations of Pro Forma Financial Information

4.04 In addition to complying with AR-C section 120, an accountant is required to comply with AR-C section 60, *General Principles for Engagements Performed in Accordance With Statements on Standards for Accounting and Review Services* (AICPA, *Professional Standards*), adapted as necessary. AR-C section 60 requires

- the accountant to comply with relevant ethical requirements.
- the accountant to exercise professional judgment in the performance of the engagement.
- the accountant to perform the engagement in accordance with Statements on Standards for Accounting and Review Services (SSARSs).
- the engagement partner to possess the competence and capabilities to perform the engagement and competence in financial reporting, appropriate to the engagement circumstances.
- the engagement partner to take responsibility for certain quality control matters.

Paragraphs .25–.26 of AR-C section 60 also include certain preconditions for the performance of the engagement.

4.05 Paragraphs 2.06–2.10 of this guide provide guidance with respect to engagement level quality control in a compilation engagement.

4.06 Paragraphs 2.11–2.12 of this guide provide guidance with respect to independence.

Acceptance and Continuance of Client Relationships

4.07 Paragraphs 2.13–2.18 of this guide provide guidance with respect to preconditions for accepting a compilation engagement.

4.08 In accordance with paragraph .07 of AR-C section 120, as a condition for accepting an engagement to perform a compilation on pro forma financial information, in addition to the requirements in paragraph .25 of AR-C section 60, adapted as necessary, the accountant should obtain the agreement of management that it acknowledges and understands its responsibility for the following:

a. The preparation and fair presentation of pro forma financial information in accordance with the applicable financial reporting framework

b. To include the following in any document that contains the pro forma financial information

  i. The complete financial statements of the entity for the most recent year (or for the preceding year if financial statements for the most recent year are not yet available) or such financial statements are readily available

ii. If pro forma financial information is presented for an interim period, either historical interim financial information for that period (which may be in condensed form) or that such interim information is readily available

iii. In the case of a business combination, the relevant historical financial information for the significant constituent parts of the combined entity

c. To ensure that the financial statements of the entity (or, in the case of a business combination, of each significant constituent part of the combined entity) on which the pro forma financial information is based have been subjected to a compilation, review, or an audit engagement

d. To include the accountant's compilation or review report or the auditor's report on the financial statements (or to have readily available) in any document containing the pro forma financial information

e. To present a summary of significant assumptions with the pro forma financial information

f. To obtain the accountant's permission prior to including the accountant's compilation report in any document containing the pro forma financial information that indicates that the entity's accountant has performed a compilation engagement on such pro forma financial information

4.09 If the accountant is not satisfied about any of the matters set out in paragraph .26 of AR-C section 60 or paragraph 4.04 as preconditions for accepting a compilation engagement with respect to pro forma financial information, the accountant should discuss the matter with management. If changes cannot be made to satisfy the accountant about those matters, the accountant should not accept the proposed compilation engagement.

Agreement on Engagement Terms

4.10 Paragraph .09 of AR-C section 120, states that the accountant should agree upon the terms of the engagement with management or those charged with governance, as appropriate. The agreed-upon terms of the engagement should be documented in an engagement letter or other suitable form of written agreement between the parties that is signed by both the accountant or the accountant's firm and management or those charged with governance, as appropriate.

4.11 Both management and the accountant have an interest in documenting the agreed-upon terms of the engagement before the commencement of the engagement. Such an understanding reduces the risk that the accountant or the client may misinterpret the needs or expectations of the other party. For example, it reduces the risk that management may inappropriately rely on the accountant to protect the entity against certain risks or to perform certain functions that are management's responsibility.

4.12 The accountant should ensure that the engagement letter includes the objectives of the engagement, management's responsibilities as set forth in paragraph 4.08, the accountant's responsibilities, the limitations of the engagement, identification of the applicable financial reporting framework for the preparation of the pro forma financial information, the expected form and content of the accountant's compilation report, and a statement that there may be circumstances in which the report may differ from its expected form and content.

4.13 An illustration of an engagement letter for a compilation of pro forma financial information is included in paragraph 4.23.

The Accountant's Knowledge and Understanding of the Entity's Financial Reporting Framework

4.14 Paragraph .11 of AR-C section 120 states that the accountant should obtain an understanding of the applicable financial reporting framework and the significant accounting policies intended to be used in the preparation of the pro forma financial information. If the entity is a combined entity, the accountant should obtain an understanding of the significant accounting policies adopted by management of each significant constituent part of the combined entity that would have been required to have been obtained by the accountant performing a compilation engagement with respect to the financial statements of each entity for the most recent annual or interim period for which the pro forma financial information is presented. The requirement that the accountant obtain an understanding of the applicable financial reporting framework intended to be used in the preparation of the pro forma financial information and the significant accounting policies adopted by management does not prevent the accountant from accepting a compilation engagement for an entity in an industry in which the accountant has no previous experience. The accountant may obtain such understanding by, for example, consulting AICPA guides, industry publications, financial statements of other entities in the industry, textbooks and periodicals, appropriate continuing professional education, or individuals who are knowledgeable about the framework or the industry.

Compilation Procedures

4.15 Paragraph .12 of AR-C section 120 states that in performing a compilation of pro forma financial information, the accountant should do the following:

a. Comply with the requirements set forth in paragraphs .13–.16 of AR-C section 80, adapted as necessary.

b. Obtain an understanding of the underlying transaction or event.

c. Ascertain that management has fulfilled its agreement pursuant to paragraph 4.08*b* of this chapter to include the following in any document that contains the pro forma financial information:

  i. The complete financial statements of the entity for the most recent year (or for the preceding year if financial statements for the most recent year are not yet available) or such financial statements are readily available

  ii. If pro forma financial information is presented for an interim period, either historical interim financial information for that period (which may be in condensed form) or that such interim information is readily available

 ©2017, AICPA

iii. In the case of a business combination, the relevant financial information for the significant constituent parts of the combined entity

d. Ascertain that management has fulfilled its agreement pursuant to paragraph 4.08*c* of this chapter to ensure that the financial statements of the entity (or, in the case of a business combination, of each significant constituent part of the combined entity) on which the pro forma financial information is based have been subjected to a compilation, review, or an audit engagement.

e. Ascertain that management has fulfilled its agreement pursuant to paragraph 4.08*d* of this chapter to include the accountant's compilation or review report or the auditor's report on the financial statements (or have readily available) in any document containing the pro forma financial information.

4.16 The requirement in paragraph .13 of AR-C section 80 that the accountant read the financial statements in light of the accountant's understanding of the applicable financial reporting framework and the significant accounting policies adopted by management and consider whether such financial statements appear to be appropriate in form and free from obvious material misstatements requires the accountant to also read the pro forma financial information and consider the following:

- Whether the underlying transaction (or event), the pro forma adjustments, the significant assumptions, and the significant uncertainties, if any, about those assumptions have been appropriately described
- Whether the source of the historical financial information on which the pro forma financial information is based has been appropriately identified

The Accountant's Compilation Report on Pro Forma Financial Information

4.17 Paragraphs .13–.14 of AR-C section 120 state that the accountant's report should be in writing and should comply with requirements set forth in paragraphs .17–.31 of AR-C section 80. In addition to the report elements required by paragraph .17 of AR-C section 80, an accountant's compilation report on pro forma financial information should include the following:

a. A reference to the financial statements from which the historical financial information is derived and a statement as to whether such financial statements were subjected to an audit, a review, or a compilation engagement

b. A reference to any modification of the audit, review, or compilation report on the historical financial information

c. A description of the nature and limitations of pro forma financial information

4.18 The accountant's compilation report on pro forma financial information may be added to the accountant's report on historical financial statements or it may appear separately.

4.19 An uncertainty about whether the underlying transaction (or event) will be consummated would not require a report modification.

4.20 An illustrative compilation report is included in paragraph 4.24.

Documentation

4.21 The accountant should prepare documentation in connection with each compilation of pro forma financial information in sufficient detail to provide a clear understanding of the work performed, which, at a minimum, includes the following:

a. The engagement letter or other suitable form of written documentation with management, as described in paragraphs 4.10–4.12

b. The results of procedures performed in accordance with paragraph 4.15

c. A copy of the pro forma financial information

d. A copy of the accountant's compilation report

4.22 In addition to the minimum requirements set forth in paragraph 4.21, documentation may include significant consultations or significant professional judgments made throughout the engagement.

Illustrative Engagement Letter for a Compilation of Pro Forma Financial Information

> **Notice to Readers**
>
> The illustrative engagement letter presented in the following paragraph is intended to show how the engagement letter can be presented, assuming that the accountant has been engaged to perform a compilation engagement on pro forma financial information. The engagement letter will vary according to individual requirements and circumstances and may be modified to include other services that the accountant may be engaged to perform. The accountant may seek legal advice about whether the proposed letter is suitable.

4.23 Circumstances include the following:

- The accountant will prepare, as a nonattest service, the pro forma financial information and perform a compilation on the pro forma financial information the accountant prepared.
- The pro forma financial information is presented in accordance with accounting principles generally accepted in the United States of America.
- The accountant expects that his or her independence will not be impaired.

To the appropriate representative of management of ABC Company:[1]

[1] The addresses and references in the engagement letter will be those that are appropriate in the circumstances of the compilation of pro forma financial information, including the relevant jurisdiction. It is important to refer to the appropriate persons.

 ©2017, AICPA

You[2] have requested that we prepare the pro forma financial information of ABC Company (the Company) and perform a compilation engagement with respect to that pro forma financial information. We are pleased to confirm our acceptance and our understanding of this engagement by means of this letter.

Pro forma financial information is a presentation that shows what the significant effects on historical financial information might have been had a consummated or proposed transaction (or event) occurred at an earlier date.

Our Responsibilities

The objective of our engagement is to

a. prepare the pro forma financial information in accordance with accounting principles generally accepted in the United States of America, and

b. perform a compilation engagement on the pro forma financial information we prepared in which we will apply accounting and financial reporting expertise to assist you in the presentation of the pro forma financial information and report without undertaking to obtain or provide any assurance that there are no material modifications that should be made to the pro forma financial information in order for it to be in accordance with accounting principles generally accepted in the United States of America.

We will conduct our engagement in accordance with Statements on Standards for Accounting and Review Services (SSARSs) promulgated by the Accounting and Review Services Committee of the American Institute of Certified Public Accountants (AICPA) and comply with the AICPA's Code of Professional Conduct, including the ethical principles of integrity, objectivity, professional competence, and due care.

We are not required to, and will not, verify the accuracy or completeness of the information you will provide to us for the engagement or otherwise gather evidence for the purpose of expressing an opinion or a conclusion. Accordingly, we will not express an opinion or provide any assurance on the pro forma financial information.

Our engagement cannot be relied upon to identify or disclose any pro forma financial information misstatements, including those caused by fraud or error, or to identify or disclose any wrongdoing within the Company or noncompliance with laws and regulations.

Management Responsibilities

The engagement to be performed is conducted on the basis that management acknowledges and understands that our role is to prepare the pro forma financial information in accordance with accounting principles generally accepted in the United States of America and perform a compilation engagement on the pro forma financial information we prepared. Management has the following overall responsibilities that are fundamental to our undertaking the engagement in accordance with SSARSs:

a. For the preparation and fair presentation of the pro forma financial information in accordance with accounting principles generally accepted in the United States of America and for the selection of

---

[2] Throughout this engagement letter, references to *you, we, us, management*, and *accountant* will be used or amended as appropriate in the circumstances.

accounting principles generally accepted in the United States of America as the applicable financial reporting framework

b. To include the following in any document that contains the pro forma financial information:

   i. The complete financial statements of the entity for the most recent year (or for the preceding year if financial statements for the most recent year are not yet available) or such financial statements are readily available

   ii. If pro forma financial information is presented for an interim period, either historical interim financial information for that period (which may be in condensed form) or that such interim information is readily available

   iii. In the case of a business combination, the relevant historical financial information for the significant constituent parts of the combined entity

c. To ensure that the financial statements of the entity (or, in the case of a business combination, of each significant constituent part of the combined entity) on which the pro forma financial information is based have been subjected to a compilation, review, or an audit engagement

d. To include the accountant's compilation or review report or the auditor's report on the financial statements (or make readily available) in any document containing the pro forma financial information

e. To present a summary of significant assumptions with the pro forma financial information

f. To obtain the accountant's permission prior to including the accountant's compilation report in any document containing the pro forma financial information that indicates that the entity's accountant has performed a compilation engagement on such pro forma financial information

g. To prevent and detect fraud

h. To ensure that the Company complies with the laws and regulations applicable to its activities

i. For the accuracy and completeness of the records, documents, explanations, and other information, including significant judgments, you provide to us for the engagement

j. To provide us with the following:

   i. Assumptions that provide a reasonable basis for presenting the significant effects directly attributable to the underlying transaction (or event)

   ii. Documentation and other related information that is relevant to the preparation and presentation of the pro forma financial information

   iii. Additional information that may be requested for the purpose of the preparation of the pro forma financial information

   iv. Unrestricted access to persons within the Company with whom we determine it is necessary to communicate

©2017, AICPA

You are also responsible for all management decisions and responsibilities and for designating an individual with suitable skills, knowledge, and expertise to oversee our preparation of your pro forma financial information. You are responsible for evaluating the adequacy and results of the services performed and accepting responsibility for such services.

Our Report

As part of our engagement, we will issue a report that will state that we did not examine or review the pro forma financial information and that, accordingly, we do not express an opinion nor provide any assurance on it. There may be circumstances in which the report differs from the expected form and content.

We have no responsibility to update our report for events and circumstances occurring after the date of such report.

If management intends to reproduce and publish the pro forma financial information and our report thereon, they must be reproduced in their entirety, and both the first and subsequent corrected drafts of the document containing the pro forma financial information and any accompanying material must be submitted to us for approval.

Other Relevant Information

Our fees for these services . . .

[*The accountant may include language, such as the following, regarding limitation of, or other arrangements regarding, the liability of the accountant or the entity, such as indemnification to the accountant for liability arising from knowing misrepresentations to the accountant by management (regulators may restrict or prohibit such liability limitation arrangements):*

You agree to hold us harmless and to release, indemnify, and defend us from any liability or costs, including attorney's fees, resulting from management's knowing misrepresentations to us or resulting from any actions against us by third parties relying on the pro forma financial information described herein except for our own intentional wrongdoing.]

Please sign and return the attached copy of this letter to indicate your acknowledgment of, and agreement with, the arrangements for our engagement to prepare the pro forma financial information described herein and to perform a compilation engagement with respect to that same pro forma financial information, and our respective responsibilities.

Sincerely yours,

____

[*Signature of accountant or accountant's firm*]

Acknowledged and agreed on behalf of ABC Company by:

____

[*Signed*]

[*Name and title*]

____

[*Date*]

Illustrative Accountant's Compilation Report on Pro Forma Financial Information

4.24 Management is responsible for the accompanying pro forma condensed balance sheet of XYZ Company as of December 31, 20X1, and the related pro forma condensed statement of income for the year then ended (pro forma financial information), based on the criteria in Note 1. The historical condensed financial statements are derived from the financial statements of XYZ Company, on which I (we) performed a compilation engagement, and of ABC Company, on which other accountants performed a compilation engagement. The pro forma adjustments are based on management's assumptions described in Note 1. I (We) have performed a compilation engagement in accordance with Statements on Standards for Accounting and Review Services promulgated by the Accounting and Review Services Committee of the AICPA. I (we) did not examine or review the pro forma financial information nor was (were) I (we) required to perform any procedures to verify the accuracy or completeness of the information provided by management. Accordingly, I (we) do not express an opinion, a conclusion, nor provide any form of assurance on the pro forma financial information.

The objective of this pro forma financial information is to show what the significant effects on the historical financial information might have been had the underlying transaction (or event) occurred at an earlier date. However, the pro forma condensed financial statements are not necessarily indicative of the results of operations or related effects on financial position that would have been attained had the above mentioned transaction (or event) actually occurred at such earlier date.

[Additional paragraph(s) may be added to emphasize certain matters relating to the compilation engagement or the subject matter.]

[*Signature of accounting firm or accountant, as appropriate*]

[*Accountant's city and state*]

[*Date of the accountant's report*]

 ©2017, AICPA

Chapter 5

Preparing or Performing a Compilation or Review of Personal Financial Statements

Introduction

5.01 Accountants may be engaged to prepare or perform a compilation or review of personal financial statements. If so, AR-C section 70, *Preparation of Financial Statements*; AR-C section 80, *Compilation Engagements*; and AR-C section 90, *Review of Financial Statements* (AICPA, *Professional Standards*), are applicable to such engagements. The purpose of this chapter is to provide specific guidance regarding how those AR-C sections are applied in Statements on Standards for Accounting and Review Services (SSARSs) engagements of personal financial statements.

Accounting Considerations

5.02 FASB *Accounting Standards Codification* (ASC) 274-10-35-1 states that personal financial statements should present assets at their estimated current values and liabilities at their estimated current amounts at the date of the financial statements. Paragraphs 4–15 of FASB ASC 274-10-35 describe the methods used to determine the estimated current values of assets and estimated current amount of liabilities. In addition, personal financial statements prepared in accordance with accounting principles generally accepted in the United States of America (GAAP) require sufficient disclosures to make the financial statements adequately informative. In accordance with FASB ASC 274-10-50-2, the following would be disclosed:

a. A clear indication of the individuals covered by the financial statements

b. That assets are presented at their estimated current values and liabilities are presented at their estimated current amounts

c. Either of the following:

  i. The methods used in determining the estimated current values of major assets and the estimated current amounts of major liabilities

  ii. The methods used in determining the major categories of assets and liabilities

d. Changes in item (*c*) methods from one period to the next

e. If assets held jointly by the person and by others are included in the statements, the nature of the joint ownership

f. If the person's investment portfolio is material in relation to his or her other assets and is concentrated in one or a few companies or industries, the names of the entities or industries and the estimated current values of the securities

g. If the person has a material investment in a closely held business, at a minimum the following:

   i. The name of the entity and the person's percentage of ownership
   ii. The nature of the business
   iii. Summarized financial information about assets, liabilities, and results of operations for the most recent year based on the financial statements of the business, including information about the basis of presentation (for example, GAAP, income tax-basis, or cash-basis) and any significant loss contingencies

h. Descriptions of intangible assets and their estimated useful lives

i. The face amount of life insurance the individuals own

j. Nonforfeitable rights that do not have the characteristics discussed in FASB ASC 274-10-35-11, for example, pensions based on life expectancy

k. All of the following tax information:
   i. The methods and assumptions used to compute the estimated income taxes on the differences between the estimated current values of assets and the estimated current amounts of liabilities and their tax bases
   ii. A statement that the provision will probably differ from the amounts of income taxes that might eventually be paid because those amounts are determined by the timing and method of disposal, realization, or liquidation and the tax laws and regulations in effect at the time of disposal, realization, or liquidation
   iii. Unused operating losses and capital loss carryforwards
   iv. Other unused deductions and credits, with their expiration periods, if applicable
   v. The differences between the estimated current values of major assets and the estimated current amounts of major liabilities or categories of assets and liabilities and their tax bases
   vi. The excess or deficit of the estimated current values of major assets or categories of assets over their tax bases

l. Maturities, interest rates, collateral, and other pertinent details relating to receivables and debt

m. Noncancellable commitments that do not have the characteristics discussed in FASB ASC 274-10-35-13, for example, operating leases

5.03 GAAP other than those discussed in FASB ASC 274, *Personal Financial Statements*, also apply to personal financial statements, and the preparer is required to consider other applicable GAAP such as FASB ASC 450, *Contingencies*, and FASB ASC 850, *Related Party Disclosures*.

5.04 FASB ASC 274 also includes an illustrative personal financial statement.

5.05 The accountant also may prepare or perform a compilation or review engagement of personal financial statements that are prepared in accordance with a special purpose financial reporting framework that presents assets and liabilities at values and amounts other than estimated current values

©2017, AICPA

and amounts. Such special purpose frameworks include the historical cost basis, tax-basis, and cash-basis of accounting.

Internal Control With Respect to Personal Financial Statements

5.06 Internal control over financial reporting includes the design and implementation of those policies and procedures deemed necessary to provide reasonable assurance that financial statements are fairly presented in accordance with the applicable financial reporting framework.

5.07 Although an individual typically does not have a formal system of internal control over financial reporting, an individual usually has some controls that provide for the preparation of his or her financial statements. For example, an individual usually has controls sufficient for him or her to identify amounts of assets owned and liabilities owed. Regardless of the formality of controls, an individual is still responsible for having those controls in place that allow for the preparation of his or her personal financial statements in accordance with the applicable financial reporting framework.

5.08 Accountants may be engaged to perform certain nonattest services that require the accountant to design, implement, or maintain certain aspects of an individual's internal control—such as financial statement preparation. The accountant should be aware that the performance of these services may impair the accountant's independence. An accountant who is not independent may perform a compilation engagement but is required to disclose the fact that the accountant is not independent in the accountant's compilation report. An accountant is required to be independent to perform a review engagement. In making a judgment about whether he or she is independent, the accountant is guided by the AICPA Code of Professional Conduct.

Agreement on Engagement Terms

5.09 The accountant is required, in all SSARSs engagements, to agree upon the terms of the engagement with management, or those charged with governance, as applicable and to document the agreed-upon terms in an engagement letter or other suitable form of written communication. The required elements of the agreed-upon terms of the engagement are included in paragraph .10 of AR-C section 70 with respect to engagements to prepare financial statements, paragraph .10 of AR-C section 80 with respect to compilation engagements, and in paragraph .11 of AR-C section 90 with respect to review engagements. The engagement letter or other suitable form of written communication is required to be signed by the accountant or the accountant's firm and management or those charged with governance, as appropriate.

5.10 In the case of a SSARSs engagement with respect to personal financial statements, *management* would be the person or persons whose personal financial statements are the subject of the engagement.

5.11 Illustrations of engagement letters for an engagement to prepare or perform a compilation or review of personal financial statements are included in paragraph 5.23.

Fraud and Illegal Acts in an Engagement to Prepare or in a Compilation or Review of Personal Financial Statements

5.12 Neither an engagement to prepare nor a compilation or review of personal financial statements contemplates assessing fraud risk. However, evidence or information may come to the accountant's attention during the performance of the engagement that fraud or an illegal act may have occurred.

5.13 With respect to personal financial statements, the client has direct control over all decisions. As such, the individual typically does not have to be concerned about employee theft or fraud. However, because of the lack of sophistication of internal control and the lack of ability of most individuals to measure assets and liabilities at fair value, there may be an increased risk of material misstatement of the financial statements or financial statement fraud.

5.14 Additionally, fraud or illegal acts may be committed by the client's agents, such as investment advisers and insurance agents. It is important that the client understand that he or she is responsible for the prevention and detection of fraud and illegal acts—and not the accountant. In addition, it is important in a review of personal financial statements that the accountant, in accordance with paragraph .22 of AR-C section 90, asks the client about the client's knowledge of any fraud or suspected fraud affecting the client.

Representation Letters

5.15 During a review of personal financial statements, a client makes representations to the accountant, both oral and written, in response to specific inquiries as part of review procedures. Such representations from the client are an important part of the information gathered by the accountant. In an engagement to review financial statements, an accountant is required to obtain written representations from the client for all financial statements and periods covered by the accountant's review report. The accountant is not required to obtain such written representations in an engagement to prepare or perform a compilation on financial statements. However, given that these representations may be the only record of fair value information, an accountant may want to obtain written representations in such engagements or at least document where or how the client documented fair value.

5.16 The requirements with respect to written representations in a review of financial statements are included in paragraphs .32–.37 of AR-C section 90.

5.17 An illustration of a client representation letter that may be obtained in a review of personal financial statements is included in paragraph 5.25. The illustrative client representation letter may be modified as appropriate for those instances in which the accountant determines to obtain a client representation letter in an engagement to prepare or a compilation of personal financial statements.

Compilation and Review Reports on Personal Financial Statements

5.18 When the accountant is engaged to perform a compilation or a review of personal financial statements, the financial statements should be accompanied by a written report. Paragraph .17 of AR-C section 80 outlines the basic

 ©2017, AICPA

elements of an accountant's compilation report. Paragraph .39 of AR-C section 90 outlines the basic elements of an accountant's review report.

5.19 The client may request that the accountant perform a compilation engagement on personal financial statements that omit substantially all disclosures required by an applicable financial reporting framework (for example, GAAP or the income tax-basis of accounting), including disclosures that might appear in the body of the financial statements. In those instances, the accountant should follow the guidance in paragraphs .24–.28 of AR-C section 80.

5.20 Also, the accountant may issue a compilation report on personal financial statements when he or she is not independent with respect to the client. When the accountant is reporting on financial statements subjected to a compilation engagement when he or she is not independent, the accountant should follow the guidance in paragraphs .22–.23 of AR-C section 80.

Departures From the Applicable Financial Reporting Framework

5.21 An accountant who is engaged to perform a compilation or review of personal financial statements may become aware of a departure from the applicable financial reporting framework (including inadequate disclosure) that is material to the financial statements. Paragraphs .29–.33 of AR-C section 80 and paragraphs .56–.60 of AR-C section 90 provide the appropriate guidance with respect to a compilation or review of financial statements, respectively.

5.22 Illustrations of accountant's compilation and review reports on personal financial statements are included in paragraph 5.26.

Illustrative Engagement Letters

Notice to Readers

The illustrative engagement letters presented in this section are intended to show how the engagement letter can be presented assuming that the accountant has been engaged to prepare or perform a compilation or a review of personal financial statements. The engagement letter will vary according to individual requirements and circumstances and may be modified to include other nonattest services that the accountant may be engaged to perform. The accountant may seek legal advice about whether a proposed letter is suitable.

5.23 The illustrative engagement letters in this paragraph are as follows:

Illustration 1—An Engagement Letter for an Engagement to Prepare Personal Financial Statements in Accordance With Accounting Principles Generally Accepted in the United States of America

Illustration 2—An Engagement Letter for a Compilation of Personal Financial Statements Prepared in Accordance With Accounting Principles Generally Accepted in the United States of America

Illustration 3—An Engagement Letter for a Review of Personal Financial Statements Prepared in Accordance With Accounting Principles Generally Accepted in the United States of America

Illustration 1—An Engagement Letter for an Engagement to Prepare Personal Financial Statements in Accordance With Accounting Principles Generally Accepted in the United States of America

To James and Jane Person:

You have requested that we prepare your personal financial statements, which comprise your statement of financial condition as of December 31, 20X2, and the related statement of changes in net worth for the year then ended and the related notes to the financial statements.[1] We are pleased to confirm our acceptance and our understanding of this engagement by means of this letter.

Our Responsibilities

The objective of our engagement is to prepare your financial statements in accordance with accounting principles generally accepted in the United States of America based on information provided by you. We will conduct our engagement in accordance with Statements on Standards for Accounting and Review Services (SSARSs) promulgated by the Accounting and Review Services Committee of the AICPA and comply with the AICPA's Code of Professional Conduct, including the ethical principles of integrity, objectivity, professional competence, and due care.

We are not required to, and will not, verify the accuracy or completeness of the information you will provide to us for the engagement or otherwise gather evidence for the purpose of expressing an opinion or a conclusion. Accordingly, we will not express an opinion or a conclusion or provide any assurance on your financial statements.

Our engagement cannot be relied upon to identify or disclose any financial statement misstatements, including those caused by fraud or error, or to identify or disclose any wrongdoing by you or noncompliance with laws and regulations.

Your Responsibilities

The engagement to be performed is conducted on the basis that you acknowledge and understand that our role is to prepare your personal financial statements in accordance with accounting principles generally accepted in the United States of America. You have the following overall responsibilities that are fundamental to our undertaking the engagement to prepare your personal financial statements in accordance with SSARSs:

a. The selection of accounting principles generally accepted in the United States of America as the financial reporting framework to be applied in the preparation of your personal financial statements

b. The prevention and detection of fraud

c. Compliance with the laws and regulations applicable to your activities

d. The accuracy and completeness of the records, documents, explanations, and other information, including significant judgments, you provide to us for the engagement to prepare your personal financial statements

---

[1] The accountant may include other nonattest services to be performed as part of the engagement, such as income tax preparation and bookkeeping services.

 ©2017, AICPA

e. To provide us with
    i. access to all information of which you are aware that is relevant to the preparation and presentation of your personal financial statements, such as records, documentation, and other matters,
    ii. additional information that may be requested for the purpose of the preparation of your personal financial statements, and
    iii. unrestricted access to persons of whom we determine necessary to communicate

The personal financial statements will not be accompanied by a report. However, you agree that your personal financial statements will clearly indicate that no assurance is provided on them.

[*If the accountant expects to issue a disclaimer, instead of the preceding paragraph, the following may be added:*

As part of our engagement, we will issue a disclaimer that will state that the financial statements were not subjected to an audit, review, or compilation engagement by us and, we do not express an opinion, a conclusion, nor provide any assurance on them.]

Other Relevant Information

Our fees for these services . . . .

[*The accountant may include language, such as the following, regarding limitation of, or other arrangements regarding, the liability of the accountant or the individuals for whom the accountant is engaging to prepare personal financial statements, such as indemnification to the accountant for liability arising from knowing misrepresentations to the accountant by the individuals (regulators may restrict or prohibit such liability limitation arrangements):*

You agree to hold us harmless and to release, indemnify, and defend us from any liability or costs, including attorney's fees, resulting from your knowing misrepresentations to us or resulting from any actions against us by third parties relying on the financial statements described herein except for our own intentional wrongdoing.]

If you request us to perform additional services not contemplated or described in this engagement letter, we will provide you with a separate agreement describing those additional services and fees.

Please sign and return the attached copy of this letter to indicate your acknowledgment of, and agreement with, the arrangements for our engagement to prepare your personal financial statements described herein, and our respective responsibilities.

Sincerely yours,

____

[*Signature of accountant or accountant's firm*]

Acknowledged and agreed on behalf of James and Jane Person by:

____

James Person

____

Jane Person

____

[*Date*]

Illustration 2—An Engagement Letter for a Compilation of Personal Financial Statements Prepared in Accordance With Accounting Principles Generally Accepted in the United States of America

Circumstances include the following:

- The accountant will prepare, as a nonattest service, the personal financial statements, including related notes, subject to the compilation engagement.
- The personal financial statements will be prepared in accordance with accounting principles generally accepted in the United States of America and will included all related notes required by accounting principles generally accepted in the United States of America.
- The accountant expects that his or her independence will not be impaired.

To James and Jane Person:

You have requested that we prepare your personal financial statements, which comprise your statement of financial condition as of December 31, 20X2, and the related statement of changes in net worth for the year then ended, and the related notes to the financial statements, and perform a compilation engagement with respect to those personal financial statements.[2] We are pleased to confirm our acceptance and our understanding of this engagement by means of this letter.

Our Responsibilities

The objective of our engagement is to

a. prepare your personal financial statements in accordance with accounting principles generally accepted in the United States of America based on information provided by you and

b. apply accounting and financial reporting expertise to assist you in the presentation of your personal financial statements without undertaking to obtain or provide any assurance that there are no material modifications that should be made to your personal financial statements in order for them to be in accordance with accounting principles generally accepted in the United States of America.

We will conduct our compilation engagement in accordance with Statements on Standards for Accounting and Review Services (SSARSs) promulgated by the Accounting and Review Services Committee of the AICPA and comply with the AICPA's Code of Professional Conduct, including the ethical principles of integrity, objectivity, professional competence, and due care.

We are not required to, and will not, verify the accuracy or completeness of the information you will provide to us for the engagement or otherwise gather evidence for the purpose of expressing an opinion or a conclusion. Accordingly, we will not express an opinion or a conclusion nor provide any assurance on your personal financial statements.

---

[2] See footnote 1.

 ©2017, AICPA

Our engagement cannot be relied upon to identify or disclose any financial statement misstatements, including those caused by fraud or error, or to identify or disclose any wrongdoing within the entity or noncompliance with laws and regulations.

Your Responsibilities

The engagement to be performed is conducted on the basis that you acknowledge and understand that our role is to prepare your personal financial statements in accordance with accounting principles generally accepted in the United States of America and assist you in the presentation of your personal financial statements in accordance with accounting principles generally accepted in the United States of America. You have the following overall responsibilities that are fundamental to our undertaking the engagement in accordance with SSARSs:

a. The selection of accounting principles generally accepted in the United States of America as the financial reporting framework to be applied in the preparation of your personal financial statements

b. The preparation and fair presentation of your personal financial statements in accordance with accounting principles generally accepted in the United States of America and the inclusion of all informative disclosures that are appropriate for accounting principles generally accepted in the United States of America

c. The design, implementation, and maintenance of internal control relevant to the preparation and fair presentation of your personal financial statements

d. The prevention and detection of fraud

e. Compliance with the laws and regulations applicable to your activities

f. The accuracy and completeness of the records, documents, explanations, and other information, including significant judgments, you provide to us for the engagement

g. To provide us with

i. access to all information of which you are aware is relevant to the preparation and fair presentation of your personal financial statements, such as records, documentation, and other matters

ii. additional information that we may request from you for the purpose of the compilation engagement

iii. unrestricted access to persons of whom we determine it necessary to make inquiries

You are also responsible for all decisions and responsibilities and for designating an individual with suitable skills, knowledge, and experience to oversee our preparation of your personal financial statements. You are responsible for evaluating the adequacy and results of the services performed and accepting responsibility for such services.

Our Report

As part of our engagement, we will issue a report that will state that we did not audit or review your personal financial statements and that we do not express an opinion, a conclusion, nor provide any assurance on them. There may be circumstances in which the report differs from the expected form and content.

You agree to include our accountant's compilation report in any document containing your personal financial statements that indicates that we have performed a compilation engagement on such personal financial statements and, prior to inclusion of the report, to ask our permission to do so.

Other Relevant Information

Our fees for these services . . . .

[*The accountant may include language, such as the following, regarding limitation of or other arrangements regarding the liability of the accountant or the individuals for whom the accountant is engaging to prepare and perform a compilation on personal financial statements, such as indemnification to the accountant for liability arising from knowing misrepresentations to the accountant by the individuals (regulators may restrict or prohibit such liability limitation arrangements):*

You agree to hold us harmless and to release, indemnify, and defend us from any liability or costs, including attorney's fees, resulting from your knowing misrepresentations to us or resulting from any actions against us by third parties relying on the financial statements described herein except for our own intentional wrongdoing.]

If you request us to perform additional services not contemplated or described in this engagement letter, we will provide you with a separate agreement describing those additional services and fees.

Please sign and return the attached copy of this letter to indicate your acknowledgment of, and agreement with, the arrangements for our engagement to prepare your personal financial statements described herein and to perform a compilation engagement with respect to those same personal financial statements, and our respective responsibilities.

Sincerely yours,

____

[*Signature of accountant or accountant's firm*]

Acknowledged and agreed on behalf of James and Jane Person by:

____

James Person

____

Jane Person

____

[*Date*]

Illustration 3—An Engagement Letter for a Review of Personal Financial Statements Prepared in Accordance With Accounting Principles Generally Accepted in the United States of America

Circumstances include the following:

- The accountant will prepare, as a nonattest service, the personal financial statements, including related notes, subject to the review engagement.
- The personal financial statements will be prepared in accordance with accounting principles generally accepted in the United States of America.

©2017, AICPA

To James and Jane Person:

You have requested that we prepare your personal financial statements, which comprise your statement of financial condition as of December 31, 20X2, and the related statement of changes in net worth for the year then ended, and the related notes to the financial statements and perform a review engagement with respect to those personal financial statements.[3] We are pleased to confirm our acceptance and understanding of this engagement by means of this letter.

Our Responsibilities

The objective of our engagement is to

a. prepare your personal financial statements in accordance with accounting principles generally accepted in the United States of America based on information provided by you and

b. obtain limited assurance as a basis for reporting whether we are aware of any material modifications that should be made to your personal financial statements in order for the statements to be in accordance with accounting principles generally accepted in the United States of America.

We will conduct our review engagement in accordance with Statements on Standards for Accounting and Review Services (SSARSs) promulgated by the Accounting and Review Services Committee of the AICPA and comply with the AICPA's Code of Professional Conduct, including ethical principles of integrity, objectivity, professional competence, and due care.

A review engagement includes primarily applying analytical procedures to your financial data and making inquiries of you. A review engagement is substantially less in scope than an audit engagement, the objective of which is the expression of an opinion regarding the financial statements as a whole. A review engagement does not contemplate obtaining an understanding of your internal control; assessing fraud risk; testing accounting records by obtaining sufficient appropriate audit evidence through inspection, observation, confirmation, or the examination of source documents; or other procedures ordinarily performed in an audit engagement. Accordingly, we will not express an opinion regarding your personal financial statements.

Our engagement cannot be relied upon to identify or disclose any financial statement misstatements, including those caused by error or fraud, or to identify or disclose any wrongdoing or noncompliance with laws and regulations. However, we will inform you of any material errors and any evidence or information that comes to our attention during the performance of our review procedures that indicates fraud may have occurred. In addition, we will report to you any evidence or information that comes to our attention during the performance of our review procedures regarding noncompliance with laws and regulations that may have occurred, unless they are clearly inconsequential.

Your Responsibilities

The engagement to be performed is conducted on the basis that you acknowledge and understand that our role is to prepare your personal financial statements in accordance with accounting principles generally accepted in the United States of America and to obtain limited assurance as a basis for reporting whether we are aware of any material modifications that should be made

[3] See footnote 1.

to the financial statements in order for the statements to be in accordance with accounting principles generally accepted in the United States of America. You have the following overall responsibilities that are fundamental to our undertaking the engagement in accordance with SSARSs:

a. The selection of accounting principles generally accepted in the United States of America as the financial reporting framework to be applied in the preparation of your personal financial statements

b. The preparation and fair presentation of your personal financial statements in accordance with accounting principles generally accepted in the United States of America and the inclusion of all informative disclosures that are appropriate for accounting principles generally accepted in the United States of America

c. The design, implementation, and maintenance of internal control relevant to the preparation and fair presentation of your personal financial statements

d. The prevention and detection of fraud

e. Compliance with the laws and regulations applicable to your activities

f. The accuracy and completeness of the records, documents, explanations, and other information, including significant judgments, you provide to us for the engagement

g. To provide us with

   i. access to all information of which you are aware is relevant to the preparation and fair presentation of your personal financial statements, such as records, documentation, and other matters

   ii. additional information that we may request from you for the purpose of the review engagement

   iii. unrestricted access to persons of whom we determine it necessary to make inquiries

h. To provide us, at the conclusion of the engagement, with a letter that confirms certain representations made during the review

You are also responsible for all decisions and responsibilities, and for designating an individual with suitable skills, knowledge, and experience to oversee our preparation of your personal financial statements. You are responsible for evaluating the adequacy and results of services performed and accepting responsibility for such services.

Our Report

[*Insert appropriate reference to the expected form and content of the accountant's review report. Example follows.*]

We will issue a written report upon completion of our review of your personal financial statements. Our report will be addressed to you. We cannot provide assurance that an unmodified accountant's review report will be issued. Circumstances may arise in which it is necessary for us to report known departures from accounting principles generally accepted in the United States of America, add an emphasis-of-matter or other-matter paragraph(s), or withdraw from the engagement. If, for any reason, we are unable to complete the review of your personal financial statements, we will not issue a report on such statements as a result of this engagement.

 ©2017, AICPA

You agree to include our accountant's review report in any document containing your personal financial statements that indicates that such personal financial statements have been reviewed by us and, prior to inclusion of the report, to ask our permission to do so.

Other Relevant Information

Our fees for these services. . .

[*The accountant may include language, such as the following, regarding limitation of or other arrangements regarding the liability of the accountant or the entity, such as indemnification to the accountant for liability arising from knowing misrepresentations to the accountant by management (regulators may restrict or prohibit such liability limitation arrangements):*

You agree to hold us harmless and to release, indemnify, and defend us from any liability or costs, including attorney's fees, resulting from your knowing misrepresentations to us or resulting from any actions against us by third parties relying on the financial statements described herein except for our own intentional wrongdoing.]

If you request us to perform additional services not contemplated or described in this engagement letter, we will provide you with a separate agreement describing those additional services and fees.

Please sign and return the attached copy of this letter to indicate your acknowledgment of, and agreement with, the arrangements for our engagement to prepare your personal financial statements described herein and to perform a review of those same personal financial statements and our respective responsibilities.

Sincerely yours,

____

[*Signature of accountant or accountant's firm*]

Acknowledged and agreed on behalf of James and Jane Person by:

____

James Person

____

Jane Person

____

[*Date*]

Illustrative Representation Letter

5.24 The following illustrative letter is intended as an illustration that may be used to comply with the requirements of AR-C section 90. The representation letter will vary according to individual requirements and circumstances.

5.25 It is assumed in this illustration that the applicable financial reporting framework is GAAP, that no conditions or events exist that might be indicative of the client's ability to continue as a going concern, and that no exceptions exist to the requested written representations. If circumstances differ from these assumptions, the representations would need to be modified to reflect the actual circumstances.

[*Date*]

To [*the Accountant*]

This representation letter is provided in connection with your review of the personal financial statements of James and Jane Person, which comprise the statement of financial condition as of December 31, 20X2, and the related statement of changes in net worth and the related notes to the financial statements for the year then ended, for the purpose of obtaining limited assurance as a basis for reporting whether you are aware of any material modifications that should be made to the personal financial statements in order for the statements to be in accordance with accounting principles generally accepted in the United States of America.

Certain representations in this letter are described as being limited to matters that are material. Items are considered material, regardless of size, if they involve an omission or misstatement of accounting information that, in the light of surrounding circumstances, makes it probable that the judgment of a reasonable person using the information would be changed or influenced by the omission or misstatement.

We represent that [*to the best of our knowledge and belief, having made such inquiries as we considered necessary for the purpose of appropriately informing ourselves*] [as of *(date of the accountant's review report)*]:

Personal Financial Statements

- We acknowledge our responsibility and have fulfilled our responsibilities for the preparation and fair presentation of our personal financial statements in accordance with accounting principles generally accepted in the United States of America.
- We acknowledge our responsibility and have fulfilled our responsibilities for the design, implementation, and maintenance of internal control relevant to the preparation and fair presentation of our personal financial statements that are free from material misstatement, whether due to fraud or error.
- We acknowledge our responsibility for the design, implementation, and maintenance of internal control to prevent and detect fraud.
- Significant assumptions used by us in making accounting estimates, including those measured at fair value, are reasonable.
- Related party relationships and transactions have been appropriately accounted for and disclosed in accordance with the requirements of accounting principles generally accepted in the United States of America.
- Guarantees, whether written or oral, under which we are contingently liable, have been properly accounted for and disclosed in accordance with the requirements of accounting principles generally accepted in the United States of America.
- Significant estimates and material concentrations known to us that are required to be disclosed in accordance with FASB *Accounting Standards Codification* (ASC) 275, *Risks and Uncertainties*, have been properly accounted for and disclosed in accordance with the requirements of accounting principles generally accepted in the United States of America. [Significant estimates *are estimates at the date of the statement of financial condition that could change materially within the next year.* Concentrations *refer to volumes of business, revenues, available sources of supply, or markets*

 ©2017, AICPA

or geographic areas for which events could occur that would significantly disrupt normal finances within the next year.]

- All events subsequent to the date of the financial statements and for which accounting principles generally accepted in the United States of America requires adjustment or disclosure have been adjusted or disclosed.
- The effects of uncorrected misstatements are immaterial, both individually and in the aggregate, to the financial statements as a whole.
- The effects of all known actual or possible litigation and claims have been accounted for and disclosed in accordance with accounting principles generally accepted in the United States of America.

[*Any other matters that the accountant may consider appropriate.*]

Information Provided

- We have responded fully and truthfully to all inquiries made to us by you during your review.
- We have provided you with
    - access to all information, of which we are aware, that is relevant to the preparation and fair presentation of our personal financial statements, such as records, documentation, and other matters;
    - additional information that you have requested from us for the purpose of the review; and
    - unrestricted access to persons from whom you determined it necessary to obtain review evidence.
- All transactions have been recorded in the accounting records and are reflected in the financial statements.
- We have [*no knowledge of any*] [*disclosed to you all information that we are aware of regarding*] allegations of fraud, or suspected fraud, affecting our personal financial statements as a whole.
- We have no plans or intentions that may materially affect the carrying amounts or classification of assets and liabilities.
- We have disclosed to you all known instances of noncompliance or suspected noncompliance with laws or regulations whose effects should be considered when preparing our personal financial statements.
- We [*have disclosed to you all known actual or possible*] [*are not aware of any pending or threatened*] litigation and claims whose effects should be considered when preparing our personal financial statements [*and we have not consulted legal counsel concerning litigation or claims*].
- We have disclosed to you any other material liabilities or gain or loss contingencies that are required to be accrued or disclosed by FASB ASC 450, *Contingencies*.
- We have disclosed to you the identity of our related parties and all the related party relationships and transactions of which we are aware.

- No material losses exist that have not been properly accrued or disclosed in our personal financial statements.
- We have satisfactory title to all owned assets, and no liens or encumbrances on such assets exist, nor has any asset been pledged as collateral, except as disclosed to you and reported in our personal financial statements.
- We have complied with all aspects of contractual agreements that would have a material effect on our personal financial statements in the event of noncompliance.
- We are in agreement with the adjusting journal entries that you have recommended, and they have been posted to our accounts (if applicable).

[*Any other matters that the accountant may consider necessary*.]

____

James Person

____

Jane Person

Illustrations of Accountant's Compilation and Review Reports on Personal Financial Statements

5.26 The illustrative accountant's compilation and review reports in this section are intended as illustrations that may be used to comply with the requirements of AR-C sections 80 and 90, respectively. The accountant's compilation or review report will vary according to individual requirements and circumstances.

Illustration 1—An Accountant's Compilation Report on Personal Financial Statements Prepared in Accordance With Accounting Principles Generally Accepted in the United States of America

Illustration 2—An Accountant's Compilation Report on Personal Financial Statements Prepared in Accordance With Accounting Principles Generally Accepted in the United States of America and the Accountant Is Aware That the Personal Financial Statements Do Not Include Provision for Estimated Taxes on the Differences Between the Estimated Current Values of Assets and Estimated Current Amounts of Liabilities and Their Tax Bases

Illustration 3—An Accountant's Review Report on Personal Financial Statements Prepared in Accordance With Accounting Principles Generally Accepted in the United States of America

Illustration 1—An Accountant's Compilation Report on Personal Financial Statements Prepared in Accordance With Accounting Principles Generally Accepted in the United States of America

James and Jane Person are responsible for the accompanying personal financial statements, which comprise the statement of financial condition as of December 31, 20X2, and the related statement of changes in net worth for the year then ended, and the related notes to the financial statements in accordance with accounting principles generally accepted in the United States of America. I (We) have performed a compilation engagement in accordance with Statements on

 ©2017, AICPA

Standards for Accounting and Review Services promulgated by the Accounting and Review Services Committee of the AICPA. I (We) did not audit or review the financial statements nor was (were) I (we) required to perform any procedures to verify the accuracy or completeness of the information provided by James and Jane Person. I (we) do not express an opinion, a conclusion, nor provide any assurance on these personal financial statements.

[*Signature of accounting firm or accountant, as appropriate*]
[*Accountant's city and state*]
[*Date of the accountant's report*]

Illustration 2—An Accountant's Compilation Report on Personal Financial Statements Prepared in Accordance With Accounting Principles Generally Accepted in the United States of America and the Accountant Is Aware That the Personal Financial Statements Do Not Include Provision for Estimated Taxes on the Differences Between the Estimated Current Values of Assets and Estimated Current Amounts of Liabilities and Their Tax Bases

James and Jane Person are responsible for the accompanying personal financial statements, which comprise the statement of financial condition as of December 31, 20X2, and the related statement of changes in net worth for the year then ended, and the related notes to the financial statements in accordance with accounting principles generally accepted in the United States of America. I (We) have performed a compilation engagement in accordance with Statements on Standards for Accounting and Review Services promulgated by the Accounting and Review Services Committee of the AICPA. I (We) did not audit or review the financial statements nor was (were) I (we) required to perform any procedures to verify the accuracy or completeness of the information provided by James and Jane Person. Accordingly, I (we) do not express an opinion, a conclusion, nor provide any assurance on these personal financial statements.

Accounting principles generally accepted in the United States of America require that personal financial statements include a provision for estimated income taxes on the differences between the estimated current values of assets and the estimated current amounts of liabilities and their tax bases. The accompanying personal financial statements do not include such a provision, and the effect of this departure from accounting principles generally accepted in the United States of America has not been determined.

[*Signature of accounting firm or accountant, as appropriate*]
[*Accountant's city and state*]
[*Date of the accountant's report*]

Illustration 3—An Accountant's Review Report on Personal Financial Statements Prepared in Accordance With Accounting Principles Generally Accepted in the United States of America

Independent Accountant's Review Report

To James and Jane Person:

I (We) have reviewed the accompanying personal financial statements of James and Jane Person, which comprise the statement of financial condition as of December 31, 20X2, and the related statement of changes in net worth for the year then ended, and the related notes to the financial statements. A review includes primarily applying analytical procedures to James and Jane Person's financial data and making inquiries of James and Jane Person. A review is substantially less in scope than an audit, the objective of which is the expression of an opinion regarding the financial statements as a whole. Accordingly, I (we) do not express such an opinion.

James and Jane Person's Responsibility for the Financial Statements

James and Jane Person are responsible for the preparation and fair presentation of the financial statements in accordance with accounting principles generally accepted in the United States of America; this includes the design, implementation, and maintenance of internal control relevant to the preparation and fair presentation of the financial statements that are free from material misstatement whether due to fraud or error.

Accountant's Responsibility

My (Our) responsibility is to conduct the review engagement in accordance with Statements on Standards for Accounting and Review Services promulgated by the Accounting and Review Services Committee of the AICPA. Those standards require me (us) to perform procedures to obtain limited assurance as a basis for reporting whether I am (we are) aware of any material modifications that should be made to the financial statements for them to be in accordance with accounting principles generally accepted in the United States of America. I (We) believe that the results of my (our) procedures provide a reasonable basis for our conclusion.

Accountant's Conclusion

Based on my (our) review, I am (we are) not aware of any material modifications that should be made to the accompanying financial statements in order for them to be in accordance with accounting principles generally accepted in the United States of America.

[*Signature of accounting firm or accountant, as appropriate*]
[*Accountant's city and state*]
[*Date of the accountant's report*]

©2017, AICPA

Appendix A

Overview of Statements on Quality Control Standards

This appendix is nonauthoritative and is included for informational purposes only.

This appendix is a partial reproduction of chapter 1 of the AICPA practice aid *Establishing and Maintaining a System of Quality Control for a CPA Firm's Accounting and Auditing Practice*, available at www.aicpa.org/interestareas/frc/pages/enhancingauditqualitypracticeaid.aspx.

This appendix highlights certain aspects of the quality control standards issued by the AICPA. If appropriate, readers should also refer to the quality control standards issued by the PCAOB, available at www.pcaobus.org/standards/qc/pages/default.aspx.

1.01 The objectives of a system of quality control are to provide a CPA firm with reasonable assurance[1] that the firm and its personnel comply with professional standards and applicable regulatory and legal requirements, and that the firm or engagement partners issue reports that are appropriate in the circumstances. QC section 10, *A Firm's System of Quality Control* (AICPA, *Professional Standards*), addresses a CPA firm's responsibilities for its system of quality control for its accounting and auditing practice. That section is to be read in conjunction with the AICPA Code of Professional Conduct and other relevant ethical requirements.

1.02 A system of quality control consists of policies designed to achieve the objectives of the system and the procedures necessary to implement and monitor compliance with those policies. The nature, extent, and formality of a firm's quality control policies and procedures will depend on various factors such as the firm's size; the number and operating characteristics of its offices; the degree of authority allowed to, and the knowledge and experience possessed by, firm personnel; and the nature and complexity of the firm's practice.

Communication of Quality Control Policies and Procedures

1.03 The firm should communicate its quality control policies and procedures to its personnel. Most firms will find it appropriate to communicate their policies and procedures in writing and distribute them, or make them available electronically, to all professional personnel. Effective communication includes the following:

- A description of quality control policies and procedures and the objectives they are designed to achieve

---

[1] The term *reasonable assurance*, which is defined as a high, but not absolute, level of assurance, is used because absolute assurance cannot be attained. Paragraph .53 of QC section 10, *A Firm's System of Quality Control* (AICPA, *Professional Standards*), states, "Any system of quality control has inherent limitations that can reduce its effectiveness."

- The message that each individual has a personal responsibility for quality
- A requirement for each individual to be familiar with and to comply with these policies and procedures

Effective communication also includes procedures for personnel to communicate their views or concerns on quality control matters to the firm's management.

Elements of a System of Quality Control

1.04 A firm must establish and maintain a system of quality control. The firm's system of quality control should include policies and procedures that address each of the following elements of quality control identified in paragraph .17 of QC section 10:

- Leadership responsibilities for quality within the firm (the "tone at the top")
- Relevant ethical requirements
- Acceptance and continuance of client relationships and specific engagements
- Human resources
- Engagement performance
- Monitoring

1.05 The elements of quality control are interrelated. For example, a firm continually assesses client relationships to comply with relevant ethical requirements, including independence, integrity, and objectivity, and policies and procedures related to the acceptance and continuance of client relationships and specific engagements. Similarly, the human resources element of quality control encompasses criteria related to professional development, hiring, advancement, and assignment of firm personnel to engagements, all of which affect policies and procedures related to engagement performance. In addition, policies and procedures related to the monitoring element of quality control enable a firm to evaluate whether its policies and procedures for each of the other five elements of quality control are suitably designed and effectively applied.

1.06 Policies and procedures established by the firm related to each element are designed to achieve reasonable assurance with respect to the purpose of that element. Deficiencies in policies and procedures for an element may result in not achieving reasonable assurance with respect to the purpose of that element; however, the system of quality control, as a whole, may still be effective in providing the firm with reasonable assurance that the firm and its personnel comply with professional standards and applicable regulatory and legal requirements and that the firm or engagement partners issue reports that are appropriate in the circumstances.

1.07 If a firm merges, acquires, sells, or otherwise changes a portion of its practice, the surviving firm evaluates and, as necessary, revises, implements, and maintains firm-wide quality control policies and procedures that are appropriate for the changed circumstances.

 ©2017, AICPA

Leadership Responsibilities for Quality Within the Firm (the "Tone at the Top")

1.08 The purpose of the leadership responsibilities element of a system of quality control is to promote an internal culture based on the recognition that quality is essential in performing engagements. The firm should establish and maintain the following policies and procedures to achieve this purpose:

- Require the firm's leadership (managing partner, board of managing partners, CEO, or equivalent) to assume ultimate responsibility for the firm's system of quality control.
- Provide the firm with reasonable assurance that personnel assigned operational responsibility for the firm's quality control system have sufficient and appropriate experience and ability to identify and understand quality control issues and develop appropriate policies and procedures, as well as the necessary authority to implement those policies and procedures.

1.09 Establishing and maintaining the following policies and procedures assists firms in recognizing that the firm's business strategy is subject to the overarching requirement for the firm to achieve the objectives of the system of quality control in all the engagements that the firm performs:

- Assign management responsibilities so that commercial considerations do not override the quality of the work performed.
- Design policies and procedures addressing performance evaluation, compensation, and advancement (including incentive systems) with regard to personnel to demonstrate the firm's overarching commitment to the objectives of the system of quality control.
- Devote sufficient and appropriate resources for the development, communication, and support of its quality control policies and procedures.

Relevant Ethical Requirements

1.10 The purpose of the relevant ethical requirements element of a system of quality control is to provide the firm with reasonable assurance that the firm and its personnel comply with relevant ethical requirements when discharging professional responsibilities. Relevant ethical requirements include independence, integrity, and objectivity. Establishing and maintaining policies such as the following assist the firm in obtaining this assurance:

- Require that personnel adhere to relevant ethical requirements such as those in regulations, interpretations, and rules of the AICPA, state CPA societies, state boards of accountancy, state statutes, the U.S. Government Accountability Office, and any other applicable regulators.
- Establish procedures to communicate independence requirements to firm personnel and, where applicable, others subject to them.
- Establish procedures to identify and evaluate possible threats to independence and objectivity, including the familiarity threat that may be created by using the same senior personnel on an audit

or attest engagement over a long period of time, and to take appropriate action to eliminate those threats or reduce them to an acceptable level by applying safeguards.

- Require that the firm withdraw from the engagement if effective safeguards to reduce threats to independence to an acceptable level cannot be applied.
- Require written confirmation, at least annually, of compliance with the firm's policies and procedures on independence from all firm personnel required to be independent by relevant requirements.
- Establish procedures for confirming the independence of another firm or firm personnel in associated member firms who perform part of the engagement. This would apply to national firm personnel, foreign firm personnel, and foreign-associated firms.[2]
- Require the rotation of personnel for audit or attest engagements where regulatory or other authorities require such rotation after a specified period.

Acceptance and Continuance of Client Relationships and Specific Engagements

1.11 The purpose of the quality control element that addresses acceptance and continuance of client relationships and specific engagements is to establish criteria for deciding whether to accept or continue a client relationship and whether to perform a specific engagement for a client. A firm's client acceptance and continuance policies represent a key element in mitigating litigation and business risk. Accordingly, it is important that a firm be aware that the integrity and reputation of a client's management could reflect the reliability of the client's accounting records and financial representations and, therefore, affect the firm's reputation or involvement in litigation. A firm's policies and procedures related to the acceptance and continuance of client relationships and specific engagements should provide the firm with reasonable assurance that it will undertake or continue relationships and engagements only where it

- is competent to perform the engagement and has the capabilities, including the time and resources, to do so;
- can comply with legal and relevant ethical requirements;
- has considered the client's integrity and does not have information that would lead it to conclude that the client lacks integrity; and
- has reached an understanding with the client regarding the services to be performed.

1.12 This assurance should be obtained before accepting an engagement with a new client, when deciding whether to continue an existing engagement, and when considering acceptance of a new engagement with an existing client. Establishing and maintaining policies such as the following assist the firm in obtaining this assurance:

---

[2] A *foreign-associated firm* is a firm domiciled outside of the United States and its territories that is a member of, correspondent with, or similarly associated with an international firm or international association of firms.

 ©2017, AICPA

- Evaluate factors that have a bearing on management's integrity and consider the risk associated with providing professional services in particular circumstances.[3]
- Evaluate whether the engagement can be completed with professional competence; undertake only those engagements for which the firm has the capabilities, resources, and professional competence to complete; and evaluate, at the end of specific periods or upon occurrence of certain events, whether the relationship should be continued.
- Obtain an understanding, preferably in writing, with the client regarding the services to be performed.
- Establish procedures on continuing an engagement and the client relationship, including procedures for dealing with information that would have caused the firm to decline an engagement if the information had been available earlier.
- Require documentation of how issues relating to acceptance or continuance of client relationships and specific engagements were resolved.

Human Resources

1.13 The purpose of the human resources element of a system of quality control is to provide the firm with reasonable assurance that it has sufficient personnel with the capabilities, competence, and commitment to ethical principles necessary (*a*) to perform its engagements in accordance with professional standards and regulatory and legal requirements, and (*b*) to enable the firm to issue reports that are appropriate in the circumstances. Establishing and maintaining policies such as the following assist the firm in obtaining this assurance:

- Recruit and hire personnel of integrity who possess the characteristics that enable them to perform competently.
- Determine capabilities and competencies required for an engagement, especially for the engagement partner, based on the characteristics of the particular client, industry, and kind of service being performed. Specific competencies necessary for an engagement partner are discussed in paragraph .A27 of QC section 10.
- Determine the capabilities and competencies possessed by personnel.
- Assign the responsibility for each engagement to an engagement partner.

---

[3] Such considerations would include the risk of providing professional services to significant clients or to other clients for which the practitioner's objectivity or the appearance of independence may be impaired. In broad terms, the significance of a client to a member or a firm refers to relationships that could diminish a practitioner's objectivity and independence in performing attest services. Examples of factors to consider in determining the significance of a client to an engagement partner, office, or practice unit include (*a*) the amount of time the partner, office, or practice unit devotes to the engagement, (*b*) the effect on the partner's stature within the firm as a result of his or her service to the client, (*c*) the manner in which the partner, office, or practice unit is compensated, or (*d*) the effect that losing the client would have on the partner, office, or practice unit.

- Assign personnel based on the knowledge, skills, and abilities required in the circumstances and the nature and extent of supervision needed.
- Have personnel participate in general and industry-specific continuing professional education and professional development activities that enable them to accomplish assigned responsibilities and satisfy applicable continuing professional education requirements of the AICPA, state boards of accountancy, and other regulators.
- Select for advancement only those individuals who have the qualifications necessary to fulfill the responsibilities they will be called on to assume.

Engagement Performance

1.14 The purpose of the engagement performance element of quality control is to provide the firm with reasonable assurance (*a*) that engagements are consistently performed in accordance with applicable professional standards and regulatory and legal requirements, and (*b*) that the firm or the engagement partner issues reports that are appropriate in the circumstances. Policies and procedures for engagement performance should address all phases of the design and execution of the engagement, including engagement performance, supervision responsibilities, and review responsibilities. Policies and procedures also should require that consultation takes place when appropriate. In addition, a policy should establish criteria against which all engagements are to be evaluated to determine whether an engagement quality control review should be performed.

1.15 Establishing and maintaining policies such as the following assist the firm in obtaining the assurance required relating to the engagement performance element of quality control:

- Plan all engagements to meet professional, regulatory, and the firm's requirements.
- Perform work and issue reports and other communications that meet professional, regulatory, and the firm's requirements.
- Require that work performed by other team members be reviewed by qualified engagement team members, which may include the engagement partner, on a timely basis.
- Require the engagement team to complete the assembly of final engagement files on a timely basis.
- Establish procedures to maintain the confidentiality, safe custody, integrity, accessibility, and retrievability of engagement documentation.
- Require the retention of engagement documentation for a period of time sufficient to meet the needs of the firm, professional standards, laws, and regulations.
- Require that
    - — consultation take place when appropriate (for example, when dealing with complex, unusual, unfamiliar, difficult, or contentious issues);

 ©2017, AICPA

- sufficient and appropriate resources be available to enable appropriate consultation to take place;
- all the relevant facts known to the engagement team be provided to those consulted;
- the nature, scope, and conclusions of such consultations be documented; and
- the conclusions resulting from such consultations be implemented.

- Require that
  - differences of opinion be dealt with and resolved;
  - conclusions reached are documented and implemented; and
  - the report not be released until the matter is resolved.
- Require that
  - all engagements be evaluated against the criteria for determining whether an engagement quality control review should be performed;
  - an engagement quality control review be performed for all engagements that meet the criteria; and
  - the review be completed before the report is released.
- Establish procedures addressing the nature, timing, extent, and documentation of the engagement quality control review.
- Establish criteria for the eligibility of engagement quality control reviewers.

Monitoring

1.16 The purpose of the monitoring element of a system of quality control is to provide the firm and its engagement partners with reasonable assurance that the policies and procedures related to the system of quality control are relevant, adequate, operating effectively, and complied with in practice. Monitoring involves an ongoing consideration and evaluation of the appropriateness of the design, the effectiveness of the operation of a firm's quality control system, and a firm's compliance with its quality control policies and procedures. The purpose of monitoring compliance with quality control policies and procedures is to provide an evaluation of the following:

- Adherence to professional standards and regulatory and legal requirements
- Whether the quality control system has been appropriately designed and effectively implemented
- Whether the firm's quality control policies and procedures have been operating effectively so that reports issued by the firm are appropriate in the circumstances

1.17 Establishing and maintaining policies such as the following assist the firm in obtaining the assurance required relating to the monitoring element of quality control:

- Assign responsibility for the monitoring process to a partner or partners or other persons with sufficient and appropriate experience and authority in the firm to assume that responsibility.
- Assign performance of the monitoring process to competent individuals.
- Require the performance of monitoring procedures that are sufficiently comprehensive to enable the firm to assess compliance with all applicable professional standards and the firm's quality control policies and procedures. Monitoring procedures consist of the following:
  - — Review of selected administrative and personnel records pertaining to the quality control elements.
  - — Review of engagement documentation, reports, and clients' financial statements.
  - — Summarization of the findings from the monitoring procedures, at least annually, and consideration of the systemic causes of findings that indicate that improvements are needed.
  - — Determination of any corrective actions to be taken or improvements to be made with respect to the specific engagements reviewed or the firm's quality control policies and procedures.
  - — Communication of the identified findings to appropriate firm management personnel.
  - — Consideration of findings by appropriate firm management personnel who should also determine that any actions necessary, including necessary modifications to the quality control system, are taken on a timely basis.
  - — Assessment of
    - the appropriateness of the firm's guidance materials and any practice aids;
    - new developments in professional standards and regulatory and legal requirements and how they are reflected in the firm's policies and procedures where appropriate;
    - compliance with policies and procedures on independence;
    - the effectiveness of continuing professional development, including training;
    - decisions related to acceptance and continuance of client relationships and specific engagements; and
    - firm personnel's understanding of the firm's quality control policies and procedures and implementation thereof.
- Communicate at least annually, to relevant engagement partners and other appropriate personnel, deficiencies noted as a result of

 ©2017, AICPA

the monitoring process and recommendations for appropriate remedial action.

- Communicate the results of the monitoring of its quality control system process to relevant firm personnel at least annually.
- Establish procedures designed to provide the firm with reasonable assurance that it deals appropriately with the following:
  - Complaints and allegations that the work performed by the firm fails to comply with professional standards and regulatory and legal requirements.
  - Allegations of noncompliance with the firm's system of quality control.
  - Deficiencies in the design or operation of the firm's quality control policies and procedures, or noncompliance with the firm's system of quality control by an individual or individuals, as identified during the investigations into complaints and allegations.

  This includes establishing clearly defined channels for firm personnel to raise any concerns in a manner that enables them to come forward without fear of reprisal and documenting complaints and allegations and the responses to them.
- Require appropriate documentation to provide evidence of the operation of each element of its system of quality control. The form and content of documentation evidencing the operation of each of the elements of the system of quality control is a matter of judgment and depends on a number of factors, including the following, for example:
  - The size of the firm and the number of offices.
  - The nature and complexity of the firm's practice and organization.
- Require retention of documentation providing evidence of the operation of the system of quality control for a period of time sufficient to permit those performing monitoring procedures and peer review to evaluate the firm's compliance with its system of quality control, or for a longer period if required by law or regulation.

1.18 Some of the monitoring procedures discussed in the previous list may be accomplished through the performance of the following:

- Engagement quality control review
- Review of engagement documentation, reports, and clients' financial statements for selected engagements after the report release date
- Inspection[4] procedures

---

[4] *Inspection* is a retrospective evaluation of the adequacy of the firm's quality control policies and procedures, its personnel's understanding of those policies and procedures, and the extent of the firm's compliance with them. Although monitoring procedures are meant to be ongoing, they may include inspection procedures performed at a fixed point in time. Monitoring is a broad concept; inspection is one specific type of monitoring procedure.

Documentation of Quality Control Policies and Procedures

1.19 The firm should document each element of its system of quality control. The extent of the documentation will depend on the size, structure, and nature of the firm's practice. Documentation may be as simple as a checklist of the firm's policies and procedures or as extensive as practice manuals.

 ©2017, AICPA

Glossary

The following is a list of terms from the AICPA Statements on Standards for Accounting and Review Services (Clarified) glossary:

Analytical procedures. Evaluations of financial information through analysis of plausible relationships among both financial and nonfinancial data. Analytical procedures also encompass such investigation, as is necessary, of identified fluctuations or relationships that are inconsistent with other relevant information or that differ from expected values by a significant amount.

Applicable financial reporting framework. The financial reporting framework adopted by management and, when appropriate, those charged with governance, in the preparation and fair presentation of the financial statements that is acceptable in view of the nature of the entity and the objective of the financial statements or that is required by law or regulation.

Basic financial statements. Financial statements excluding supplementary information and required supplementary information.

Comparative financial statements. A complete set of financial statements for one or more prior periods included for comparison with the financial statements of the current period.

Designated accounting standard-setter. A body designated by the Council of the AICPA to promulgate accounting principles generally accepted in the United States of America pursuant to the "Compliance With Standards Rule" (AICPA, *Professional Standards*, ET sec. 1.310.001) and the "Accounting Principles Rule" (AICPA, *Professional Standards*, ET sec. 1.320.001) of the AICPA Code of Professional Conduct.

Emphasis-of-matter paragraph. A paragraph included in the accountant's compilation or review report that is required by Statements on Standards for Accounting and Review Services (SSARSs), or is included at the accountant's discretion, and that refers to a matter appropriately presented or disclosed in the financial statements that, in the accountant's professional judgment, is of such importance that it is fundamental to the users' understanding of the financial statements.

Engagement partner.[1] The partner or other person in the firm who is responsible for the engagement and its performance and for the report that is issued on behalf of the firm and who, when required, has the appropriate authority from a professional, legal, or regulatory body.

Engagement team. All partners and staff performing the engagement and any individuals engaged by the firm or a network firm who perform procedures on the engagement.

Error. Mistakes in the financial statements, including arithmetical or clerical mistakes, and mistakes in the application of accounting principles, including inadequate disclosures.

---

[1] This term is also defined in paragraph .13 of QC section 10, *A Firm's System of Quality Control* (AICPA, *Professional Standards*), for purposes of the Statements on Quality Control Standards. Refer to QC section 10 for specific language.

Experienced accountant. An individual (whether internal or external to the firm) who has practical review experience and a reasonable understanding of

a. review processes;

b. SSARSs and applicable legal and regulatory requirements;

c. the business environment in which the entity operates; and

d. review and financial reporting issues relevant to the entity's industry.

Financial reporting framework. A set of criteria used to determine measurement, recognition, presentation, and disclosure of all material items appearing in the financial statements (for example, accounting principles generally accepted in the United States of America [U.S. GAAP], International Financial Reporting Standards promulgated by the International Accounting Standards Board, or a special purpose framework).

Financial statements. A structured representation of historical financial information, including related notes, intended to communicate an entity's economic resources and obligations at a point in time or the changes therein for a period of time in accordance with a financial reporting framework. The related notes ordinarily comprise a summary of significant accounting policies and other explanatory information. The term *financial statements* ordinarily refers to a complete set of financial statements as determined by the requirements of the applicable financial reporting framework but can also refer to a single financial statement.

Firm. A form of organization permitted by law or regulation whose characteristics conform to resolutions of the Council of the AICPA and that is engaged in the practice of public accounting.

Fraud. An intentional act that results in a misstatement in financial statements.

Generally accepted accounting principles (GAAP). References to *generally accepted accounting principles* in SSARSs means generally accepted accounting principles promulgated by bodies designated by the Council of the AICPA pursuant to the "Compliance With Standards Rule" and the "Accounting Principles Rule" of the AICPA Code of Professional Conduct.

Historical financial information. Information expressed in financial terms regarding a particular entity, derived primarily from that entity's accounting system, about economic events occurring in past time periods or about economic conditions or circumstances at points in time in the past.

Interpretive publications. Interpretations of SSARSs; exhibits to SSARSs; AICPA Guide *Preparation, Compilation, and Review Engagements*; guidance on preparation, compilations, and review engagements included in AICPA Audit and Accounting Guides; and AICPA Statements of Position, to the extent that those statements are applicable to such engagements.

Management. The person(s) with executive responsibility for the conduct of the entity's operations. For some entities, management includes some or all of those charged with governance (for example, executive members of a governance board or an owner-manager).

©2017, AICPA

Misstatement. A difference between the amount, classification, presentation, or disclosure of a reported financial statement item and the amount, classification, presentation, or disclosure that is required for the item to be presented fairly in accordance with the applicable financial reporting framework. Misstatements can arise from fraud or error. Misstatements also include those adjustments of amounts, classifications, presentations, or disclosures that, in the accountant's professional judgment, are necessary for the financial statements to be presented fairly, in all material respects.

Noncompliance. Acts of omission or commission by the entity, either intentional or unintentional, which are contrary to the prevailing laws or regulations. Such acts include transactions entered into, by, or in the name of, the entity or on its behalf by those charged with governance, management, or employees. *Noncompliance* does not include personal misconduct (unrelated to the business activities of the entity) by those charged with governance, management, or employees of the entity.

Other-matter paragraph. A paragraph included in the accountant's compilation or review report that is required by SSARSs, or is included at the accountant's discretion, and that refers to a matter other than those presented or disclosed in the financial statements that, in the accountant's professional judgment, is relevant to users' understanding of the compilation or review, the accountant's responsibilities, or the accountant's compilation or review report.

Other preparation, compilation and review publications. Publications other than interpretive publications.

Professional judgment. The application of relevant training, knowledge, and experience, within the context provided by SSARSs, accounting, and ethical standards, in making informed decisions about the courses of action that are appropriate in the circumstances of the preparation, compilation, or review engagement.

Prospective financial information. Any financial information about the future. The information may be presented as complete financial statements or limited to one or more elements, items, or accounts.

Pro forma financial information. A presentation that shows what the significant effects on historical financial information might have been had a consummated or proposed transaction (or event) occurred at an earlier date.

Report release date. The date the accountant grants the entity permission to use the accountant's review report in connection with the financial statements.

Required supplementary information. Information that a designated accounting standards-setter requires to accompany an entity's basic financial statements. Required supplementary information is not part of the basic financial statements; however, a designated accounting standards-setter considers the information to be an essential part of financial reporting for placing the basic financial statements in an appropriate operational, economic, or historical context. In addition, authoritative lines for the methods of measurement and presentation of the information have been established.

Review documentation. The record of review procedures performed, relevant review evidence obtained, and conclusions the accountant reached (terms such as *working papers* or *workpapers* are also sometimes used).

Review evidence. Information used by the accountant to provide a reasonable basis for obtaining limited assurance.

Special purpose framework. A financial reporting framework other than GAAP that is one of the following bases of accounting:

a. **Cash basis.** A basis of accounting that the entity uses to record cash receipts and disbursements and modifications of the cash basis having substantial support (for example, recording depreciation on fixed assets).

b. **Tax basis.** A basis of accounting that the entity uses to file its tax return for the period covered by the financial statements.

c. **Regulatory basis.** A basis of accounting that the entity uses to comply with the requirements or financial reporting provisions of a regulatory agency to whose jurisdiction the entity is subject (for example, a basis of accounting that insurance companies use pursuant to the accounting practices prescribed or permitted by a state insurance commission).

d. **Contractual basis.** A basis of accounting that the entity uses to comply with an agreement between the entity and one or more third parties other than the accountant.

e. **Other basis.** A basis of accounting that uses a definite set of logical, reasonable criteria that is applied to all material items appearing in financial statements.

The cash-basis, tax-basis, regulatory-basis, and other-basis of accounting are commonly referred to as *other comprehensive bases of accounting* (OCBOA).

Specified parties. The intended users of the accountant's compilation or review report.

Subsequent events. Events occurring between the date of the financial statements and the date of the accountant's compilation or review report.

Subsequently discovered facts. Facts that become known to the accountant after the date of the accountant's compilation or review report that, had they been known to the accountant at that date, may have caused the accountant to revise the accountant's compilation review report.

Supplementary information. Information presented outside the basic financial statements, excluding required supplementary information, that is not considered necessary for the financial statements to be fairly presented in accordance with the applicable financial reporting framework. Such information may be presented in a document containing the reviewed/compiled financial statements or separate from the reviewed/compiled financial statements.

Those charged with governance. The person(s) or organization(s) (for example, a corporate trustee) with responsibility for overseeing the strategic direction of an entity and the obligations related to the accountability of

 ©2017, AICPA

the entity. This includes overseeing the financial reporting process. Those charged with governance may include management personnel (for example, executive members of a governance board or an owner-manager).

Updated report. A report issued by a continuing accountant that takes into consideration information that the accountant becomes aware of during the accountant's current engagement and that re-expresses the accountant's previous conclusions or, depending on the circumstances, expresses different conclusions on the financial statements of a prior period reviewed by the accountant as of the date of the accountant's current report.

Written representation. A written statement by management provided to the accountant to confirm certain matters or to support other review evidence. Written representations in this context do not include financial statements, the assertions therein, or supporting books and records.

Index of Pronouncements and Other Technical Guidance

A

C

Title	*Paragraphs*
Code of Professional Conduct	
ET section	
1.200.001, "Independence Rule"	1.22, 2.03, 3.09
1.210.010, "Conceptual Framework for Independence"	1.22, 2.10
1.295, "Nonattest Services"	1.23, 2.03, 3.09
1.295.030, "Management Responsibilities"	1.23, 2.11
1.295.040, "General Requirements for Performing Nonattest Services"	1.23, 2.11
1.320.001, "Accounting Principles Rule"	1.188

F

Title	*Paragraphs*
FASB ASC	
205, *Presentation of Financial Statements,*	
205-40	1.202, 1.204–.205
220, *Comprehensive Income*	2.46
230, *Statement of Cash Flows*	1.144
274, *Personal Financial Statements*	
274-10	5.02–.04
450, *Contingencies*	1.159, 1.193, 5.03
740, *Income Taxes*	1.144, 1.159
810, *Consolidation*	1.159
850, *Related Party Disclosures*	5.03
855, *Subsequent Events*	
855-10	1.170, 2.36
FASB ASU No. 2014-15, *Presentation of Financial Statements—Going Concern (Subtopic 205-40): Disclosure of Uncertainties about an Entity's Ability to Continue as a Going Concern*	1.202

©2017, AICPA

G

I

Q

Subject Index

A

C

 ©2017, AICPA

F

 ©2017, AICPA

I

 ©2017, AICPA

J

©2017, AICPA

©2017, AICPA

©2017, AICPA

 ©2017, AICPA